I0521738

as good as the best

as good as the best

POWER AND
POSSIBILITY
BEYOND C-PTSD

D. NOVO

ONLY
GOLDEN
NARRATIVES

E-Book ISBN: 979-8-218-91279-6

Only Golden Narratives LLC
Website: OnlyGoldenNarratives

Copyright © 2026 by D. Novo

All rights reserved.

No portion of this book may be reproduced in any form without written permission from the publisher or author, except as permitted by U.S. copyright law.

This book is intended for informational purposes and to provide personal insights through narrative only. This book draws on a range of publicly available sources, research, and the author's personal experience. The author has made reasonable efforts to ensure that the information presented in this book is accurate and current at the time of publication. However, the author and publisher make no guarantees regarding outcomes or results from the use of this information. Each reader's experience is unique, and progress and outcomes may vary. Readers assume all risk associated with the use of this information. To the fullest extent permitted by law, the author and publisher disclaim any and all liability for any loss, injury, or damage arising from the use of or reliance on the information in this book.

All opinions expressed are solely those of the author and should not be interpreted as statements of fact or professional advice. The author is not a licensed professional, and the content of this book should not be considered professional, legal, medical, psychological, or financial advice. The reader is advised to consult a qualified professional regarding their specific circumstances.

The personal stories in this book are drawn from the author's experiences. No real names are used, and identifying details have been omitted or generalized to protect privacy.

*I may be as bad as the worst, but thank God **I am as good as the best**.*

Walt Whitman

Contents

Introduction

Thank you for opening this book. Welcome to a story where you are the hero.

A story where your dreams become reality.

A story where you believe your potential is without limits, and your possibilities are endless.

A story where you begin to feel a wholeness that once seemed out of reach.

A story where you believe you're as good as the best, and that you can live a life as good as the best.

And it becomes true. All of it.

Here's the catch: This story is not a fairy tale. Fairy tales hide the truth, and this story is grounded in truth.

And here's the other catch: You're not just the hero; you're also the villain. Or, more precisely, your limiting beliefs are the villains—the thoughts of shame, guilt, fear, and worthlessness that keep you from attaining what you truly want and living a life that is free and fulfilling.

While many people from all sorts of backgrounds have limiting beliefs that can benefit from transformation, this book is specifically meant to validate, inspire, and empower those who have C-PTSD from childhood trauma, and the resultant (and particularly toxic) limiting belief patterns.

Most people are familiar with PTSD. I have C-PTSD—complex PTSD, the result of chronic, long-term childhood trauma. For me and many others, C-PTSD results from ongoing and repeated mistreatment that involved betrayal and a loss of safety and trust. This mistreatment is typically perpetrated by a parent or caregiver, and it may take the form of emotional or physical abuse, neglect, inconsistent and conditional affection, a lack of attachment, or invalidation or denial of feelings. To say that unconditional love is lacking in such circumstances is a dramatic understatement.

This trauma lacerates the emotional wholeness we are all born with. A dark, interfering wound forms, and our mind and body are wired in response, without our consent. The darkness can lead to all kinds of difficulties: feeling unseen; struggling to trust others; being easily triggered; or having trouble regulating emotions (and the breath). Our existence may be overwhelmed by a deep precariousness, as if we're perpetually at the edge of chaos, deprivation, and powerlessness. We may use hypervigilance to grasp onto ever elusive stability. We may seem normal, or even like we have it all together on the outside, while we're breaking apart on the inside.

The wound is dark, but we are light.

You are light.

The crushing weight of trauma and abuse may have made you want to give up many times, yet *here you are*. You have been at the bottom (or may still be there), and you may even have been told you only deserved the bottom. And yet, a part of you still believes more is possible—and that part of you opened this book.

You're rare, but not as rare as you may think.

You're not alone.

You are loved, even if you were not loved as a child.

You are forgiven, if only you forgive yourself.

You have dreams—rich, textured dreams.

And those dreams can come true.

This book is designed to give you permission to pursue your dreams and reclaim everything that was unfairly denied to you: your self-worth, sense of abundance, connection to your imagination, trust in the universe and yourself, and ability to authentically connect to others.

This book is my love letter to you, to myself, and to the universe.

Our origin stories are dysfunctional in a way that we thought no one could ever understand, but we're not alone. We were harmed in ways we thought no one could ever understand, but we're not alone. Somehow, we escaped. Somehow, we looked for answers, meaning, recovery, redemption—anything. We spiraled and collapsed at times, made mistakes, hurt others. Somehow, we kept going, driven to heal, learn, express, grow, and connect.

This book, by necessity, must address darkness. But this book is about light.

Let's start here:

You are worthy, exactly as you are.

You are as good as the best.

Your life can be as good as the best.

Your potential is without limits. Your possibilities are endless.

You will heal more than you ever thought possible, and you will begin to believe this.

All that is required to know and realize your dreams is already within you.

This book is about light, but this book cannot solve for everything or everyone. I've tied myself up in knots over the years trying to make it work for everyone, but it's impossible.

This book is not for the profoundly pessimistic. Defenses of pessimism have been written and make good points, but pessimism is a privilege. Pessimism doesn't survive trauma. Pessimism doesn't survive poverty. Pessimism doesn't survive brutal unfairness. If you've gone through trauma, you're likely already more of an optimist than not, because it was really, terribly, horribly hard—and you are alive and interested, here, reading this book. The fact that you're here is a miracle.

This book is also not for those struggling with serious mental illness. I'm not a therapist; I'm only someone who has been through a lot and likes to think and write. Professional help can assist everyone on their journey, but if you are struggling with serious mental illness, therapy is imperative.

This book suggests a practice similar to manifesting, but it's not a manifesting book. Classic manifesting books, such as those written by Napoleon Hill and Neville Goddard, changed my life. They taught me the power of unassailable conviction. But their explicit demand for conviction and accompanying lack of nuance are why they work—and also why they don't. If the reader doesn't manifest their desires by following the advice of a particular book, it's the reader's fault, either due to a lack of faith in the philosophy or a lack of effort. This implicit (and sometimes explicit) blame, combined with the lack of additional tools, insights, and therapies, can make readers with C-PTSD feel worthless, which only leads to more failure in the practice of "manifestation", contributing to a cycle of worthlessness. These books don't wrestle with the uncomfortable realities of trauma recovery or our inequitable starting places, and especially not the fact that affirmations don't heal limiting beliefs instilled over years of a difficult childhood. Manifesting, as traditionally conceived, leaves behind so many of us who desperately want to believe in it.

This book discusses pathways to healing, but it alone will not heal you (nor will any other book). Books about healing from trauma provide fantastic tools and can make us feel seen, but they typically end—perhaps unintentionally—focused on pain rather than expression of the authentic self. They often leave me stuck in a victimhood mentality. What we focus on becomes our existence, so it's not a surprising effect. This book aims to instill in you a belief that you *can* heal and you *can* realize your dreams. Having C-PTSD doesn't limit your possibilities; engaging in healing only adds to the possibilities available to you. Given what you've been through, you have unique insights, the potential to empathize and understand, and a creative, deeply felt view of the world.

This book will not give you simple rules for success, nor promise that this "one thing" will ensure you achieve your goals. The truth is never "one thing" that can be distilled into a 200-page book, although many books are promoted as such one-stop solutions. Books about success lay out helpful steps, but they don't address limiting beliefs around motivation or confidence. Whenever I read these books, I wonder about motivation. Why would anyone bother to begin a new habit? Why would anyone start counting down before taking action? Why would anyone take the leap to change their life and embrace the attendant discomfort? Where does intrinsic motivation and purpose come from? I believe most of these books speak to those who are already motivated, secure, and stable, with solid internal resources that they can summon—even if those resources are temporarily buried.

In fact, books from all the previously mentioned genres are often written from a perspective of oblivious privilege. Many types of privilege exist. Privilege is having your needs met. Privilege is not worrying about money. Privilege is experiencing unconditional love and feeling safe. It's so much easier to heal from trauma when you have the time and money to work with excellent practitioners. It's so much easier to manifest your desires when you're connected to a network of wealthy, educated, and successful individuals (and not scared to ask them for help). It's so much easier to improve your mental and physical health when you're not focused on survival. I know this because I have been on both sides: lacking much of the foregoing as a child and young adult and having many of these privileges now.

Everything is easier when you've been made to feel worthy and loved from a young age. This book is for those of us who were not. That ship of unconditional love has sailed, but we still have a life to live. It's our responsibility to heal and take back everything that was refused to us.

This book assumes you've read books about trauma, healing, manifesting, and achieving your goals, or are at least familiar with their ideas. This book is indebted to the writers of those books, but this book also assumes you want something more.

This book is for *us*, in those times when we feel lost, on the edge, crushed, confused, or deeply and profoundly worthless. This is the book I wish I'd had when I was younger, deep in the struggle and patching together approaches, therapies, and advice in a desperate attempt to occupy my mind and body with ease. When being seen, loved, and empowered would have felt like a miracle.

The way we were treated as children had nothing to do with us. The life we choose to live today has everything to do with us.

No matter what you've done or what you're currently doing, no matter what's been said or done to you, no matter what you've said or done to yourself: *You are worthy as you are, right now.*

Instead of bippity-boppity-boo, instead of three wishes, I give you this:

You will heal.

Your potential is limitless.

Your possibilities are endless.

Not *if* you're perfect. Not *if* you stop making mistakes. Not *if* you work hard. Not *if* you suffer. Not *if* you prove yourself to others, or impress others. Not *if* you "win." Not *if* you save your family from themselves. Not *if* someone else seems to give you the validation you never had. Not *if* you forgive. Not *because* of your career, or your social media likes, or the number in your bank account.

IN THIS MOMENT, AS YOU ARE, YOU ARE WORTHY OF A LIFE AS GOOD AS THE BEST.

This book prioritizes the forest over the trees. It sets out several "practices" that are intended to guide you to a life as good as the best by transforming your limiting beliefs—but each practice could make up its own book, or several. I don't have all the answers; I only have the practices that have brought me to a place far better than I ever thought possible. They have begun to reconnect me to everything I thought I had lost or never had in the first place.

I've aspired to make the practices clear, but they also contain inherent complexities and contradictions. The truth is irrevocably messy. I won't simplify things so they sound neat and easy. Nor will I fall back on aphorisms or tell you what's right or wrong. Anything too simple, too black/white, is a lie. A digestible, comforting lie, but a lie, nonetheless.

You were lied to many times.

If you experienced childhood trauma, you were lied to about what it meant to be loved. You were lied to about your fundamental worth. You were lied to by the people who were supposed to make you feel loved, accepted, and validated. You internalized all of it, but you don't need it anymore.

You were also lied to by society. One of the most pernicious lies you've been told is that you are your production and output, your compliance and conformity, and that working hard and following the rules will make your dreams come true. Worth and hard work seem to be inextricably tied together in our history, culture, and language. In fact, in the language of my ancestors, the word "vredan" means both worthy and hardworking. And it makes sense that when tribes and later villages and communities had to feed and protect their members, members had to contribute to the survival of not only themselves but also the group. It makes sense that members in such a group would want to discourage a lack of contribution. And it also makes sense that under capitalism, hard work is encouraged as a way of feeding into the system, enriching the already rich and motivating entrepreneurship, while also being held out as a carrot, as a sliver of hope to the lower and middle class that they might also increase their own status.

Unfortunately, this cultural ethos of hard work as the path to success is sustained by the trauma many of us experience as children. Our parents or caregivers didn't show us unconditional love, only *fake love* earned through achievement, performance, hard work, submission, or appeasement. We had to earn love, and love that has to be earned isn't love at all. This experience was even more fraught for those of us who were told (or who had conveyed to us) that we were worthless, that our feelings didn't deserve attention, that we were a nuisance, or that we were a tool to make others feel good.

And so, we continue "earning" love, seeking external validation to feel whole. Hard work is a salve for the wounds of trauma, and it's easily manipulated by everything from corporate culture to consumerism to marketing to social media. Many career and financial "successes" seem fueled by the very self-hatred instilled by childhood trauma. Some people numb the pain with work and believe, subconsciously, that work will heal them and make them feel whole, loved, and deserving. They work and work, and perhaps advance their careers. Unfortunately, it's a house of cards. Work setbacks can be a whole new trauma, but even work successes can be accompanied by a surprising emptiness, the shocking hollowness of the promise that everything would finally be okay. When work doesn't work anymore, it's hard not to restart the cycle of worthlessness all over again.

You don't need to achieve to be loved or treated with dignity. Love you have to earn is not love. This "yearning to earn" energy disconnects us from our true desires and gifts. It places us in a vicious cycle of brief gratification followed by discontent and feelings of emptiness, followed by more mindless effort and suffering in a futile attempt to alleviate the despair. You don't have to earn the right to exist as yourself.

This book is about living your most authentic dreams. Living your dreams is distinct from "success" in the eyes of society, although they can overlap. People who have unresolved trauma and feel inauthentic, disconnected and deeply afraid succeed all the time. You can absolutely "succeed" while lacking self-worth or pursuing a dream that has nothing to do with what you really want—I did it for many years. You can "succeed" feeling as if you must prove your worth to the world, as if you're nothing without honors and accolades, as if you must earn the love of the universe, all the while projecting ruthless invulnerability. You can fight your way to the top and feel invigorated doing it.

You can also absolutely fail, too—sometimes in a way that is spectacular, and other times in a way that is quite ordinary. The acute pain of failure felt by those of us who rely on success for validation can cause us to lose motivation, bury our gifts, embrace mediocrity, and fade into the background. It can seem to substantiate the belief that we'll never be good enough. The pain can cause us to settle for something that doesn't feel right or true to us.

Even if your "success" continues, when you lack self-worth, you are vulnerable to self-sabotage. Self-sabotage takes many forms: personal drama mucking up your dream life; living in a world in which a fight is always required, because that's all you've known; or never experiencing calm and ease. Your body or mind can undermine you, sometimes catastrophically, right when you feel like you're at the top. Or, more mundanely and very commonly, when you lack self-worth, your life may be harder and more complicated than it needs to be.

You were lied to in another way, as well. A particular person will not save you. No one person can fill the emptiness your parents or caregivers left you with. So many songs, books, and movies are based on the idea that you're not whole until you meet your soulmate. It's a nice thought, but once you're an adult, no one person can make you feel worthy or whole in a way that's sustainable and true. It has to come from you. In fact, if someone feels like your "savior," they're probably triggering your childhood wounds through their mix of personality and physical characteristics, creating a beautiful illusion that finally, through relationship with them, everything will be okay.

Although one person won't save you, healthy relationships contribute to your healing. As we'll discuss in Chapter 3, the only way to have healthy relationships with other people is to recognize and respect their wholeness and your own, whether they are your partner, child, or friend. Through this experience, you'll also learn to love yourself.

You are your own hero, but you live in relationship.

I know all of this because I learned it the hard way, and I continue dismantling the lies that formed the limiting beliefs I held for so long. My unresolved trauma continuously blocked me over the years, and I didn't recognize it because it was so integrated within me. Although I had achieved goals, those achievements tended to be fraught with obstacles. Things that I wanted to happen for me did, more often than not, but they took a long time, and it felt like an uphill climb. I thought I deserved that uphill climb—I thought I proved my worth through the climb. I believed I needed to prove myself through pain. I believed a public spectacle of attainment would one day finally make me feel worthy. And I never dared set my sights too high.

I tried every self-help approach imaginable, but I realized that I couldn't avoid engagement with my trauma, that I couldn't just replace limiting beliefs by repeating mantras because those beliefs were so deep, so buried, so integrated into my blood, muscle, bone, and movements. I had to own the past and recognize its awkward imposition on my body and mind. I had to heal, regulate, and integrate to converge on well-being and possibility, connection, creative expression, and authenticity.

Although none of the practices in this book came naturally or easily to me (and many still don't), it's not an uphill climb for me anymore. It's more of a labyrinth in which I'm steadier and more assured.

You can have steadiness and assurance in your own labyrinth. *Your labyrinth is yours.* Only you have the privilege and responsibility of living in your skin. Only you know what it feels like. Only you live with your decisions. You can't be someone else, and no one else can be you, and that's an amazing thing. Only you can express and experience your authentic dreams. Healing, regulating, and integrating will connect you to your authentic self. And in turn, expressing your authentic self through your dream will be healing, regulating, and integrating.

I'm writing because it's the way I feel compelled to express myself and give back. Writing makes me feel alive and true, which is healing in itself. What makes you feel alive and true?

Authentic expression brings meaning to your life, whether that's through a work of art, a business, a loving relationship, or a garden you grow in your backyard. If your dream is aligned with your authentic self, progression toward your dream will unfold naturally. Work won't feel like work (most of the time), and it definitely won't feel like suffering. Belief in what's possible won't be forced but rather will live in the body—believing will be like breathing. Everything will flow in a way you never thought possible. You will not be susceptible to following the vagaries of others' approval, hoarding money so you feel whole, pursuing power to feel important enough not to be destroyed, striving for physical excellence to prove you can't be hurt, or attracting others so you can feel validated.

Dreams come true all the time. We live in a world that will try to convince you otherwise—convince you that you must be practical, work yourself to the bone (whether physically or energetically), follow the rules, and blend in with the crowd as much as possible. The mainstream considers it "rational" and "logical" that your life will not be too different from the one lived by your family and those in your immediate community, that you will not invent or create, make leaps in wealth accumulation, heal from disease, or provide an aspirational example of excellence.

But look around you. If dreams didn't come true, would we have works of art in our world—physical, musical, or otherwise—that inspire joy and awe? Would we have extraordinary technological advances, or insights, or social movements that lead to real change? Would we see examples of incredible athletic performance? And, also, just as importantly, would we see people with careers, families, friends, hobbies, and homes that they love?

Can you name people who have attained what you want? Whether in your community or farther out in the world, I promise you people have attained what you desire. Whether it's wealth, health, a job they love, a sense of peace, a partner, or something else, it's been done, and it has been done by people whose starting points have been just as rough as yours.

What makes you so different that it can't happen for you?

I can almost hear that voice in your head, because I still sometimes hear it in mine. It's an ugly voice saying you are unworthy of your dreams, of stability, dignity, belonging, or happiness. It says you're too poor, too uneducated, too unconnected; your thoughts are too negative, your pain is too deep, and your trauma is too unhealed. It says your pain was earned, you're irredeemable, and there's nothing you can do about it.

That voice isn't the real you. That voice is the voice of your wounded narrator. Our wounded narrators protected us when we had no protection, with limiting beliefs that kept us from being mentally obliterated by childhood trauma. Those limiting beliefs that once kept us together now threaten to prevent us from living a life as good as the best. Those limiting beliefs will block us at every chance and sabotage us once we're halfway there. Those limiting beliefs, awash in the legacy of fear, shame, and helplessness, are at the root of our most damaging mistakes.

Limiting beliefs contain a lot of energy, and so they must be transformed, rather than replaced or repressed. Until they are transformed, our external worlds will reflect them. Until they are transformed, our lives will be defined by them. Limiting beliefs hold together a cruel and invisible prison, and the practices in this book are intended to begin to dissolve that prison, and to funnel all the energy left behind into a life as good as the best. Once the prison is dissolved, our wounded narrators no longer have a role to play. They can rest, in peace.

You may think that where you stand today is an impossible starting point. It isn't. I don't know your circumstances, but I know what it's like to be stuck, trapped in a toxic environment or in a toxic mentality. I have felt powerless, suffocated, and alone. It's not fair that it feels so much harder for you than others, but I hope this book makes it a little easier.

You have a right to goodness—right now, no matter your circumstances, shame, pain, or regret. You have a right to safety, security, love, trust, confidence, mental and physical health, and opportunity. You have a right to express your authentic self and realize your dreams through such expression. You don't need to work harder or manifest better or pray more or perform for others or pay for online classes or in-person retreats in order to "earn" love or worth or success. You don't need to convince others of your worth, of your right to feel, to experience stability and peace. It's you who needs to know, who needs to integrate these beliefs into your body and mind.

Life is our gift, power, and obligation. As adults, we create our own world, whether we like it or not. We become what we believe and the actions we take based on those beliefs. Until we transform our limiting beliefs, they will dictate our possibilities and dilute our power. And so we start by shifting our focus to limitless possibilities.

Chapter 1

Practice Abundance

When you realize there is nothing lacking, the whole world belongs to you.

Lao Tzu

Where do you see scarcity? What do you believe will always be lacking in your life or in the world? What do you conserve, hoard, or ruminate over? Whether it's money, health, time, freedom, love, success, well-being, or any manner of tangible things, your choice to perceive immutable limits is the foundational limiting belief, and the first to be dismantled, through the practice of abundance.

Practicing abundance means choosing to recognize unlimited resources and opportunities. It's choosing to believe that anything and everything is possible.

A belief in possibility is foundational to healing and to realizing your dreams. You find what you look for, and people tend to look for things they believe are already present. If you believe limits and barriers are present, you'll find them. If you believe resources and opportunities are present, you'll find them instead. You'll have an open mind that recognizes obscure opportunities and a relentless drive to unearth hidden resources. An abundant mindset will transform your life, and it will feel like magic.

Is this hard to believe? I've been there; I spent my life in and out of a scarcity mindset, which is the opposite of an abundant mindset. A scarcity mindset is a focus on what is perceived as scarce rather than what is abundant. A scarcity mindset is caused by feelings of lack, worthlessness, and anxiety about never being able to have enough, and once it dominates, it leads to ever greater feelings of lack, worthlessness, and anxiety about never being able to have enough. It's a never-ending, dark, and depleting feedback loop. A scarcity mindset—and its attachment to lack and mediocrity—leads to the bleak and barren perpetually threatening your life.

If we're looking for evidence of limits, we can find it. Budgets. Stagnant or fixed incomes. Environmental degradation. Marathons with one winner. Tournaments with one winner. Hierarchies at work. Limits on how much we receive and how far we can go. These are all indubitable constructs shaping our perception of the world. We can only take away their power by shifting our attention, reframing, or breaking them down. Instead of focusing on limits, we can focus on possibilities to ease into limitlessness. Anything is possible. Every problem has a solution, or multiple. Every ceiling can be shattered. Every pool and every pie can be expanded. *A way through and beyond always exists.*

If we're looking for evidence of abundance, we can find it too. The universe—and its resources and opportunities—expand all the time, through technological innovations, more efficient distribution, more effective communication, and other tangible products of ideas. Solutions, advancements, and breakthroughs are all products of ideas. The Fed prints money or lowers interest rates. Immigrants fill population needs, allowing countries to continue to function. New jobs replace old ones absorbed by new technology. Agriculture expands to feed more people. A person breaks out of the hierarchy by leaving their current job for a better opportunity.

A person moves to a new state for a fresh start. A person finds a new income stream to supplement their finances.

To see or find the way through and beyond limits requires conviction, tenacity, a sense of humor, and the power of the imagination. Critically, *ideas dissolve limits*. The more we appreciate the power of ideas, both on a macro and individual level, the more likely we'll believe in and experience abundance. We'll consider the implications of this in more detail in the following chapter, but let's celebrate ideas here in relation to abundance.

Suddenly, with an idea, we see a path or source where we once saw limit or lack. I believe that as long as humans have imaginations, they will innovate their way out of many supposed constraints. Of course, it's not all sunshine and roses. Some of the most amazing discoveries, innovations, expansions and improvements occur after a galvanizing hardship or tragedy is experienced. Humans are imperfect, and our timing is imperfect. Civilizations fail before they're replaced. We run out of something right before we discover an analogue. But innovation has never ceased.[1] Problem-solving has never abated. Resources are shared in one way or another. Humanity marches forward. Despite some rough troughs, quality of life (by most metrics) improves.

Despite challenges, I don't believe we live in the worst of times. Maybe that's because if I had been born a hundred years earlier, I'd be a peasant in the home of my ancestors, never learning to read, dominated by a husband arranged for me, and acutely vulnerable to war and famine. People are still living a similar existence to the one I imagine here, but they are a far smaller percentage than they once were. Humanity has survived, adapted, and innovated out of difficult times—and it will continue to do so. Believing this doesn't lull me into complacency, but rather motivates me to do more to make the world a better place.

Cultivating an abundant mindset is a choice to dissolve limits. It's not up to abundance to show up; it's up to you to see it. Observation is existence. Observation is unequivocal. I can choose to observe how little time I have to write today, or I can choose to observe how much time I have to write today, and demonstrate gratitude for that time by seeing it and using it. Neither is technically inaccurate, but the former is likely to lead to anxiety, inefficiency, and negative thoughts and the latter is likely to lead to a sense of power and capability, energy, and focus—bringing me closer to my dreams.

Abundance will not come knock you over the side of the head while you're perceiving a world of lack, mediocrity, and stagnation, or even one of collapse, destruction, and doom. It's up to you to find and observe the light, the spark, the movement, the excellence. The universe abounds with goodness, love, creativity, and success. The universe abounds with unlimited opportunities and resources to find love, generate wealth, create art, solve problems, and change your life. More than enough opportunities and resources exist for me, and more than enough opportunities and resources exist for you.

We can dig deep to determine why we struggle with an abundant mindset. We may rationalize that we're being realistic, but that's usually a cover for deeper challenges centered on fear. These challenges typically fall into three categories, which we'll discuss in the following sections: guilt and shame (about having enough or having more than enough, a common condition among those of us with C-PTSD); a scarcity mindset (which might be due to childhood trauma but is also commonly caused by societal conditioning); and envy or jealousy (also commonly encouraged by societal conditioning).

Let Go of Guilt and Shame

You won't experience abundance if you've been conditioned to feel guilt or shame for it, or to think it has to be earned or deserved, or that it makes you spoiled. Guilt and shame are the most significant impediments to abundance. Those of us with C-PTSD as a result of traumatic childhoods may have experienced literal scarcity or a psychology of scarcity. Our experiences have led us to struggle to believe that abundance is available to us now, with no strings attached.

Some of us may feel shame about possessing bounty of any sort, whether it's wealth, freedom, peace, community, or love. If we believe we're worthless, we'll think we don't deserve anything, and receiving will feel unsettling. Our wounded narrator will say: You haven't earned it. Our wounded narrator will say: You only have value for your achievements, for your place on the (illusory) hierarchy, and what you receive will be limited to the bare minimum for such achievement. Our wounded narrator will say: You belong on a treadmill, forever running to nowhere.

Our wounded narrator will also say: How dare you enjoy your day when your parents are struggling? Our wounded narrator will say: How dare you have ease and abundance when they don't? Our wounded narrator will say: You should be worried, struggling, making sacrifices, and scraping by—and even if you're not, you should be engaging in rhetoric that suggests you are.

Some of us may have been conditioned to think "enough" or even "close to enough" is too much, and that we're selfish for not giving as much as possible away (especially to our narcissistic parents).[2] Whenever I received money from a relative as a child (from the time I was four until my high school graduation celebration), my parents would take it from me, because, as they said, they needed it. I learned that having something for myself was not the *right* thing. If I had anything at all, I owed it to my parents to give it to them. It made no sense, and I knew it didn't, but it's how I felt. In my twenties, I struggled with that same feeling of never wanting to have too much money, because with it came a sense of obligation and guilt. If I somehow had enough, I felt guilty for holding onto it. This was after making my way through college on my own and barely scraping by before law school, where I once again struggled while relying on massive amounts of loans. My parents' conditioning worked: I gave my family money and emotional support, while receiving none in return. If I had even a little extra, I felt overwhelming guilt. I felt selfish for enjoying money or freedom from worry. I gave and gave, not from a spirit of true abundance but from fear, guilt, and shame.

In fact, I was terrified of the freedom of abundance. I was terrified of *having*. I told myself I didn't need money. Hadn't I found happiness without it? As enlightened as it may sound, I realized later that this rationalization came from guilt for having obtained so much beyond what my family had. I thought I deserved to live hand to mouth while serving others in the nonprofit sector, because I was worthless unless I continually served without having. The community replaced my "family." Through an act of transference, I let the public good become what I'd sacrifice everything for.[3]

Other people may experience this trauma-inflicted scarcity mindset with respect to time, love, or other resources (and I have, as well). They may feel lazy when they take time to relax, having been given the impression they should always be working in one way or another. They may feel frivolous for taking a vacation for similar reasons. They may feel selfish for enjoying their freedom instead of getting caught up in family drama. They may feel guilty for finding the kind of love no one in their family ever experienced and ultimately sabotage the relationship. They may feel self-indulgent for taking the time to heal. They may feel guilty simply for having a great day. Some of this is internal, and some of this is perpetuated by dysfunctional families who don't want any one member to break out and experience something wonderful. For example, my family of origin shamed me, accusing me of being on a high horse, when I used time and resources to begin my healing journey.

Think about your past and what may impact your ability to maintain an abundant mindset. Process and release any feelings of guilt or shame with respect to wealth, health, love, freedom, success, luck, and all the other gifts of the universe. Notice when you feel bad and excavate the trigger. Consider the way your family of origin reacted and spoke to you about having, experiencing, and enjoying. Consider the language they used. My triggers around abundance are most activated after I've gone through a challenging time, processed it, and am feeling great afterward. The guilt and shame set in immediately, lying to me that I don't deserve to have peace. I notice these low-frequency beliefs and recognize them as a vestige of my conditioning that is irrelevant and debilitating now. I acknowledge the wounded narrator as separate from the part of me that is as good as the best. And I let go.

Unearth the toxic and sabotaging guilt and shame and let it go.

It never made sense—but it *really* doesn't make sense now.

Don't sacrifice your life to lack and stagnation just because those around you have made that choice. You can't make them believe in abundance, as much as you may wish to. They want things to never change. Dysfunctional families rely on the status quo and are tremendously afraid that you'll leave them and the dysfunctional dynamic holding the family together will implode. Abundance is about growth, and they don't want growth. You may be guilted and shamed (sometimes subtly, sometimes overtly) into feeling that your abundant life is an affront to them. After all, don't you deserve to live in scarcity and fear, on the precipice of oblivion?

No. *You are inherently deserving of abundance.*

We all are.

Believe, go after it, and don't stop until you experience it.

One way to beat back the guilt and shame is by being generous with yourself. Gift yourself small, pleasurable items that you associate with abundance—a fancy chocolate bar, flowers, a massage, anything to brighten your day—but also occasional luxury items, like jewelry, a coat, or a work of art. If spending makes you uncomfortable, you can also gift yourself a chunk of time (especially when you feel like you have no time to spare) to do something relaxing.

Experiencing something that symbolizes abundance for you is an investment in yourself and your future. Your mind doesn't like cognitive dissonance (the mental discomfort of conflicting beliefs), and so accepting a symbol of abundance forces your mind to reconcile scarcity and abundance in favor of abundance. Your mind will be more inclined to believe abundance is available to you.

It's about practicing feeling abundance—working through the discomfort of it, the guilt and shame of it—not about receiving a dopamine hit, distracting yourself from reality, or flaunting a status symbol. A status symbol doesn't emanate abundance but rather insecurity, conformity, and people-pleasing.

This is not about excess; excess is not abundance. Going on a shopping spree where you buy massive amounts of cheaply-made, inferior goods only tells the universe that you deserve scarcity, waste, and poor quality. This is also not about consumption; consumption is not an investment in yourself. Scarcity tells us that mindless consumption will fill lack, but it never will.

It's okay to have enough. It's okay to have plenty. It's *not okay* to feel bad about having. If you feel bad about having, you'll struggle to attain and struggle again to keep what you attain.

Eliminate Your Scarcity Mindset

Scarcity is the great lie. Scarcity generates fear, desperation, regret, anxiety, and envy. Scarcity keeps us weak, unfocused, and striving, perpetually grasping for instead of expressing our dreams. Scarcity triggers mindless consumption in a futile attempt to numb the bottomless feelings of deprivation. Believing in scarcity traps us in perpetual struggle and lack.

Lack itself is not a lie. Lack—the experience of not having enough of something, such as food, love, or freedom—is a real human experience, and a particularly brutal one. However, lack is a momentary, transient, and visceral experience. Scarcity is a conviction that lack is an enduring, inescapable state. Scarcity is thinking everything will be okay as soon as you get more of something, but never thinking you have enough, and never thinking you are worthy of having enough (or more than enough).[4] Scarcity exists only in the mind, and only the mind can eliminate it.

Ask yourself: What do I think is out of reach? What am I waiting for? What do I think I'm running out of? What do I unquestioningly assume is the truth? Most importantly, what am I making excuses about?

People often make excuses for actions they subconsciously don't want to take. Excuses of not having enough "time" or "money" are particularly common and conceal a scarcity mindset. For example, when someone says they are waiting for stock prices or real estate prices to fall before buying in, they're not focused on what they can do to create the wealth needed to buy; rather, they are focused on something going badly for others. This places them in a scarcity mindset. Scarcity mindsets tend to lead to negativity, dread, and inertia. Other examples are people bemoaning global warming and not trying to innovate out of it, or thinking that merely complaining about the president will lead to changing half the country's mind.

A scarcity mindset accepts depletion as a natural state. Instead, *choose to believe expansion is a natural state.*

I know it can be challenging. As a child with limited options for autonomy, lack was my reality. I grew up living in an 800-square-foot duplex with four other people, sharing a bed with my siblings and a bathroom with my entire family, wearing clothes bought from garage sales (although my underwear was from Kmart and my shoes from Payless), and owning only books that cost less than fifty cents at said garage sales. We used food stamps and were on and off welfare over the years. I worried my family could become homeless at any time. I would watch my mom pleading with our landlord not to evict us, crying and hysterical. I rarely received gifts for Christmas or my birthday. It was the only existence I knew, on the edge of a bottomless pit of nothingness—the edge of not breathing, of having nothing, of being nothing. When my step-grandfather bought me a ten-speed bike for my birthday, a tremendous upgrade from my previous bike, I spent the entire day riding it. It was stolen the very next day right from the front of our home (I had nowhere else to put it). I wasn't getting another one.

Experiential lack saps the soul, demanding much of its energy, but experiential lack is transitory. I lived in lack, but the real prison I lived in was a scarcity mindset. I lived in a context full of people who believed abundance wasn't available to them and therefore shouldn't be available to their children. I was conditioned to grovel. My mother told me that we would be homeless if I, a child, didn't convince my father not to gamble once he received his paycheck. Manipulating people into giving us things for free by subtly (or maybe not so subtly) presenting ourselves as struggling, pathetic, and/or pitiable was an art form. The main tools were asking (or not saying anything at all, but presenting ourselves sadly), avoiding eye contact, looking down when saying thank you, and never allowing our bodies to betray any hint of confidence. The charity we received that way was apparently worth sacrificing our dignity. Any way we could obtain something to survive another day was valid because survival seemed to be all that was available to us. And so I clung to anything generous and free—a meal, a ride, a hand-me-down dress—while feeling deeply unworthy of having anything at all.

To be clear, groveling is bad and reflects a scarcity mindset, but *help is good*. Assistance is a form of abundance. Dignity is not degraded but rather blossoms when you accept support with gratitude, a sense of your worth, and a recognition that the help itself is proof of abundance. Know that your state of needing help is temporary, and commit to pay it forward once you (inevitably) have enough.

That child was taught a scarcity mindset, but the scarcity mindset didn't win. Over time, I recognized the sources of abundance available to me. At school and in the public library, I could access so much of what I cared about: books, knowledge, and caring teachers and friends. Forms of abundance are always available to us, and when we are in situations characterized by lack, we can still be relentless in unearthing them.

When I went to college, I finally had the freedom to be myself and not live in fear. Money flowed to me through scholarships, grants, and jobs that were much easier than the waitressing I did in high school. I wasn't wealthy, but I had enough—and it didn't matter at a college where wealth was stealth (I was later told I passed as middle class). I made friends. I had amazing discussions and learned so much. My time was my own. I was the happiest I'd ever been, and it felt marvelous.

I felt literal abundance, but remnants of a scarcity mindset remained. I carried habits that are common for those growing up with lack. For example, when going out to eat, I was terrified of wasting food by leaving any leftovers on my plate. I obsessed over supposed bargains even when they were meaningless (the latter is still a struggle to avoid). Even after law school when I had a relatively high-paying job, I was scared to buy myself things that were "too" beautiful or expensive. And billing hours in an intensely hierarchical system is not conducive to an abundant mindset. Certain careers feed off people with scarcity mindsets, and the law is one of them.

Suggestions from the universe as to how to live with an abundant mindset entered my life from time to time. My first boss would take me out to meals and assuage my guilt for leaving food on my plate. I dated and befriended people who were generous without strings attached. But I wasn't convinced of the reality of abundance by any of those, or a book, or love, or a beautiful scene. I was convinced by the economy in the spring of 2020. After a dip, stocks, bitcoin, and real estate skyrocketed. Money was made out of nothing during a time when people were terrified of a virus. Money was made out of nothing when nothing was happening. It dawned on me that *anything* could be made out of nothing. It was all a matter of perception. It was all a matter of observing the opportunity or resource and capitalizing on it.

It's challenging not to succumb to a scarcity mindset when the news is full of tragedies and there are real concerns about wars and environmental degradation. The practice of abundance is not about closing your eyes to those occurrences or pretending they don't exist. You can influence such occurrences, but you can't control them. And they should never control you by defining your mindset. Problems are inevitable. No utopia awaits us (although I believe a better, healthier universe does). Some things may get worse—but more things will get better, and you can be part of them getting better. In fact, it's your responsibility to be. But the people who make a difference aren't those who are swept up in fatalistic, fear-based narratives, thinking the sky is falling or the world is ending. The people who make a difference are those who believe a solution to every problem exists.

Here are some tangible ways to eviscerate your scarcity mindset:

- Be generous to yourself.

- Invest your money. Investing is a figurative abundance generator before it becomes a literal abundance generator. By investing, you're telling the universe you have more than enough, so now you're investing in the future. You're demonstrating your trust in abundance and your trust in your own wisdom and abilities. Do some research and find a way to invest that's in your wheelhouse. Be thoughtful, gather good advice, and take your time. The right place to invest may change with the times: the stock market, cryptocurrency, real estate, luxury items, a local business. No amount to start with is too small.

- Find public, open sources of abundance. It might be a coffee shop in the nicest or coolest neighborhood in your town, a lush hotel lobby, a library, an art museum, a public park, or a beach that's exclusive but still open. You are worthy of being there.

- Enjoy and derive meaning from physical items you value (we'll discuss art and beauty's capacity to enrich our environment in Chapter 8). Hold them loosely, however. Obsessing over the possibility of something being lost, broken, or stolen reflects a scarcity mindset.

- Use abundant language, because your language defines your perception. Language can either impose limits or shatter them. Never say anything is "too expensive," or even "expensive" at all. Never say things like, "There are no good men/women left." Such statements demonstrate a frame of reference grounded in scarcity. Everything you dream of exists or will exist.

- Practice the following mantras:

  ○ *Time is plentiful.*

  ○ *Wealth is plentiful.*

  ○ *Love is plentiful.*

  ○ *I own the energy I send out into the universe.*

  ○ *I will always find a way.*

  ○ *So much is available to me.*

  ○ *I give, and I receive.*

  ○ *I am abundant.*

  ○ *My gifts are abundant.*

Release your hold on time. Time is abundant and flexible, as we'll discuss in Chapter 10. The more you hurry and worry, the scarcer time will feel, and the more you'll fumble and bungle. The next time you're feeling short on time and in a hurry, stop. Stop completely for five minutes and tell yourself: I command time. Time doesn't control me. Carving out a few moments when time seems oppressive tells the universe that you believe time is abundant. And time *is* abundant. *We make time for what we want to make time for.*

The most powerful way to eliminate a scarcity mindset is practicing generosity toward others. It's impossible to hold a scarcity mindset in the moment you're performing a generous act.

I define being generous as giving to enrich the recipient, without expectation. It's the absence of expectation that affirms abundance. As soon as you give with an expectation—of reciprocation, of love, of acceptance, of a thank you note, of finally feeling whole—you have failed at generosity and succumbed to a scarcity mindset. Giving based on enriching yourself, or what you think the recipient should appreciate (an attempt to control their perspective), is not the practice of generosity. Generosity is about helping someone, but it's also about helping someone *while knowing more than enough is available to you, as well*. The absence of expectation is what conveys to the world how strongly you believe in abundance.

Generosity is about the recipient's perception. As with any loving act, intentions don't matter. The recipient's perception of enrichment without reciprocal obligation matters. You don't get to give someone a gift they don't want, and that you should know they don't want, and call yourself generous. *It's not your call.* The intention might be to add joy to the world generally, or provide reward for hard work, or to fulfill an ethical obligation. You may have no intention at all except for following the guidance of this book. It's all good. The only corrupt intentions are those that expect or desire a particular response from the recipient or the universe. Generosity enriches the recipient (usually in an obvious manner), the giver (not because the recipient will express gratitude or give back, but because the giver is demonstrating that they believe more than enough is available), and the universe (because it literally adds to abundance).

Generosity isn't only about spending money by buying someone a coffee or a meaningful gift, or donating to charity, although those are certainly generous acts. Generosity can be simple, and it is available to even those of us without. You always have something you can give: your spirit; your intellectual, creative, interpersonal, or other gifts; your kindness; or your ability to listen, empathize, and encourage. Gifts to others can include a smile, compliments, and social invitations; introducing someone to new music, a new friend, or a new way of looking at things; helping someone with a move or a job search; and the time you spend listening to someone in pain without glancing at your phone or watch. It's all meaningful. It all adds to what's available for everyone and serves as an exemplar of what's possible.

For those of us raised to hoard and exploit, generosity can be challenging. For example, those who experience a lack of love develop a scarcity mindset around love and can have trouble getting in the habit of giving love freely. We may be stingy, desperately holding on to any crumb we've obtained. We may not want to make anyone feel better than we did or do. We may be suspicious or possessive, or behave like bullies. We may find comfort in thinking others are suffering through the same lack. Even once doing well, we may tend toward greed because our newfound well-being is precious to us and we're worried it could be taken away in a blink.

I've found the only way out of the fear of generosity is to start with moments when the body and mind are at ease, when fear is as absent as possible. It might be being generous to a stranger, or anonymously, or any other manner that contains no potential triggers related to any way your generosity may have been exploited as a child. For example, I grew up in a family where we never threw parties, so throwing parties is one of my favorite ways to practice expressing generosity.

You're capable of generosity. Start small, but celebrate the abundance inherent in your act. Over time, you'll be more motivated to perform generous acts you might not have previously been ready to perform.

Here are some ways you can practice generosity:

- Give big tips.

- Give small gifts whenever you can, wherever you go.

- Embrace opportunities to express congratulations or sympathy.

- Donate to charity (with money, time, used goods, or promotion).

- Host parties, dinners, or picnics.

- Make food for others, or share what food you have.

- Compliment people authentically, especially about things you know they care about.

- Always give with composure and without expectation.

If you make it out of tough circumstances—whether those are financial, emotional or physical—give back to others facing similar challenges, with no expectation of gratitude or reciprocation. Giving back once you've "made it" demonstrates that you're neither desperate to hold onto nor fearful of losing your current well-being. By giving of something generously—your money, your resources, your time, your service, your cheer, your love—you're telling the universe you're not worried about that particular thing being scarce. It shows you're confident in your ability to generate more of whatever it is. The looser your hold is on what you have, the more confidence you'll radiate. You'll start to feel empowered and limitless, and more than enough will become available to you. Everything, good or bad, only multiplies when given.

An important caveat for those of us with C-PTSD is that generosity never demands self-sacrifice. Generosity is about giving *while* taking care of yourself, not after or before. It can be a tough line for us walk. Ensure you're taken care of—materially, emotionally, physically—always. Certain individuals take advantage of generosity. Extricate them from your network quickly.

Scarcity is a lie. A never-ending pool of kindness, love, inspiration, and engagement is available. Tap into it and contribute to it. Remain fully engaged with it, and over time, you'll see it everywhere.

Eliminate Envy by Recognizing It as Inspiration

I grew up in a community where jealousy thickly laced every interaction, unseen but always felt. Immigrants who came from little desperately aimed to prove to others that they had worth and status in this new world. People bragged, judged, showed off, competed, and put others down—both behind their backs and to their faces. These immigrants and their ancestors had lived through horrific times of war, poverty, political upheaval, and rapid industrialization. They grew up feeling as if they were less worthy than citizens of the West, and they fought among themselves for a status they believed was limited.

My community was not unusual. Envy is a part of many communities. Individuals attempt a shortcut to self-worth by comparing themselves to others in their immediate context in hierarchical terms. When they sense that they don't measure up, they feel envy. This leads to a lack of gratitude for how much they have; a failure to share their gifts with members of their community, out of fear of not being good enough; and a sabotaging of themselves as they sabotage their community. As a result, abundance is completely undermined. Envy keeps people distracted, sad, and fearful when they could be working cooperatively to lift up their communities to a higher level of connection and abundance, success, and wealth. Desperation, anxiety, fear about losing status, and even hate all relegate the envious to a prosaic despair. So much goodness is lost to dark competitive energies, when what could be used to build up is used to tear down.[5] And the envious are never a threat to the dominant power structure. As long as people remain short-sighted, addicted to consumption, and fighting among themselves for crumbs of status, they won't band together, hold the elites accountable, or fight for deeper changes in society.

Envy is complicated. Experiencing actual, literal abundance doesn't obviate envy (let alone lead to a sense of abundance); in fact, at times, abundance may inflate it. If someone defines themselves by their wealth, their surface-level sense of self (they are probably disconnected from their authentic self) is acutely vulnerable to any perceived threat. Many people in wealthy communities compete over everything possible, desperate to stand out among other similarly wealthy people.

Envy is a strong natural emotion that some struggle with more than others. It's also one of the most irrational emotions, grounded in scarcity and a lack of self-worth. You may choose to think limits of abundance exist, but even so, it's utterly irrational to believe that the supplies of wealth, love, creativity, and well-being are so limited that if one person has them, you can't also have them.

Of course, envy has nothing to do with rationality. Envy arises from not feeling good enough, and from thinking what someone else has makes *them* good enough, which in turn reminds you of why you don't feel good. If you permit envy to drive your thoughts, beliefs, and ideas, you won't see abundance.

Choose to believe that perpetual opportunities exist. You may not be able to have exactly what someone else has, but anything exact should not be coveted. You want the authentic thing. If you envy someone for having an attractive, fun, loving spouse, go out and find one yourself. You can't have theirs, but you can have someone just as great. You may not be able to be as talented a painter as someone else is, but maybe you can be a talented designer within a niche market. If someone has a material possession you'd like, make a plan to earn the money to purchase it or find a substitute you like as much. Maybe you didn't get the starring role in this play, but you could get it in the next one. Plays are a good model because there are multiple productions every year at multiple theaters. You won't have it tomorrow (or maybe you will), but if you believe in perpetual opportunities, *you'll have it*.

Envy, like all strong emotions, carries energy that can be transformed from depleting to expansive. We can transform envy into inspiration by choosing to be motivated by what we initially envy—a practice that, over time, dissipates instances of reflexive envy.

The fact that someone has what you want means it's *doable*. If they have it or can do it, *so can you*. While envy is internal, dark, and distracting, a mire of resigned mediocrity, inspiration is—well, inspiring. Inspiration stimulates thoughts and ideas that demand embodiment. Inspiration can even be harder than envy because it demands action, while envy is inert.

Ask: What do I want that this other person has? Awareness of what you want is the first step to attaining it. And then: Why do I think I can't have it? Become aware of the role of your limiting beliefs, and then choose to take action that aligns with your ultimate goals instead. If you're feeling envious, project admiration and inspiration—or, at the very least, be appropriately congratulatory and courteous. Choose to act like, and thereby become, someone who is not threatened by others' success.

Find people to inspire you, whether they are famous or in your community. Think of what you admire about them and know you can cultivate the same. This may be a character trait like confidence, or a certain style of dress or lifestyle. Of course, inspiration is *not* copying. Copying is creepy and inauthentic, and it will set you back. You can be inspired and informed by someone else's path, but always make your own. When you know what you actually want, not what society or a particular social group tells you to want (we'll discuss this in Chapter 7), your desires and intentions become manifestly distinct to you.

It doesn't matter if someone arrives at the place you'd like to be more quickly than you. It's only a moment. It's unproductive to think that a moment in time defines who you are. When you arrive at that same place, the past will be a memory and won't matter. Sometimes you have to wait and they don't. Sometimes they take a turn you don't want to take, or vice versa. It's not always "fair," but it's not exactly unfair either. Envy is focused on a moment in time, as if that moment is the end all be all. There is no "end." Life moves on, moment to moment. There is "happy," but there is no "ending."

Most areas of life are ripe for expansion, adaptation, and transformation. Create, and don't compete for what's been created. Abundance means you could write a book tomorrow on the same topic as this book, and your book would not take away from my book; your book would add more healing and empowerment to the universe, and our ideas could interact in turn, helping readers all the more. For you to do something good, something creative, something brave, would take nothing away from me. It would only add to the abundance of the universe.

Choose to believe that *success is contagious*. You can do anything. And the more successful people you have in your life, the more their success will influence you positively. The more success people find, the more they can give to the people around them. Be grateful that people you know and/or love are succeeding. Be admiring. Be inspired. YOU CAN DO ANYTHING, TOO.

The most effective way to obviate envy while facilitating abundance is experiencing and expressing gratitude. Gratitude is an abundance accelerator. Gratitude displaces feelings of envy, shame, and scarcity. When you appreciate what you have, you're telling the universe what you enjoy while adding to total abundance.

Everyone has something for which they can express gratitude. It may be large things, such as your health, loved ones, wealth, opportunity, travel, stability, or adventure. It may be small things, such as a good meal, the sun shining, a stranger holding the door open for you, or a hug from a loved one. Your circumstances may be truly awful in this moment, or you may feel imprisoned in an overwhelming darkness that has little to do with your circumstances. Start small. Find something for which to be grateful. For example, the fact that you are willing to read these words shows that you have an open mind and a flourishing belief that more is possible than what you see. Be grateful for your access to information. Be grateful that you are not alone on your journey. Break down every element of your being and existence, because you undoubtedly have gifts you take for granted.

Use your object of envy as a starting point for what you should actually be grateful for:

- Instead of being envious of a young person, be grateful for your age.

- Instead of being jealous of someone with generational wealth, be grateful for the opportunity to build your own wealth on your own terms.

- Instead of being jealous of someone else's beauty, identify the beautiful aspects of yourself and emphasize and celebrate them. Beauty is a mindset.

- Instead of being jealous of someone's wonderful family, build up your network with good people. Eventually, you'll create your own wonderful family.

- Instead of being jealous of someone's seemingly perfect childhood, be grateful that you're aware and healing.

Gratitude journals are popular and a great way to set gratitude into motion, but they can be hard to maintain over time. Jot down what you're grateful for (almost) every day, at whatever time works best for you. Evening is often suggested, as it can be a time to look back at the day. I prefer writing down what I'm grateful for in the mornings, as I tend to feel more inspired and as if the universe is my oyster in the early hours. Practicing gratitude also infuses the beginning of the day with positive energy. If you find it hard to commit to gratitude as an everyday practice, write an email to yourself with the object of gratitude as the subject line and remind yourself to look back at it. This practice can be done anywhere and anytime, interweaving feelings of appreciation throughout your day. Write about a fun time with friends, finding a great parking spot, or receiving a compliment from a stranger. Over time, you won't have to note your gratitude because it will become an indelible part of how you approach each day.

Have gratitude for what you have and what you know you will have. Have gratitude for your dreams, as if they were already realized. For example, I could write the acknowledgments to this book, thanking all the people who have supported and encouraged me on my journey.

Expressing meaningful gratitude to another person is a powerful propellent within the network of connection. Appreciate people for what they spent time and thought on, and for the risks they've taken. They will feel seen and empowered. Your relationship with them will be enriched. And the more you celebrate the good people in your life, the more good people will enter it.

If something surprising, annoying, or frustrating happens, express gratitude for the resolution, particularly if it's quick. Just yesterday, I broke a glass bottle in the garage and was extremely frustrated that I had to spend time picking up pieces of glass under and around the car. Ultimately, it only took about five minutes. So instead of focusing on the disturbance, I focused on and expressed gratitude for the quick resolution. You may have an uncomfortable interaction with someone; express gratitude that it's over.

Some of us with C-PTSD, particularly those with narcissistic parents, may have had gratitude used against us like a cudgel. My father frequently told me I wasn't "grateful"—for having a roof over my head and food to eat, for not being more severely abused, and for not being thrown out of the house the day I turned eighteen. Never mind everything else going on; I was to be effusively appreciative. If you were raised in a similar way, let go of this distorted view of gratitude. Acknowledge it as profoundly unhelpful. Never say "thank you" because you're afraid—never say *anything* because you're afraid. Say "thank you" because you mean it. You know, intuitively, deep down within yourself, what you should be grateful for, just like I knew then (and knew they weren't the things held over my head). Gratitude should never be used in a manipulative fashion, by you or anyone else.

***

When we barely have the reserves to survive, physically and emotionally, it takes a tremendous mindset shift and enormous strength to turn to abundance. And once we're healing, the healing process can crowd out visions of abundance as we focus on achieving the stability and safety that feel so good. Healing can feel like such an ordeal that we may convince ourselves simply having peace is enough. *More than enough is never too much.* Let abundance in now, in tandem with the practices in this book. Believe that what you want and need exists, and use your imagination to see it making its way to you.

Chapter 2

Practice Imagining

Truth is a matter of the imagination.
Ursula K. LeGuin, Left Hand of Darkness

Imagination will often carry us to worlds that never were, but without it we go nowhere.
Carl Sagan, Cosmos

The most powerful way to let abundance in is to reconnect to your imagination. Our imaginations are the greatest power in the world. Our imaginations generate the ideas that lead us to know and bring forth our dreams, ideas that dissolve limits and fuel abundance. Ideas heal us. And I don't think it's an overstatement to say ideas save us.

Discussing the imagination is challenging for me, because for a long time I thought my imagination was dead, or at least deadened by a wounded narrator who was adamant that I didn't need it. I also thought that attaining goals was a matter-of-fact, rational process. I still can't claim to be a highly imaginative person, but reconnecting to my imagination led me to write again, to find healing through my writing, and to share this book with you.

Practicing the imagination means empowering the part of you that comes up with ideas, and then using those ideas to shape your perception of what's possible.

While perception and imagination are generally thought of as distinct from each other—one based on "reality", and the other based on "fantasy"—they're intimately connected. Ideas are simply thoughts of new possibilities. Perception, on the other hand, is what we observe and feel through our mind and our body's senses. The only way we can see the world is through the intermediaries of our senses, and these intermediaries are informed by our genetic propensities, the conditioning of our culture, our adaptations to our particular environment, and our instinct to survive and thrive. We see through our rose-colored glasses, or Asperger's, or anxiety. Or our trauma.

We don't live in an objective "reality." Each of us lives in a perception of reality created by our own thinking. If a different version of reality exists, it's unknowable to us. Our human (imperfect, fallible, and extraordinary) minds are our only means of perceiving reality. The human mind is full of biases and heuristics that compromise its "accuracy", while often aiding its pure survival. Mountains of scientific data reflect that our minds are constantly missing things while exaggerating others, and are indelibly shaped by our insecurities, traumas, proclivities, and neurodiversity. Numerous philosophers—from Plato to Descartes to Kant to the postmodernists—have also explored the idea that a reality exists that is not known.

Our perceptions have been shaped (inexcusably so, for those of us with C-PTSD) by forces outside of our control. We can accept that reality, and also embrace the fact that to the extent we're open to experience, insight, and ideas, we can transform our perception. Our perceptions are inherently changeable. Think about the way your mindset has changed over the years after different types of experiences. Think about the way someone in a cult perceives the cult's messaging and culture as ethical and true, but after escaping can't comprehend how they used to think the way they did. Think about how immersing yourself in a different culture can reshape your perception of the world.

Understanding that reality is made through perception and that you can shape your perception allows you to direct your reality in the only way possible. Our thoughts, beliefs, and ideas—and the actions they inspire—are the only type of control we can exert over what we make happen for us.

So, if we believe our dreams are possible and that life tends to go well for us, we'll see the sunny side, the opportunities, the resources, and the relationships. We'll be brave and pursue them. We won't give up. More often than not, the universe will respond in kind.

Keep in mind the following:

- You own your thoughts, beliefs, and ideas.

- Your perception is a gift, a power, and a responsibility.

- Aspire to believe you are worthy.

- Aspire to believe you will heal.

- Aspire to imagine endless possibilities.

"Aspire," because if you have C-PTSD, it can be hard to perceive these things. We don't have the complete control over our perception that some other self-empowerment authors espouse. Nothing is 100 percent. Everything is a spectrum. Instead of thinking we should control 100 percent of our perception and berating ourselves when we have negative thoughts, we should aim to ensure that about 85 percent of our thoughts, beliefs, and ideas trend toward the positive, the boundless, and the empowered.

The 85 percent rule was originally developed from analyzing the performances of elite sprinters. It states that doing something at 85 percent of maximum effort will produce better results than doing it at 100 percent effort. Counterintuitively, that means to reach maximum output (here, maximum results), you actually refrain from giving maximum effort. Operating at 100 percent effort all the time results in exhaustion, burnout, and less optimal results. Like most athletic performance, owning your thoughts, beliefs, and ideas is more about relaxation, form, and optimizing your positive energy than it is about working hard. Being overly tense, fixated on perfection, or obsessed with an annoying thought that refuses to submit keeps you from aligning with your highest self.

In some ways, this process is circular, because your perception of effort—how hard you *feel* you're working to steer your perception towards the aspirational—is what matters. You should feel as if you are proceeding at a steady pace, always with room to breathe, always holding yourself accountable while not being too hard on yourself. You can't feel as if you are struggling or desperate to catch up.

Aspire to master 85 percent of your perception. Let the remaining 15 percent go. Recognize the 15 percent and hold it tight for a moment—be curious about it, ask it questions (for example, what triggered the limiting belief, or why is the limiting belief more comfortable than the aspirational one?)—and then let it go. Let it go, because the energy you would spend trying to rein it in would deplete you and undermine the entire effort. Funnily enough, letting go of the 15 percent makes it more likely you'll eventually transform it as well, as it will only live on in a weaker, more dissipated form.

Maybe even believing at an 85 percent level that you can heal and bring forth what you want seems impossible to you. Choose to start to believe that *it's possible*. Practice believing that *it's possible*. ANYTHING AND EVERYTHING IS POSSIBLE.

To start, you can say (aloud or in your mind) or write affirmations like these:

- *I am worthy of a life as good as the best.*

- *I am capable of extraordinary acts.*

- *I welcome love.*

- *I am open to ideas.*

- *I am open to opportunity.*

- *Things work out well for me.*

- *I am treated well.*

- *I trust myself.*

- *I have compassion for myself.*

- *Anything is possible.*

You can find many more examples online. Practice using your affirmations over and over again. I like writing mine down from time to time. I also like repeating them while doing breathwork (more on that in Chapter 6), taking a walk, running, or riding a bike, and especially when gazing up at a blue sky or beautiful trees. Your own perception-shaping affirmations should be the background music to your life. If you experience resistance to an affirmation, acknowledge, question, and release it. You may want to journal about it, thinking through why you find a particular affirmation so hard to believe. Repeating the affirmations a million times will never be enough if you're doing so while holding internal resistance. The practice will become easier over time as this internal resistance dissolves.

When I place certain statements in this book, I'm practicing affirmations with you, weaving them in as we go along. Affirmations are critical to shaping your perception, but they aren't enough. To know and see what you want, to believe it's real and true, you'll need your imagination.

The imagination is the space where thoughts exist unencumbered from the constraints of old trauma, conditioning, and adaptations to your environment. These thoughts can nourish what's possible for you, your community, and the universe. Your imagination is the most fertile and vibrant element of your mind, and harnessing it can make your reality all the more fertile and vibrant. Even if you're not so sure about the power of perception, think about the way ideas fuel reality. Ideas turn to form, or visible things, all the time—whether it's an invention or an invitation design, a dish you're cooking for dinner, or a route you're taking to work. Ideas enter your perception and are realized when you decide to act upon them. Ideas lead to the creation of something—anything—real.

Using your imagination means giving your mind the freedom to think without limits. It means letting thoughts run a little wild. It means not judging your ideas but being curious about them and seeing where they take you. Using your imagination will lead you to gain the insights, epiphanies, ideas, and moments of wonder that will inspire you; show you what's possible; reveal your best and most authentic dreams and the paths to realizing them; and ultimately give you a positive, visionary perception of yourself and the universe. Using your imagination allows you to sideline the wounded narrator in favor of the authentic self.

Your imagination is a gift that begets gifts. Gifts of the imagination are all around us. Everything you experience with your senses is a result of someone's imagination, or several interconnected imaginations. Every innovation, every technology, every advancement, every book, and every work of earth-shattering art and life-changing music is the result of the human imagination.

Take yourself out of your suspicion about what's possible, take yourself out of any questions about your self-worth and whether you're good enough to create, and take yourself out of all judgments, fears, and even excitement about these words. Just marvel at the human capacity for imagination.

Frida Kahlo's paintings. The mural on the side of a city building. One World Trade Center. Artificial intelligence. Cars. Electric cars. Airplanes. Space ships. Taylor Swift's music. Tupac Shakur's music. Mozart's music. The music your kids sing at preschool. The coffee shop down the street. The playground down the street. Your house. Your clothing. Every television show or TikTok video you waste your time watching. The chair you're sitting in right now. The book in your hands—its content, its font, its cover design, the way it feels in your hands. It all came from imagination. All of it started inside the mind of an individual, or several individuals who worked together, or was built on top of what came before. And so on and so on, resulting in the universe we have today, and on it continues.

These creators made real what was once only in their minds. They made real what others may never have thought possible. They showed people something they never knew they were missing, and nothing was ever the same. That's the power of ideas. Ideas break through what is currently true and bring forth what *will be* true.

You are a creator. We are all creators, whether we like it or not. Even by deciding to do nothing, to imagine nothing, we're choosing to create nothingness. You are better than nothingness. You are capable of creative acts.

Do you feel disconnected from your imagination? Do you not even see the point in using it as an adult? Is it hard for you to think of much that seems interesting, or do you internally rebuke yourself for wasting your time with frivolity? Do you think you should be "realistic" and "practical"?

It's easy to think according to appearances, routines, and what is right in front of you. It takes work to break down the limits formed by cultural conditioning, which can take many forms. For example, imagination is suppressed by conservative cultures or communities that place undue pressure on their children to "succeed." Sadly, this suppression is prevalent in most social classes in modern society, in different variations. Depending on your environment, you may be pressured to become a lawyer, a doctor, an influencer, a nursing assistant, a mechanic, or a stay-at-home wife and mother—whatever appears most reliable to the superficially powerful in your community. You may have been encouraged by your family or community to make money in the most predictable way possible, even by well-meaning parents. They were conditioned to think that way, to focus on survival (which may have differing definitions itself), and to be fearful of the worst-case scenario (which also has highly variable definitions), and now they can't see beyond their constrained view of reality. The worst-case scenario may be prison in one community and working at a fast-food restaurant in another. These dynamics are heavily influenced by the ruthless nature of capitalism. Capitalism oils its wheels on feelings of unworthiness that lead to individuals striving to succeed in the hopes of feeling whole, loved, and deserving.

For those of us with C-PTSD, imagination is sometimes subsumed in service of the drive to survive or escape. Someone existing in a perpetual state of hypervigilance doesn't have the real-time capacity to engage their imagination. Living in fear of rageful attacks or episodes of disoriented drunkenness, while being held responsible for the well-being of my entire family, did not leave much space for my imagination as a child. Sometimes reality is too full of pain to make easy room for the imagination. In hard times, when we are stuck, for whatever reason, the idea of using the imagination can be devastating. It's too full of hope. Entertaining aspirational visions only to be repeatedly disappointed can be soul-crushing and leave us feeling stupid and weak.

I remember using my imagination at times, and I think those experiences in many ways saved me. Reading, riding my bike while making up stories in my head, and playing imaginative games with neighborhood children (like creating pretend kitchens out of other people's garbage) brought me joy, escape, and the feeling that other ways of being and living were possible. Maybe those experiences eventually led me out and into the world of greater possibility. I can't be sure, though; at some point, I chose the comfort of "realism" and "practicality" over my already tenuous connection to my imagination.

So, if you struggle to connect with your imagination, I hear you. If you are stuck, I hear you. I'm no longer living under the threat of emotional and physical pain, but I still struggle with imagination, play, visualization, and even remembering my dreams. My body and mind are deeply, subconsciously programmed for survival and to "protect" me in dangerous circumstances I no longer live within. It has taken the practices described here to begin to undo that programming and to value and honor my imagination, and everyone else's.

I now think of my imagination as my partner. Whenever I have an idea, I'm using my imagination. It's there with me. I'm innovating all the time—from scheduling my day, planning a vacation, or writing an email. That baseline imagination is a part of me, and all I have to do is expand upon it. I have a robust force of will that saved my life, but I know it is only through creative acts that I not merely settle for survival but live a life as good as the best.

Bringing your mind and body into a regulated and integrated state through the practices and integration therapies discussed in this book will help liberate your imagination from the darkness of your injury. But even those who have gone through life relatively unscathed by trauma are taught not to waste time on their imaginations. For example, if your parents have a toxic relationship or go through an ugly divorce, and you didn't see happy families in real life while you were growing up, how could you even begin to imagine one? If you grew up in urban poverty, would you dream of being an entrepreneur? If you grew up in rural Iowa, would you dream of being a transgressive artist? If you grew up in a hyper-privileged big-city suburb full of doctors, lawyers, and CEOs, would you ever imagine being a political activist? Even economically privileged people, even people with good-to-great parents, even people who had a sitcom-style childhood, may have been conditioned to reject their imagination. But no matter how lost or nonexistent your imagination feels, you can connect to it.

Regardless of what your circumstances are or have been, *you have a right to ideas.*

You have an inherent right to dream.

You have a right to dream big or small, to daydream, to envision, to play inside your mind. That is your right, and don't dare let a cruel parent, poverty, bias, unspeakable hardship, a conservative culture, or even the double-edged weight of privilege take that right away from you. You don't have to be "serious" or "practical" all the time. You are not controlled by false, fear-based constructs.

Therefore, the first step is to eliminate the words "realistic" and "practical" from your vocabulary. Remind yourself that the idea of being "realistic" is extraordinarily limiting. It speaks to the lowest common denominator. "Realistic expectations" are a way the powerful keep the less powerful down. Capitalism is fueled by the generative and entrepreneurial, but it is also fueled by a larger population agreeing to serve as minions. Don't be a minion.

In fact, most people are not unrealistic enough. One study demonstrated that a reason male entrepreneurs succeed more often than female entrepreneurs may be precisely because they are more unrealistic.[6] Entrepreneurs frequently fail before they find success, and unfortunately, in the study, disproportionately more women than men were discouraged from trying again after such failures. As "rational" as it may seem to give up after multiple failures, more men succeed because they don't.

One of my favorite childhood books and present-day musicals is *Matilda*. Matilda is an extraordinarily gifted young girl trapped in terrible circumstances. She has mean parents who don't see her for who she is, and a horrific headmistress at her school who scapegoats her. Her only life rafts are books and her teacher, Ms. Honey, until she discovers the power of her imagination. First, she uses her imagination to play tricks on those who are cruel to her, but eventually she realizes she can move physical objects with her mind. Ultimately, Matilda uses her imaginative gifts to free herself and her classmates from the evil headmistress, and to free herself from her family.

Matilda saves herself through a shift in her perception and the awakening of her imagination. She takes ownership of her life the only way she can, by honoring her imagination. The initial spark is reading, which inspires awe and stimulates her curiosity. Her imagination and confidence flourish with Ms. Honey's support. With practice and experimentation, she follows her imagination to surprising and beautiful places. I interpret the story as not being about whether it's possible to move objects with one's mind or not, but rather as being about what we let ourselves *believe* is possible. Matilda doesn't engage in self-pity, even though she is consistently shamed by those entrusted to care for her. She knows she must write her own story. As a child, her only power is her mind, and she uses it to free herself.

Our ideas reveal potential, what can be if we allow it to emerge and choose to believe in it. Once we see what can be, we're motivated to perform creative acts that add to the abundance of the universe. These creative acts also help us regulate and integrate, to connect to others, and to reaffirm beliefs in power and possibility. Our creative acts make anything possible.

Daydream

Yes, daydream. The fun kind of daydreaming is good for you.

Clinical psychologist Jerome Singer established three main styles of daydreaming: Positive-Constructive Daydreaming (playful, wishful, and constructive imagery), Guilty-Dysphoric Daydreaming (obsessive, anguished fantasies), and Poor Attentional Control (difficulty directing and sustaining focus). While the latter two can be problematic, Positive-Constructive Daydreaming had enormous benefits. It's associated with creativity, planning, problem-solving, openness to experience, curiosity, sensitivity, memory consolidation, self-reflection, and the exploration of ideas, feelings, and sensations. Positive-Constructive Daydreaming uses the default mode network, which is comprised of functional, multi-regional brain activity that becomes most active when the brain is at rest (and not engaged in an external task). A healthy default mode network plays a critical role in healthy mental functioning.

Singer's research suggests that daydreaming, imagination, and fantasy are essential elements of well-being. Mind-wandering is often characterized as a mistake, a mental mishap, or a cognitive failure. At times, our mind wanders without our permission or awareness, but mind wandering can also be exquisitely volitional. Volitional mind wandering is the conscious choice to disengage the mind from external tasks and perceptions and focus instead on an internal stream of thought. It involves "meta-awareness"—consciousness the whole way through, from the choice being made to focus inward to the awareness of what arises. Positive-Constructive Daydreaming requires the ability to switch easily back and forth between different streams of consciousness. It's a form of the inward reflection that was extolled by Enlightenment philosophers, who believed such reflection empowered people to direct their own lives. Inward reflection is a skill, and therefore it can be practiced and improved.

Given its myriad benefits, it's appalling that we don't learn how to engage in Positive-Constructive Daydreaming while we're children in school. Instead of encouraging healthy daydreaming, modern society conditions it out of us for the sake of culturally-approved "productivity." We're taught that this productivity requires high attentional demand. The rigid structure of the modern education system labels children who struggle with high attentional demand (but may excel at daydreaming) with ADD/ADHD. These children are considered neurodivergent as a result of engaging in an activity that would benefit us all.

High attentional demand and focus have their place, but they exhaust the brain. Remember the 85 percent rule. Your mind needs to be released from these demands before it can even begin the process of Positive-Constructive Daydreaming.

The best way to start the practice of Positive-Constructive Daydreaming is to begin a low-key activity, like knitting, gardening, walking, cycling, or even light housework. First, embrace the mental boredom of it. Second, allow your mind to wander. Imagine something playful, like swimming, traveling to a new city, or attending a concert by your favorite artist. Hold the wishful image in your mind while continuing the low-key activity. See if more images take shape and where they take you. Be conscious of your stream of thought, but don't be controlling. Allow yourself to follow your stream of thought while remaining mostly unfocused. If thoughts arise that you enjoy, or if you think of an intention or dream, enjoy it. Delight in the thought and take your time with it. See where else it leads. If you're afraid (as I often was when I began this practice), remember that you were born knowing how to do this.

If a negative or even practical thought inserts itself, label it as unhelpful. When we reappraise our thoughts, we reduce activity in the amygdala, the part of our brain responsible for processing our memories and emotions—especially fear and anxiety. Stay present and accept any uncomfortable sensations instead of rigorously fighting them; they will pass if you let them. This is not the time to question or analyze these thoughts, because the aim is to daydream. Circle back to the original image. Stay in a resting, unfocused state, where your mind will recharge, give birth to and connect ideas, and gently excavate memories. When you're ready to conclude your daydreaming, acknowledge the compelling ideas that arose and tuck them back into the focused part of your perception for keeps. Your thoughts, beliefs, and ideas will be enriched and refined.

Maybe your life is super hard right now, requiring high attentional demand. Maybe you're stressed about paying your bills, keeping a roof over your head, or supporting an ill family member. Maybe you're in physical or mental pain. Daydreaming sounds like a ridiculous proposition with reality so full, with the demands on your attention so high.

Trust that your mind is free if you believe it is, no matter what your circumstances. *It's all yours.* Even if you're physically trapped, your mind can travel anywhere, across time and space.

Find twenty minutes and begin the low-key activity in the safest and calmest environment you can find. Disengage from your present and let—or force, if you need to—your mind to wander. If your present is a horror, your daydreaming stream will inevitably fall off track. It will be harder for you than it is for someone with fewer worries. Whenever the stream falls off track, label the thoughts as unwelcome and gently guide your mind back to rest. If you're stuck, picture a dolphin, a dog, or a cat. Pick whichever animal you like best, and think about his or her day. It's awkward, but the transition to daydreaming is inherently awkward for some of us. Compel this thought, as many times as you need to, and then see where your daydream goes. Keep trying over and over again. Daydream your way out of the horror.

Positive-Constructive Daydreaming is magical. It allows your mind to escape a horrific present before your body can—and eventually, in combination with the practice of bringing forth discussed in Chapter 4, will pull your body through to escape as well. Telling people to accept the present, to think of it as an outcome of their thoughts, is an absolutely awful thing to do to people in a challenging circumstance. If "now" is terrible, you should absolutely not accept it. If "now" involves suffering, wholeheartedly reject it. Acknowledge the temporary nature of the "now." Use your imagination to escape "now" before your physical body is able to do so. Let your imagination carve the escape path. Give your mind the permission to push you forward.

Embrace Ambiguity

Embrace the power of uncertainty. In the 1990s, researchers Arie Kruglanski and Donna Webster introduced the concept of "need for cognitive closure" (NFCC). A person's NFCC represents their need for an answer, on any given topic, versus their inclination to embrace ambiguity (and the accompanying confusion). Someone with high NFCC is more likely to: want to reach a conclusion quickly; enjoy black and white stories with simple morals; quickly form judgments about other people or groups; and feel uncomfortable lacking a definitive answer to a question, issue, or plot in film or book.

In contrast, someone with lower NFCC is more likely to: accept nuance and ambiguous endings (for example, understanding that good people can do bad things and vice versa); be comfortable not knowing something; and score higher on creativity assessments. Other researchers have demonstrated that groups comprised of people low in NFCC produced a higher quantity of ideas and more original ideas than groups comprised of people with high NFCC, resulting in more productive outcomes to projects.[7]

For some of us, high NFCC is our trauma response. NFCC naturally goes up when someone is threatened, and it goes down when they feel safe. If you had a stressful childhood during which you were required to remain on high alert to danger at all times to protect yourself, you may experience high NFCC as an adult. If mistakes were dangerous (either emotionally or physically), you probably didn't feel safe making them, and feeling it's safe to make mistakes is required for low NFCC. One study found that high NFCC was significantly positively correlated with maladaptive perfectionism,[8] which can also be a consequence of childhood trauma. Maladaptive perfectionism entails setting extraordinarily high standards and then punishing yourself with harsh criticism when failing to meet them—when failing to be "perfect". This leads to low self-worth, feelings of distress, anxiety, and depression, and sometimes the withholding of subsequent effort in order to preserve the false belief that being perfect is a requirement for existence.

It may be hard for you to accept that you don't have all the answers, let alone that answers aren't always the answer; it was for me. High NFCC can lead to quick and resolute decisions, which are not only conducive to survival in a tough environment but also generally celebrated in our culture. Decisiveness is considered a positive attribute, but evidence suggests that high NFCC contributes to suboptimal processing strategies and poor decision-making. A discomfort with nuance, complexity, and uncertainty can lead to decreased creativity and rationality—and ultimately, bad decisions. As just one example, with respect to investing, investors with high NFCC tend not to update their investment portfolios in line with their risk preferences in changing circumstances, due to a lack of openness to new information and discomfort with re-evaluating a decision that's already been made.[9]

Uncertainty is powerful and forces us to work through the answers we originate on autopilot. This is the only way to reach deeper truths. Acknowledge uncertainty's beauty, power, and inevitability, and then try to surrender to it, for as long as you can. As uncomfortable and unnatural as processing nuance and complexity may be for some of us, only if we try can we cultivate a belief in limitlessness. If we reject ambiguity, we reject possible nuanced paths. If we form a black-and-white, judgmental outlook, we close off refreshing perspectives, inspiring relationships, and unconventional approaches. *Answers aren't always the answer.*

The good news is that NFCC can be lowered to a more advantageous level through the following:

- Read—anything, but fiction works particularly well. One study involved 100 participants assigned to read either a nonfiction essay or a short story. The participants' NFCC levels were assessed after their reading was completed. Those in the short story group experienced a significant decrease in the self-reported need for cognitive closure. The effect was particularly strong for participants who were habitual readers of fiction.[10]

- Foster your psychological safety through the practices set forth in this book. To the extent your drive to seek definitive answers is a trauma response, healing can help you accept the tentative or indeterminate. Recognize that the part of you that demands clear-cut answers is not you, but the wounded narrator programmed from your injury, trying to protect you in a context where it's no longer necessary or conducive. Answers feel good in a momentary, shallow way, but they don't change anything. Embrace insights just as much as you embrace definitive answers.

- Learn to embrace and even revel in problems. Working through problems leads to insights and epiphanies, and your response to a problem tells the universe what you want (and what you're capable of). Becoming comfortable with open, unsolved issues doesn't mean you don't work to solve these problems; it means taking your time with the information, valuing insights as much as determinacy, and not rushing toward resolution. It means letting the solutions emerge, instead of anticipating a particular outcome. Closure is a prison; emergence is freedom. Embrace that resolution is a fleeting moment, quickly dislocated due to the dynamic nature of reality.

- Tell yourself, over and over again, that you're okay with open-endedness, nuance, and complexity—that they are safe and that you are safe. Wrap yourself in these words. Eventually, they will become true. Find ways to bring open-endedness, nuance, and complexity into everyday conversations, whether they concern thinking about the behavior of a friend or the state of politics or the economy. One of the easiest ways to do this is to simply ask questions. Things won't look black and white anymore, but you'll come closer to the truth.

Lowering your NFCC may seem demanding and even terrifying, but it prepares you for the journey to healing and realizing your dreams, which can also feel demanding and terrifying in new ways. The known may feel safe, but it's also often confining and even unsettling. The journey to a life as good as the best exists in the unknown and unpredictable, the space of possibilities within which freedom, contentment, and everything else you want can be reached. Become comfortable in this space, as it is where the possibility of anything different than the life you're leading right now exists. Become comfortable with a lack of determinacy, because it will always be with you, even when you attain what you want. Our culture encourages us to button up our attainments in a way that can be reflected on a holiday card or in a LinkedIn post, but attainment is one moment on a journey, and that moment quickly shifts under our feet. It's terrifying—but also beautiful.

Be Curious

One extraordinarily helpful way to facilitate acceptance of open-endedness, nuance, and complexity is to embrace and encourage your own curiosity. Curiosity is desiring to know, seeking to understand, and enjoying the journey to knowing and understanding. While ambiguity means that some questions are unanswerable or may have multiple answers, curiosity means wanting whatever answers we can get whenever we can get them, anyway. By enjoying the journey to understanding, we take the pressure off ourselves to immediately know all the answers, and we reside in the space of receptivity. Not knowing means having a reason to seek knowledge, and *seeking* knowledge makes life interesting. Making sense of the unusual elevates us mentally and emotionally.

Curiosity enriches and refines our thoughts, beliefs, and ideas through many paths. For example, curiosity is associated with a wide scope of attention (the curious tend to explore more of a visual scene with their eyes).[11] A wide scope of attention means gathering more diverse information, creating a more expansive perception and a richer ground for learning and ideas. Curious people also tend to be happier and less stressed.[12]

Here are some ways to facilitate curiosity:

- Ask people (or the world—i.e., use books, the Internet, or AI) questions. As hard as it may seem at first, you can and will think of a question. It can be about absolutely *anything*. If you see something new mentioned in a news article or program, seek more answers and information. Ask people questions about themselves—their hobbies, their interests, their travels. Even if part of you doesn't care, ask. You may be surprised by what you learn.

- While asking people questions, don't be annoying or invasive, and suspend all judgment. Imagine your mind is open, and it will be. Imagine yourself trying to understand the world better by engaging with one extraordinary person at a time.

- Actively listen to others. Don't spend your time thinking of what to say next or rushing to speak.

- Seek out novelty. Simply changing the lighting or temperature in the place you work all day can trigger a surge of curiosity and creativity. On the day I wrote this page, I went to a new coffee shop and changed seats three times while there. You can also change your route to work or your evening routine, try a new cuisine, or go to an art exhibit outside of your comfort zone.

- Use a journal or a notebook. Write down your thoughts, observations, feelings, and insights. Write down dreams you remember. Writing something down compels us to slow down and stimulates curiosity.

- Find enjoyable learning and dive in. It could be anything in which you have the slightest interest. For example, I recently read an encyclopedia of cocktails.

- Explore your environment.

- Welcome boredom. For those of us with C-PTSD, boredom is the best break our mind gives us.

- Try to understand multiple viewpoints. Take an issue and consider it from all sides. Be curious about the arguments for and against it.

- Don't make assumptions. The only healthy assumption is that there's always more to learn.

Visualize

Visualization is integral to the imagination. The world without words is a powerful means to ideas that can become reality. Andre Breton, the founder of Surrealism, noted that "the man who cannot visualize a horse galloping on a tomato is an idiot."

Can you visualize it?

It's okay if you can't. You may just be someone with C-PTSD.

The first time I tried, I struggled. I saw the horse, and I saw the tomato, but it was incoherent. As I wrote this book, I'd return to the image each time I reviewed this section. And each time, the image became easier to visualize. I began to experience it as a full scene (for example, I pictured the tomato juice spraying out of the tomato as the horse galloped, and I heard a few neighs from the horse).

Here are a few other practice images to visualize:

- A teddy bear driving a dump truck

- A sheep sleeping on an orange

- A baby orangutan eating an ice cream cone

These examples are purposely silly and without stakes. The point is practice. Even in these examples without stakes, note where your imagination struggles. When I visualized the horse galloping on the tomato, my struggle was in picturing the movement. And I frequently, without even realizing it, imagined the scene as a cartoon. For you, the struggle may be the horse's color or eyes, or the sound that's made when the horse gallops.

The struggle you have points to a specific weakness in your visualization abilities. Be curious about such weaknesses, which are places of resistance formed by fear, discomfort, or simply a belief that visualizing is a waste of time. Make an effort to determine where these beliefs come from. Awareness is the origination of transformation. Gently work in the missing visual or auditory elements. Take time to fully realize a simple vision, and then add more complexity over time.

Fear affects visualization in another way, as well. Thoughts that push up against the culturally approved or personally acceptable can feel untamed and scary. We may see images in our own visualizations that feel wild and outside of the bounds we, in a knee-jerk reaction, want to impose. We may see images related to trauma. If you see images that disturb you, for whatever reason, don't panic, don't choose anxiety, don't struggle, don't shut down, and don't judge yourself. Suppression never works. Berating yourself never works. Acknowledge your thoughts and any discomfort, darkness, or lack of intention on your part. Label the image as unhelpful or unwelcome. Let it dissipate or transform into something better.

Before turning to the visualization of something more personal with stakes, you can start small, or at least with something adjacent to your comfort zone. You can imagine a particular bird you like, such as a hawk or a blue jay. You'll be surprised how quickly one is brought into your real-life view purely through imagining it. But even if it isn't, it's just a bird. Enjoy the visualization of it. Allow your imagination to feel playful and powerful.

Next, find a subject area that is a good mix of high and low stakes. I have fun imagining my kids' birthday parties as I plan them. I don't focus on every detail, but rather the details that are important to me. For my son's first birthday, I visualized the food truck I wanted in our driveway. Getting the food truck to our home required various steps, but I found the vision motivated me through mundane planning and ensured a successful outcome.

Another great way to force visualization is to read fiction, or narrative nonfiction, and visualize what you're reading. The beauty of reading is that visions aren't imposed on you as they would be while consuming media with a visual component, such as television, movies, websites, and social media. Instead, partial details provided by text encourage you to construct a vision. Reading also shows you what's possible (something other forms of media can do, as well). When I was a child, feeling trapped in my circumstances, reading not only made me feel less alone, but it also opened up possibilities. Reading generated and fed the ideas that saved me. The power of reading terrifies those who would rather shut down the imagination. Fight for books. A whole world of possibility, inspiration, and empathy lives in the written word.

Consider a Social Media Pause

As much as the Internet and social media have engendered new forms of connection, community, and the sharing of arts and knowledge, the bulk of their content is antithetical to the imagination. I'm going to say something that's controversial for a writer who wants their book read in today's age: The Internet and social media do more harm than good to the imagination. The Internet and social media are crowded with crude and common data, language, and images. They are rife with imitations, simulations, desperation, despair, envy, denigration, and sloppy spelling and grammar. Much of the supposed creativity on display online entails conformity in disguise, the following of a trend that only contains minor, insignificant alterations from the mainstream.

If you feel stuck and disconnected from your imagination, or if you feel unmotivated, or as if your energy is weak or watered down, remove yourself from social media and maybe even the Internet—ideally entirely, but at least for the most part. Even if it's where you imagine the audience for your creative expression, take a step away first.

It's a form of dopamine detox. A dopamine detox entails avoiding any kind of pleasure triggers that stimulate dopamine production. Dopamine is a neurotransmitter that affects learning, motivation, sleep, mood, and attention. Dopamine inspires us to act, and due to dopamine, when you perform an act you perceive as pleasurable, your brain is set up to repeat the experience continually.

Phone alerts, texts, and social media provide quick hits of dopamine. They are hyper-stimulating; engaging with them can become addictive. Addictive behaviors generally are not only physically and mentally harmful, but they also consume our thoughts, leaving little room for imagination. Doing a dopamine detox—taking a break from these hyper-stimulating forms of technology and allowing yourself to feel lonely or bored, and then engaging in simpler activities to alleviate those feelings, such as going for a walk, writing in a journal, or reading a book—can bring awareness to your dopamine triggers so that you are less affected by them, encourage more flexible thinking, and help you become more centered and balanced. A dopamine detox resets your brain and creates more space for the imagination.

Facilitate Awe

Awe is a sense of wonder inspired by the sacred, reverent, grand, or sublime. Awe is looking at a sunset, or hearing a choir sing, or seeing the earth from outer space. It's hearing someone brilliant speak, or giving birth to a child, or being blessed by the random kindness of a stranger. The feeling is so vast that it transcends normality, even if only for a moment. The experience of awe may even include a feeling of fear—the kind of fear inspired by something so amazing and beyond us it can't be fully explained or understood. Moments that defy expectation, explanation, and classification inspire awe.

Awe has been called the "emotion of transformation." In his book *Awestruck*, researcher Jonah Paquette defines the experience of awe as primarily involving two components: encountering vastness and experiencing transcendence.[13] Vastness is experienced when we perceive something through our mind or senses that is too astounding to fit into our current worldview, shattering our preconceptions of what's possible. Transcendence is experienced when we try to make sense of what inspired awe and realize we can't. According to Paquette, "awe blurs the line between the self and the world around us, diminishes the ego, and links us to the greater forces that surround us in the world and the larger universe."

Through vastness and transcendence, awe broadens our relationship with the universe. Studies have shown that when people experience awe, the default mode network becomes more loosely connected. As we discussed with respect to the benefits of Positive-Constructive Daydreaming, a loose default mode network facilitates imaginative thinking. Part of this loosening occurs because we stop thinking so much about ourselves when in awe, which—in somewhat of a contradiction—humbles us *while* empowering us to dream big. Researcher Jia Wei Zhang found that the experience of awe can lead to an open mindset as well as a propensity to explore and approach experiences with unconventional perspectives—all processes critical to creativity.[14] Other research has demonstrated that the experience of awe, even for only five minutes, can boost the immune system, slow the heart rate by activating the vagus nerve, calm the nervous system, and reduce pain.[15]

Awe is a feeling that can be pursued and cultivated even in difficult environments. One of my most vivid experiences of awe growing up was attending Orthodox Christian church services. The churches are ornate, full of gold plating and décor; enormous, gorgeous icons of Jesus, Mary, and the saints; lush red carpeting; and finely-crafted wooden pews. The choir sings beautifully, with the priest chanting in harmony. Incense fills the room. My senses were so inundated during the services that at some point, after the daydreaming turned to boredom, I would feel transcendent. I would experience insights and epiphanies, while also feeling free and grounded at the same time. Even though I didn't agree with many of the rules, restrictions, and practices of the church, this tremendous, escapist experience sustained me every Sunday.

Awe can sustain (and even save) you, too.

Pursue the sublime. It's all around us, in varied places—in nature, the arts (paintings, sculpture, architecture, poetry, literature, theater, music, film, photography, music, and dance), food, religion, fashion, design, speeches, sex, friendship, and fellowship.

Here are some specific ways to facilitate awe:

- Slow down. Eat slowly, walk slowly, look around slowly. Appreciate your senses.

- Engage in something collective. Engaging in any kind of

synchronized movement at an event—such as cheering for a sports team, moving to the music at a concert, dancing at a club, participating in a demonstration, or worshiping at church—generates an intense, positive shared feeling referred to as "collective effervescence" by sociologist Emile Durkheim. Our emotional connection with others during collective effervescence generates awe in ourselves and in those to whom we are feeling connected. Consider joining a performing arts group, running a marathon, volunteering with a group, or attending a dance party.

- Spend time in nature. Enjoy a calming forest or a mountain view, a creek or the ocean. Really observe and notice. One of my favorite things to do is spot bugs with my kids—to notice the cricket hop and truly marvel at it; to hold a ladybug and watch it fly away; to see the magic in these tiny animals. Bugs, trees, plants, and toads were readily available marvels to me as a child when little else was. Nature is available to all of us, in one way or another.

- Watch the sunrise or sunset. The more beautiful the view, the better—but any will do. Notice the colors. Let yourself be immersed in this everyday ritual of nature.

- Look at photos or watch a documentary about something awe-inspiring: outer space, wild animals, rock climbing, or the most beautiful places on earth.

- Look at art. Go to public installations, art museums, or art galleries. If you have financial difficulties, check online for special dates with free or reduced-price admission. Many cities will offer free days at museums.

- Listen to music.

- Grow and water your plants. Examine their leaves. Notice the way the sunlight bathes them. Notice their stage of growth.

- Go swimming (or just take a bath). Float. Focus on the feeling of the water on your skin.

- Watch a live performance—music, dance, theater, comedy, anything.

- Meditate (we'll discuss this practice in more detail in Chapter 6).

- View architecture.

- Visit parks.

- Ride a bike.

- Value the ordinary, extraordinary moments, like a smile from someone on the street.

- Go to a farmer's market and appreciate the variety of colors and textures of produce.

- Watch rain or snow fall.

- Feel the sun on your skin.

Awe teaches us to appreciate the magical moments that can never be replicated. Awe teaches us that we are just a small part of a bigger universe. Awe teaches us that limitlessness is real. After all, if such moments of awe are possible, how could your dreams not be?

Travel

We've discussed visualizing, daydreaming, embracing ambiguity, exercising curiosity, taking a break from social media, and experiencing awe as ways to serve the imagination. Working on all of them may seem overwhelming, but one tool—travel—can hit all of them at once.

Travel supports visualization, daydreaming, ambiguity, curiosity, and awe because it breaks up your day-to-day routine and your cycle of repetitive thoughts, refreshing the stale corners of your mind. We all have those stale corners. Travel washes them all out. Travel of any kind will jump-start your life, shake up your perception, and fire up your imagination. It will give you new things to visualize, aspire to, and be curious about. It will generate ideas.

Change the environment that surrounds you as dramatically as possible for as long as possible. Lack of funds should not be a barrier or excuse. Start where you can. If you can afford to go to Kenya, or Alaska, or Fiji, do it; but if you can't, somewhere you can drive or bus to for a hike or a camping trip is great. Even visiting a nearby town you've never seen for an afternoon positively influences the imagination.

While you're in this new location, immerse yourself in the environment. Stay off your phone as much as possible, don't use social media, and don't engage in conversations about what's going on back home any more than absolutely necessary. Spend time with old friends and/or meet new people, asking questions and engaging with them. If you're in nature, let yourself go, enjoying the sun on your skin, the stars at night, the views, the trees, the plants, the mountains or ocean or desert. If you're in an urban environment, let yourself go, enjoying the views of the skyscrapers, the energy, the examples of creativity, and the gritty beauty emanating from the clustered buildings. Rural areas, with their peace and quiet, are often thought of as the best places to recharge, but urban environments can be just as inspiring for some of us. For example, if you're currently in a rural or suburban area and enjoy theater and the arts, or nonconformity generally, a trip to the city to see shows, visit art museums, attend a free festival, or just walk around might be tremendously healing and inspiring. Simply being in the mix in dynamic outdoor communal spaces encourages ideas.

No one place is better than the other. The key is not where you go, but the fact that you have removed yourself from your routine and environment, from everyday eyes and expectations on you, from the known and predictable. You have given your mind something new and pure to react to.

I grew up never traveling with my family. I knew there was a world different from my own because I saw it in books and on television, but it didn't feel real. I couldn't see what was possible for me or why I would even want it. Then, in high school, driven by a need for stimulation and to be away from home as much as possible, I joined as many clubs and activities as a nonathletic person could, which led to travel opportunities. I traveled to other towns to compete with the speech team and visited Orlando with the marching band. I would travel to Chicago with friends, visiting downtown as well as more dynamic neighborhoods such as Chinatown. My social studies class took a field trip to the Art Museum of Chicago. These baby steps ripped open my world. *There was more.*

And yet when it was time to apply to college, I was terrified of being too far away from my dysfunctional family. I was scared to apply to competitive schools and be rejected, to set my sights too high. I felt guilty for leaving my siblings behind and was bizarrely worried about paying for plane tickets, despite staring down private college tuition. I ended up visiting small Midwestern liberal arts colleges on my own in a beat-up sedan. I told my parents I was going and I went, with no cell phone. Sometimes I'd just visit for the day; other times I would stay the night with a host student. I experienced both discomfort and expansion. I felt freer than I ever had before.

I went to college and used it as a springboard to travel more. I led volunteer trips to diverse regions in the U.S. and spent semesters and summers interning in different cities. Each experience shifted my soul. I was never the same again.

I was broke, but my college had resources. This was the way for me. A way for you exists as well. Uncover the resources and opportunities that facilitate meaningful travel.

While you're there, wherever it is, engage your imagination through the practices discussed in this chapter. During or after, write down ideas that pop into your head, descriptions of things you've observed, and insights you've gained. Look up, not down. Find awe. Be curious. Ask questions and take in the experiences of others. Also ask yourself questions, such as: How do I feel when I'm here? What do I miss from home? What am I happy to be away from? How would I describe the people here? How would I describe the energy here?

Realize the way people in your family or your community live is not the only way to live.

Realize that anything and everything is possible.

***

If you don't like where you currently are, your ideas can take you elsewhere. Treasure and nurture your ideas, however minor or common they may seem, and allow them to shape your perception towards abundance and possibility. Allow them to unfold into creative acts that help you break out of the current conditions of your life.

Don't let yourself be haunted by the past, or what your life was like as a child, or the mistakes you may or may not have made as a young (or older) adult, or the way others may or may not see you, or what your family's history is, or your community's. Your imagination doesn't care. Your imagination is so regenerative that it remains pristine. Your imagination, if you let it breathe, will overpower the low-frequency feelings attached to the past.

Nothing is just "the way it is." Certain elements of your character or your physicality may need to be accepted at a foundational level, although they can be improved or better integrated with the rest of you. In any event, those elements, whatever they are, are not barriers to making your life what you want it to be by performing creative acts.

Your imagination is all yours. You are the gatekeeper of your ideas and the resulting creative output. It's up to you to decide when to share the fruits of your imagination with the universe, and in what capacity. You'll never feel 100 percent ready to do it. Take a leap anyway. I've decided to share this book with you. I'm terrified, and I'm leaping. Whatever else happens, the act itself is transformative. Acting based on thoughts, beliefs, and ideas inspired by my imagination and cultivated by my highest self (rather than the limiting ones held by my wounded narrator) is validating and empowering.

Don't be overly concerned with the opinions of others. We can try to manifest our ideas in the most appealing way possible, and be thoughtful and empathetic of our audience, but we can't control others' reactions to our creative acts.

Don't take it personally if someone criticizes your ideas or creative output—because it's not. It isn't about you. It's about them and their inner world. They may be pessimistic, or lack self-worth, or feel unimaginative themselves. Or, very commonly, they just see things differently than you do. Maybe you'll gain an insight from them, or maybe you won't. You'll never agree with everyone, and anything expressing a deeply personal view of the world is likely to resonate with some and not others. Some of the greatest art is deeply polarizing, and that's okay. If you attempt to mold your product into something that will win over everyone, you'll win no one.

Any worry I may have about your reaction to this book—to anyone's reaction to this book—sullies my ability to be authentic, creative, and expressive. It's a constraint arising from my wounded narrator, who still desires to be perfect and loved by all. What's the point of destroying my imagination to try to control a reaction I can't control? Instead, I focus on authenticity, expression, and my love and empathy for all of us dreamers. Love and empathy are acts of connection, which form another powerful practice.

Chapter 3

Practice Connection

In the kingdom of love, there is no competition; there is no possessiveness or control. The more love you give away, the more love you will have.

John O' Donohue, Anam Cara

Connection—relationships with others, of all kinds—can be fraught for those of us with C-PTSD. Yet without connection, we can't heal, receive opportunity, or give back. We are left static in our wounding. We can't live a life as good as the best.

The practice of connection involves performing acts of love, empathy, acceptance, service, or creativity to create connections that heal yourself *and others*.

We form connections with others through any and all interactions with them (good, bad, and neutral acts, omissions, and verbal and nonverbal communication, whether in-person or digital, whether momentary or enduring). These connections create an invisible network that pulses and vibrates with energies that touch our lives. I call this the "network of connection," and I believe that it makes up the universe (the Universe, the Source, Consciousness, Oversoul, or Universal Mind are similar but distinct concepts). We are a part of a network, and the network also surrounds us. We are immersed within the network like we are immersed in the atmosphere. Sections of this network are dark, injurious, and/or depleting. Other sections are brilliant, restorative, nurturing, and conducive to greater abundance. And still others can be a composite.

The connections making up the network are based on acts, not individuals. The nature of our interactions with other people—the acts done to another—determines the frequency of energy discharged by the connection. These energies stack upon each other repeatedly, in multiple directions, creating a multilayered network across dimensions of space and time that connects us to others and to our environment. Our section of the network determines our context (the implications of which will be discussed in Chapter 8), and we simultaneously determine our context through our actions. It's a two-way street—people will change their ideas, thoughts, and beliefs based on the context in which they find themselves, but they also inevitably influence that very context.

The invisible network cannot be proven, only felt. We all know that some interactions are depleting and other interactions are energizing. Depleting interactions induce tension, frustration, or anxiety, and/or make us feel worried or disconnected, whereas energizing interactions enliven and invigorate, create a sense of connection, and leave us feeling good. We can't always point to a reason these interactions affect us the way they do. We have a seemingly inexplicable ability to sense the vibes of others, or in a room. This may have something to do with electromagnetic fields; the heart (which is deeply affected by thoughts and emotions) produces an electromagnetic field that projects from 3–12 feet outside of the body. Or it may have something to do with pheromones (chemicals that animals and humans release that trigger a social response from members of our own species); a queen ant can be temporarily removed from her colony and everything runs smoothly because the ants can follow her pheromone trails, but if she is killed, the ants won't know what to do anymore. Or it could be some other unseen process of which we are not yet aware.

The network comprises the "universe" to which traditional manifesting appeals are made. The network might be God, or at least the closest to God any of us will ever be (notably, spiritual experience often includes a sense of "oneness" with all). We have no way of knowing, but we do know that most religions agree that *our acts matter*. The most empowering approach to life is centering on the universe we create through our thoughts, beliefs, and ideas, and the actions and resulting connections they inspire. The vibrations of our connections not only have a direct influence on others but also create ripple and snowball effects, feeding back into the network, over and over again, giving birth to additional vibrations and influences. The result is a powerful, magical, all-knowing, and all-seeing "universe." The network is not "us," but the network is all of the positive, negative, and neutral vibrations we generate and into which we are unavoidably immersed.

If we want our context to serve our dreams, we choose to generate and immerse ourselves in positive frequencies to the extent possible. We can do this by practicing something akin to the Golden Rule. The Golden Rule—"Do onto others as you would have them do to you"—is an enduring precept, appearing in many religions and ethical teachings across cultures and history, from the Vedas to the Tao Te Ching to Jesus to the meditations of Marcus Aurelius, that guides behavior in the right direction *most* of the time. It motivates the individual to treat others well—as, presumably, they would want to be treated—and it provides greater assurance that the individual will be treated well, because most (but not all) people treat others the way they are treated (most of the time).

The practice of connection adds a critical corollary to the Golden Rule: The way you treat people (including yourself) is the way *you* will be treated. People will absorb how you are in the universe—consciously or subconsciously—and will tend to react in kind, whether they realize it or not. As a result, *others* will treat you the way they see you treat *yourself and others*. We are all one, interconnected within a network.

We all want love, empathy, and acceptance. We all appreciate service and creativity. We all want dignity and the benefit of the doubt. We all want to be seen and appreciated. And so we should give this back, when we can. On the other hand, none of us wants to be abused, so none of us should tolerate abuse. There are people who want to break others through abuse; do all you can to avoid them. Don't play their game, because you'll never benefit, let alone win.

For some, it may sound easy; for those of us with C-PTSD, it can be challenging even when we have the best of intentions. Many of us have attachment wounds and toxic people in our lives, and we struggle to belong. We may have a broad mistrust of people, a disinclination to rely on others. We can begin to heal these aspects of ourselves through the practices in this chapter. It will take effort at first, but one day healthy connections will stop feeling like work. We won't be perfect, but we will be mostly conscious of what we contribute to each interaction.

No matter how much those of us with C-PTSD may wish otherwise, we can't bring forth our dreams outside of the network of connection. We mobilize the network of connection in our favor to express—make real—our dreams. None of us can do it alone (believe me, I've tried). No one makes their dreams come true without human interaction. By appreciating that the network of connection is the driving force behind what happens to us, we can more easily take ownership over our lives. It takes time, but it becomes easier. If we feel worthy, we are more likely to treat ourselves and others well. If we treat ourselves and others well, we are more likely to feel worthy and more likely to invite opportunity, resources, and positive energy into our lives.

The way you treat others, and the way you allow yourself to be treated, will define your context, the garden bed in which your dreams bloom. When others feel the positive frequencies of your acts, they will respond more positively to you. They may give you a smile, a generous gesture, or an invitation. You may attract a new friend, potential love interest, or job opportunity. Many times, the results of the acts will be more subtle, but they will still create light that shines on you and into the lives of people to whom you are connected, even when you can't see it. These acts create your universe, your context, and you. You are not one act, but you are what you repeatedly do.

Address Attachment Wounds

Your context—and the entire network—wants to unfold organically based on the best of you. It naturally seeks to be coherent, creative, energizing, supportive, and full of light. Unfortunately, it is impeded by the reality of pain, trauma, and even evil. When we think or act based on our trauma, we rupture the unfolding of our context and shatter our opportunities for greatness.

A sense of self-worth is fostered when a child feels that it's safe to be vulnerable, and that the child's expression of their feelings—and their vulnerability—will not threaten their attachment to their caregivers. Attachment wounds result when that doesn't happen—when we are raised by caregivers who are not attuned, or are super stressed or emotionally unreliable, and we feel our relationship is threatened by our expression of our authentic self. I believe that if everyone grew up securely attached with present and loving caregivers, *almost* everyone would feel loved and worthy, and the universe would be a kinder and more empathetic place.

Attachment wounds are both the most common cause of low self-worth (and they can also be our interfering wounds, which are discussed in detail in Chapter 5) and the most common cause of ruptures in the network of connection.

Dr. Gordon Neufield, a Canadian developmental psychologist, advocates a relationship-based approach to attachment and that healthy emotional balance comes from the expression of emotions, not from reason and perception. In the book he co-wrote with Gabor Maté , *Hold On To Your Kids*, the authors note that healthy attachment results from children feeling an invitation to exist in their caregivers' presence, exactly the way they are.[16] *They are permitted to simply exist, as themselves.* They are loved, regardless of the parent's expectation or need.

If healthy attachment sounds like a fantasy, I'm right there with you. I didn't experience unconditional love as a child, and I still struggle to recognize and appreciate it when I receive it today, from my partner, my children, and dear friends.

When we don't receive mirroring, attunement, and validation from our caregivers, we're not only left feeling unworthy, but our interactions with individuals other than our caregivers are deeply impaired. When we're not taught to relate to others from a place of trust, empathy, and healthy boundaries, we can become distrustful, mean, or narcissistic, or overly solicitous, self-effacing, or conformist. These qualities don't produce healthy vibrations. We may push people away or hold them overly close, consciously or unconsciously. Certain people may be drawn to us for these qualities because of their own attachment wounds—but their attraction doesn't come from a healthy place either. Our interactions can become corrupted and confusing, even when we believe we're trying our best.

I was physically and emotionally abused as a small child. I was not comforted, and I was not seen. I was lied to, put in dangerous situations, and told I was worthless. Academic success helped me gain attention, accolades, and conditional approval (from teachers and, to a much lesser degree, from my parents). Attention, accolades, and conditional approval can feel like love to someone who has never had it. I'm not sure if my academic success saved me or made everything worse—most likely, it was a little bit of both. Everything I did at home seemed to inspire rage, but academic success made me feel special; it was a refuge, delivering me from a devastating deprivation. As I grew up, I used career success and success with the opposite sex in a similar manner. Winning began to feel like I thought love was supposed to feel. This "fake love" was my solace. After all, even if they aren't treated as they should be by their parents, winners still get to win and receive the perks that go along with it. Those perks sustained me, as they sustain many of us, but they only give us a weak, distorted sense of wholeness. We may finally feel good enough to deserve to exist, but our self-worth remains fallow.

Of course, when we view the world as a hierarchy, not winning—not being told we are extraordinary—feels like death by oblivion. That's how I felt, anyway, and this mindset kept me away from healing and kept me away from my dreams. The truth is, a network is not a hierarchy. In a simple network, no nodes of control exist. No one is on top or on the bottom. You can't practice connection effectively if you allow yourself to view the world as a hierarchy.

My raw attachment wound complicated my relationship with teachers and professors, and even fitness instructors. If I wasn't the favorite, if I didn't receive extra attention, I assumed I was hated, and I'd tie myself in knots trying to please a teacher who had neutral feelings toward me. Neutral wasn't good enough for me. Neutral made me feel like I didn't deserve to exist. Neutral crushed me more than rejection ever could. Through the therapies and practices discussed in this book, I realized that not being the favorite wasn't personal (and that even having favorites was problematic), that I was stuck in a cycle from my past, drawn to these individuals so I could relive versions of my pain with hope for a happier outcome. Of course, I subconsciously *knew* that happier outcome wouldn't arrive, and therefore my profound lack of self-worth—disguised by my superficial grandiosity—would be validated. I learned that fake love—attention, accolades, and conditional approval—was just an energizing dopamine kick. I only began to heal when I appreciated it as only that, nothing more.[17]

I also sought fake love in relationships and avoided intimacy. True connection to others for those of us who experienced childhood trauma can be so fraught, so complex. Some people with trauma (especially abandonment) are desperate to feel needed by others. I felt so needed as a child in a perverse, parentified way that feeling needed by another adult made me feel panicked, trapped, and suffocated. I couldn't bear neediness. Many of my friends, and my partner, don't present as needy, for a wide variety of reasons. I was the fun and nonjudgmental friend, not the friend you called in tears. I've learned to be more emotionally available for the sake of my children and my healing, but at times, emotional availability still feels excruciating. I want to solve everyone's problems quickly and move on, and I have to stop myself. I'm still somewhat terrified of needing someone, and I'm not sure I'll ever be able to admit that I do.

Attachment theory categorizes the types of insecure attachment as anxious, avoidant, and fearful avoidant (a combination). Like all categorizations, these groupings are imprecise and inaccurately static; people shift from anxious and avoidant depending on the relationship and can demonstrate mild or severe forms of attachment trauma. To determine whether you are insecurely attached, consider yourself and your relationships in terms of consistency, open communication, authenticity, positive self-worth, and the ability to trust and be intimate with others. I'm a halfway healed fearful avoidant: my tendency is to seek intimacy, but immediately after experiencing it pull back and create distance. As a child, I was randomly engulfed by my parents' emotions; I had to take in and validate or regulate their emotions, only to be abandoned with respect to my own. And so as an adult, I felt powerful when I did what I wasn't permitted to do as a child, keeping others at bay and even ruthlessly rejecting them, and thereby keeping myself from falling apart. I believe I caused a great deal of pain to those in any kind of relationship with me over the years due to my push-pull, hot and cold inclinations—inclinations I didn't understand at the time, inclinations that felt like survival. For that, I'm deeply sorry.

Awareness and intention allow us to avoid the negative relationship spirals into which our attachment wounds pull us. Unfortunately, awareness and intention don't erase pain, although they do limit it. They are life rafts in the storm. They give us something to grasp onto and a closer relationship with reality. We may turn anxious or avoidant, but by being aware—and having the intention to cultivate a healthier response—we mitigate the multitude of potential negative effects.

Determine if you have an attachment wound (if you have C-PTSD, you probably do) and how it affects your life. Whether you're avoidant, anxious, or both, by remaining at the level of a powerless child emotionally, by operating as if you still haven't met the requirements of being loved, you ignore that you are now an adult with resources. Realize you may be replicating patterns in your relationships in some form or another. Honestly assess your past with respect to any fake love for which you settled. Contemplate, journal, talk with a therapist, and talk with your partner and friends. Practice the therapies you'll read about in Chapter 6, as interfering wounds and attachment wounds are often synonymous (or at least entangled).

Remember, you always deserved to be seen, heard, and comforted—and you still do.

You were always worthy of connection.

You were always worthy of dignity and validation.

You were and are always worthy of love.

You are imperfect, and perfectly lovable.

One of the most challenging aspects of healing attachment wounds is recognizing that connection is imperfect. You will never be protected from perpetual rupture and repair. Even when feeding connections with people who are empathetic and trustworthy, people who are engaged in healing, we risk hurt. We risk rupture. Connection gives us the world but also necessarily challenges us. Seek connection, because you can't avoid being immersed in the network of connection anyway. Seek connection, because you can't heal without being vulnerable in the way healthy connection demands. You heal when you allow yourself to accept a kindness, to feel something that you previously felt too broken to be capable of, or to express something that was once terrifying.

You heal when you try.

Avoid Relationships with Toxic People

If you allow people to treat you badly, you tell the universe that you accept and deserve poor treatment. If someone is harming you and expects you to adapt to that behavior, they shouldn't get to be in your beautiful life. They shouldn't get to be in your context. That includes your family. That includes your supposed soulmate.

Everyone makes mistakes from time to time and inadvertently hurts someone's feelings. Even mostly kind people may occasionally hurt someone else's feelings (sometimes even on purpose). The network of connection is complicated that way. Toxic people, however, are those who harm you emotionally and/or physically (consistently, more than a few times), don't take accountability for such harm, and don't make appropriate efforts to change their behavior. These people have a pattern of toxic interactions. The acts these people perpetrate suggest they want to break you to avoid confronting their own trauma. No one is born toxic; it's a decision to not question low-frequency beliefs and to continue to perform the lowest-frequency actions, over and over again.

Don't return poor treatment—but never accept poor treatment, either. If a person continues to demonstrate harmful behavioral patterns, your choices are to either establish strong boundaries or stop engaging with that person entirely. If appropriate and safe, you might directly confront that person and tell them that their behavior is unacceptable. If they do not make a genuine effort to change, or if you cannot dramatically limit the negative connection, sever it.[18] We should never feed injustice, cruelty, or evil. We must starve it.

Keeping toxic people in your life will leave you questioning your worth, cloud your view of what's possible, and sap your time and energy. You can still perform positive acts towards others while toxic people are in your life, but your proclivity to do so will be limited. You'll spend too much energy in the wrong place. This process is perpetual and complex—you'll continuously meet or be exposed to toxic people. Quickly identify them and narrow their influence over you to the greatest extent possible.

People either love you the way we all should be loved (or are trying to—doing the difficult work to learn how) or they don't. You can set all the boundaries in the world with certain people, and they will kick down the door completely at random. You can communicate your hurt, and they will respond with lies, gaslighting, and manipulation. You can give them chance after chance, only to have your heart shattered over and over again.

Some of these people have personality disorders like narcissism; others may be addicts; and others may simply be reacting based on their own trauma. It doesn't matter. It's not up to you to figure them out; it's their responsibility to figure themselves out and heal. I've read numerous books in an effort to understand the personality disorders that very likely afflicted my parents.[19] Although I found books helpful and many of the anecdotes validated my own personal experience, these books were predicated on my efforts to understand, empathize, and create boundaries for people who had zero empathy for me or respect for boundaries. I was supposed to understand *them*. It was just another way I was permitting their context, their imaginations, their ways of being to overwhelm my own.

Beyond what you need to heal, stop wasting your time trying to understand toxic people.

It doesn't matter why they do the things they do.

It will never make sense.

You cannot subject yourself to repeated abuse, no matter what your culture or conditioning says. You'll find it close to impossible to heal when you keep a toxic person close. They will drain your energy and dim your light. Meanwhile, when someone believes in you, when someone treats you with empathy, compassion, and understanding, when someone sees you or tries to see you, power and possibility enter your life.

Not everyone with a mental health issue or disorder is "toxic." It's about consistency, accountability, and communication. It's about whether they respect boundaries. It's about whether they are getting the help they need to get better. The toxic people are the ones who, although they may generally apologize from time to time, don't actually believe they need to change. They believe *you* need to change to appease *them*. I was told as much many times by my father. And when you're in appeasement mode, you can't heal or express your authentic self. You're limiting your life to the vagaries of someone's poisonous imagination. You're nothing but a cipher to them, and nothing you do will change that fact. You won't express your dreams in appeasement mode. You can barely connect to your authentic self in appeasement mode.

I'm taking a harsh approach because I know how bad some of us have it. I'm taking a harsh approach because I'm sick of being asked to spend my time asking the universe why someone abused me.

Life is unfair, and there is no answer. I accept that no resolution exists.

I accept that it doesn't matter. I matter. You matter.

If, after a good faith effort of empathy and understanding on your part—a good faith effort to turn the connection positive—an individual continues to mistreat you, limit or sever the connection.

I realized I had to go no contact with my parents—to shift away from perpetual appeasement mode—embarrassingly slowly myself. Due to the deluge of emotional abuse, drama, lies, and chaos I struggled against every time I saw them, I stopped talking to my parents at various times. At one point in my early twenties, when I was living in the city about an hour away from them, I went an entire six months not speaking to them. This was after my father exploded at me on Christmas, screaming that I was garbage and throwing things in my direction. I don't remember what the reason was, but likely it was disagreeing with him about something trivial—it was always something trivial that led to the rage. I left immediately and drove back to the city. Six months went by, and I received no phone calls from either parent.

I was at the beginning of young adulthood, making my way in the world. And I was treated as if I did something wrong because I didn't take the rage submissively. I was treated as the one who had to adapt to the dysfunction, to lie, and to suppress.

It was an extraordinarily difficult experience, and I'm sad and embarrassed to say that when my father called me six months later, acting as if nothing had happened, I also acted as if nothing had happened. These episodes—these negative frequencies that intruded on a context I was trying so hard to improve—had happened many times before and continued to happen, despite my being an adult able to separate myself physically. I learned to never spend a Christmas at my parents' home again, but I didn't learn that the behavior would never stop. My six months of no contact was not a punishment; my agreeing to re-engage without an apology was acceptance. I accepted the abuse.

A few years later, my husband and I traveled to the area for Thanksgiving. While at work in the city close to my family's home, I received a call from my parents telling me that my father was going to go to jail unless I sent them several thousand dollars.

I said no. I said it didn't make sense, and even if it was true, it was their fault. I told them I was at work and they were interrupting me. They didn't care.

When all of us converged at my late childhood home for Thanksgiving a few days later (after each of my siblings was asked for money, and after the issue had somehow gone away—not sure if he was scammed or wanted to extract money from us), my father's rage was irrepressible. In his view, he had done nothing wrong and we were horrible children. After being called out on his behavior, my father verbally attacked us. He told us that if we were actually good children, we'd be taking him on cruises and buying him cars. Most of what he said was much, much worse. Most painfully, he had debased the one happy holiday my family celebrated (Christmases were horrible, and birthdays were the worst days).

I stopped talking to my parents, again. Again, I didn't hear from them. I became pregnant. Then, one day in April, I received a call that my father had been in a horrible accident at the manufacturing plant where he worked. He was in surgery. He might die. And so again, I entered appeasement mode. I immediately hopped on an airplane and visited the hospital for multiple days, opening my heart, being supportive, acting like the past had never happened. I bought him a stuffed dog. Briefly, I was validated. I was the rescuer. I had done the right thing, and I felt really good about it. My father even told me I should write a book.

I don't regret spending time with my father during that difficult time. His accident was truly horrendous. So horrendous that I thought if he was ever going to change, if he was ever going to appreciate his life and the people in it, now was the chance. And he did have a brief period of calmer behavior for a year or so. He had become a grandfather and had a new opiate prescription. He didn't really listen or show empathy, but at least he didn't rage. Slowly but consistently, however, the controlling, narcissistic, unaccountable, and rageful behavior returned, especially when his psychiatric meds were "off."

I had thought the tragedy would change him. I learned that tragedy doesn't change people. People change because they want to change. People change because they believe they are changeable and believe they are worthy of a better life. People change because they know they *must* change. Change is a personal choice.

And our love will never change anyone. It might help someone who is already on the path to change, through their own volition, but it alone will change no one. Change can be inspired, but change cannot be bestowed.

After multiple difficult interactions, my father sent me a text telling me *I* had to change. I had spent my entire life trying to appease him while struggling to discover my own identity and achieve well-being. I had my own family now, and after every interaction with him, I felt depleted and in despair, utterly emptied of the calm, patience, and flexibility I needed so much as the mother of a young child. I was DONE appeasing. I was done suppressing my emotions out of the irrational fear of two people who had no real power over me anymore. I was done speaking to two people who continuously hurt me, invalidated me, and blamed me, for whom my feelings and boundaries were utterly meaningless.

I told my parents that I would engage with them again if they went to therapy. My mother's response (which I heard secondhand) was: "How would she know if we went to therapy?" They very obviously didn't go. Their texts—that I ignored—would quickly shift from love bombing to abuse (rage, hostility, and cruelty from my father; blame and shame from my mother; and zero accountability from either of them).

And yet, even now, it's hard for me write these words. It's extraordinarily difficult to disentangle yourself from toxic people, especially if they are the ones who were supposed to love you unconditionally or the ones you loved (and feel pathetic for loving). I didn't want "no contact" to be the answer. I was a problem solver, and I wanted a resolution with all of my heart. I wanted to be the rescuer. I wanted to be the one who convinced them to obtain the help they needed. I wanted to be the one to convince them that they were worthy, to find a way for them to feel their worth, to lead a pleasant and peaceful life. I wanted them to heal or at least chill out. None of that happened.

None of it happened because those aren't the kinds of dreams that are attainable. We can't solve for or save other people. We can't control them in any manner. The good news, however, is that they can't control us either.

My rescuer fantasy was destroyed, and out of the ashes I forged a path to being the person I had always wanted to be. Out of the ashes, I set out on the journey of writing this book.

Instead of worrying about fixing, helping, appeasing, or rescuing toxic people, focus on your healing. You're not responsible for the thoughts, feelings, and actions of others; you're only responsible for you. Their toxicity has nothing to do with you. They can't see you—they can only see a projection of all of their repressed pain, unhealed trauma, and everything they hate about themselves but don't have the courage to change. They hurt you to ameliorate their own pain in the short-term. They attempt to define you so as to define themselves. They are lost in a tangle of their own childhood trauma, suppression, repression, and projection, fears, shame, self-hatred, biases, fantasies, and nightmares. They can't see you—the beautiful, vibrant, worthy you.

You will not be rewarded for drowning in someone else's darkness. You will not be rewarded for letting someone else's projection define you. Please don't squander your sacred time.

Pain is not love. "Your" toxic person is not an exception. Never make excuses for other people. We want to convince ourselves so badly that people who cause us pain actually love us. We will turn our mind and body upside down trying to convince ourselves, consciously and subconsciously. If you call poor treatment love, you will continue to receive poor treatment from the network of connection. You will attract people who treat you poorly, and it will feel like connection to you. Your context will be plagued by this problem even as you otherwise make powerful strides toward healing.

If you're in an abusive relationship, make plans to leave in the safest, most effective way possible and *leave*. This feat takes more planning, work, and courage than anything else in this book. Stay safe. Ensuring your departure is effective may require patiently saving money and gathering resources. Reach out for any kind of help you possibly can. *You will need help.* Know you are worthy of such help. Tell people what's going on if you need to.

You must save yourself, because no one else will.

The freedom from toxic people, and especially abusers, can be overwhelming when the prison they built is all you've ever known. The freedom means you get to write your own story and decide what happens to you. The freedom means you can't retreat into the fallback identity of victimhood. The freedom means power and accountability. Patiently let the freedom wash over you. The open space of freedom can feel like an abyss. It's a space with no constraints, where the rules your wounded narrator created for survival no longer apply. It can induce panic or paralysis. As a result, some people go back to their toxic prisons. The freedom feels immense and overwhelming or the familiar voice of the wounded narrator promises them the comfort of predictability. I hope the practices discussed in this book will put you in a position where that return isn't tempting. You are more than your past.

One last note: Don't desire "revenge," "karma," or "payback." Never allow these ideas to occupy more than a fleeting thought. Don't desire any type of ill will or harm toward anyone, or to control anyone in any manner. These desires have negative frequencies. Revenge can and does hurt the target, but the cost is an infusion of dark energy into your own life. The dark energy takes you down with the target, eventually and always. I have chosen it before gladly, only to regret it later. Perhaps, at times, the cost of dark energy may seem worth it to you. It's your choice, but you should be aware of the cost: The fullest expression of power and possibility will be blocked from reaching you. I don't like the concept of "enemies", but I've always appreciated the modern proverb: "If you wait by the river long enough, the bodies of your enemies will float by." Sever, and let go.

Cultivate Intimacy, Healthy Connections, and Authentic Social Belonging

We all want to be seen, loved, and accepted, and we thrive when we learn to admit it. Our emotional and physical health and function emerge from the relationship between body and mind, but also from relationships with each other. We're influenced by the people with whom we surround ourselves, for better or worse. We all rely on the energy of others—and without good energy from others, we have a harder time healing. According to psychologist Bruce Alexander, each of us needs "psychosocial integration": a combination of individual autonomy and social belonging. We may think we're protecting ourselves by not opening up to others, but we are ultimately rendering ourselves more vulnerable.

Daniel Siegel, clinical professor of psychiatry and director of the MindSight Institute, introduced the distinct but related concept of "interpersonal neurobiology." According to Siegel, we're connected internally (we'll discuss the implications of this in Chapter 6) and also externally, with the people around us, and these internal and external connections should be integrated for the healthiest outcomes.[20] No way exists to separate our brain and nervous system from the universe in which we exist. Emotions affect nerves, and nerves affect emotions. Nerves act on hormones, hormones act on the immune system, the immune system acts on the brain, the brain acts on the gut, and the gut acts on the brain—and all of these parts and systems act on the heart, and vice versa.

The boundaries between us and our outer world are immutably notional, always fluid. We are all one. What the other people around us do influences our bodies and minds, as well as our thoughts, beliefs, ideas, and actions. What we do influences them too, in ways that are seem both logical and magical. For example, compassion activates the vagus nerve, a key part of the parasympathetic nervous system responsible for calming responses.[21] Childhood asthma is directly affected by the mother's and father's emotions.[22] Holding hands with a loved one moderates the negative influence of receiving a shock.[23] Today, I woke up from a dream at the exact moment as my toddler across the hallway did. We are connected to each other in infinite and inexplicable ways.

I see intimacy and social belonging as two sides of the same coin; intimacy relates to the connection to a particular person, and social belonging is feeling a part of a larger entity such as a partnership, team, community, or organization. They both entail emotional safety, trust, openness, reciprocity, and vulnerability met with compassion and support. They both entail being able to be yourself without judgment or fear of rejection, being able to relax your defenses as you know you won't be judged or controlled, and being unafraid of being hurt because you know you can repair any conflict or misunderstanding.

Some of us with C-PTSD, especially with avoidant attachment, want to withdraw from connection and believe we are doing so to protect ourselves, particularly during the healing phase. Some might believe they are introverts (I consider myself an extrovert, but I carefully manage my connections much like an introvert) or even accept loneliness as a natural state. For some of us, avoiding toxic people is easy because we start avoiding everyone. We are so scared that engagement with others will lead to pain again. We are so scared that healthy social relationships and belonging don't exist for us. We are so scared to believe that it might be possible to feel safe and seen, to be vulnerable enough to believe and then have our hopes crushed all over again.

We can't let the fears win. As traumatized as our hope is, it's a yearning for something we need. You will not be your best self energetically if you're in a state of perceived social isolation. A great deal of data indicates that social isolation is deleterious, emotionally and physically. Loneliness leads to fight-or-flight stress signaling, which rouses the nervous system, promotes inflammation, and negatively impacts immune system functioning.[24] The perception (as always) of loneliness or social isolation carries more weight than any outside judgment of it. Evidence suggests that perceived social isolation is linked to depression, poor sleep quality, impaired executive function, accelerated cognitive decline, poor cardiovascular function, and impaired immunity at every stage of life.[25] Meanwhile, frequency and quality of contact with others are major predictors of happiness.[26]

Interventions focusing inward that address negative thoughts underlying loneliness tend to be more helpful than those designed to improve social skills, enhance social support, or increase opportunities for social interaction. In one study, the researchers used cognitive behavioral therapy to address maladaptive social cognition (distorted beliefs combined with misinterpreting social cues), which empowered patients to recognize and work through their negative thoughts about self-worth and how others perceive them, ultimately reducing their loneliness.[27] We too can cultivate the belief we're worthy of connection. We can't live lives completely devoid of loneliness, but we can recognize loneliness as a temporary condition that has nothing to do with our fundamental worth.

Here are some ways to build social engagement:

- Try to engage with people in person as much as possible. Most people are better and more likable in person. You won't find true social belonging online.

- Join a choir. Sing in groups. Oxytocin is secreted during group choral and improvisational singing. Cortisol is decreased during group listening and singing.

- Get a dog and take them on walks or to dog parks.

- Find a sport or physical activity you enjoy that involves interaction.

- Join a running group.

- Find a group based on your hobbies.

- Do low-stakes dating.

- Volunteer.

- Join a church, temple, synagogue, mosque, or other religious community.

Connection is sustaining, but a caveat for all of us with C-PTSD is that we can't be so desperate for connection that we accept any form of it, even if it depletes or damages us or clouds our light. You deserve healthy, supportive, and restorative connections. You deserve attunement. Don't settle for less. You can't force anyone to like you, value you, treat you right, or be anything but what they are. I've tried many, many times. It doesn't work. You may occasionally be lonely until you find your people, but your people exist. Believe they exist. Keep looking for them.

Your people demonstrate kindness, empathy, and generosity. They're creative and brave, thoughtful and open-minded. They listen to you. They see you. It may be scary at first, but the only way to bring good into your life is by insisting on it. Be calm and cool but friendly and kind to people who try to exclude you, because they aren't the people you'd want to be around anyway. Build a few strong friendships, and they will sustain and nurture you through this journey.

Of course, a lack of trust in others and a belief that we are broken can cause us to constantly search for signs that someone will hurt us. Healthy connections *should* feel mostly good, sustaining, and comforting. However, those of us with C-PTSD may experience distressing responses in our bodies whenever our safety feels threatened, including by a simple feeling of closeness or an innocent act or statement that reminds us of our past. Our nervous system can feel completely wrecked by ordinary intimacy. During healing, we are learning to know and trust ourselves, to understand our bodies, and should take all negative reactions seriously. We can pay attention to our body and mind before, during, and after any interaction. If someone elicits a negative reaction from your physical system more often than not, avoid them (to the extent possible) during healing. A negative reaction may entail a racing heart, an aching belly, or a physical flood of negative emotions.

Even an ostensibly positive reaction that's too stimulating for our nervous system is a red flag. Some of us with C-PTSD—who are not in a great position to trust our programmed gut—may mistake a dopamine rush for connection or rescue. As we've noted, a dopamine rush is a brief, intense release of dopamine in the brain that feels like intense reward—excitement, happiness, and even euphoria. Dopamine rushes are invigorating and can lead to an amazing feeling of catharsis. Other than the energy and catharsis, which can be exploited positively, a dopamine rush is meaningless. For many of us with C-PTSD, a dopamine rush is simply a trauma response, the result of past conditioning; it's the thrill of a situation that mirrors our past trauma, laden with childlike hope for a different outcome. It's a throwback: This time, this person will love me. This time, this person won't abandon me. This time, I'll be seen.

Another common reaction to others is trauma bonding. This has different interpretations. In my personal experience, it functions as a re-traumatization, an echo of our wounding. We may be drawn to someone whose behavior triggers (or reactivates) the unhealed attachment (or interfering wound) from our childhood. There is something about this person's combination of looks, manner, and behavior that is on the same frequency as the abusive parent, or it otherwise provokes our buried pain. To our subconscious core, to our wounded narrator, it's like fantasy time travel. The person provoking this may be abusive, or they may be struggling with their own attachment wounds and behaving in an unhealthy manner without realizing it. They may love bomb us (and become a sort of surrogate parent in this way) and idealize us. Being idealized by this person can feel like the unconditional love we never had. They may seem to see us as perfect, to love us as perfect, and it feels amazing. They love us as perfect. Our wounded narrator is (briefly) in paradise. It's addictive. Only later does this person begin to withhold and reject, which feels very abrupt and deeply familiar. They reject us as imperfect. We feel flawed, or even worthless. And so we do everything we can to return to their idealization of us, even if it means accepting poor treatment and being inauthentic. We now have anxiety, but the relationship also feels safe in this new corrupted context. We can manage this, because we've managed something similar before. We experience a fantasy of control.

I want to give attention to this dynamic because many of us with C-PTSD who crave intimacy fall for it, over and over again. Even being aware of it isn't enough to stop it from happening. And I want to emphasize it's not always abusive, just unhealthy. You may even be in a relationship where both people are treating each other with idealization followed by rejection, over and over again. You might be the one doing it. These relationships create feelings of shame, anxiety, and fear, but are also deeply familiar.

It's not our fault. As children, we lost out on someone taking an interest in our inner world and mirroring and validating our emotional truth. When someone does these things (and especially if we also find them physically attractive), the resonance can feel like nirvana. The promise of paradise. If they have elements we are drawn to rescue, fix, or affirm, it can feel even more exhilarating. We find the illusion of redemption and rebirth. Finally. We will be seen for how we are, not for how we perform, while also saving someone else. The possibility is intoxicating.

It's an illusion.

Dopamine lies. Our past conditioning lies. Our fantasies and projections lie.

I can't tell you whether it's truly love, but I'll say most of the time it's not. Most of the time it's an illusion, and a particularly brutal one. It's the lie of love that, even with tremendous healing, is a perpetual threat. It's not fair. You live with your attachment wound. Even after tremendous healing, it will reassert itself at unpredictable times. You can only develop and maintain healthy connections by first questioning your responses to others through the lens of your trauma response.

It starts with the awareness that there is, there is no "permanent, omnipotent other" who will heal your wounds. As James Hollis writes in the *Eden Project: The Search for the Magical Other* (a life-changing book about relationships, rooted in Jungian philosophy), no one is going to "repair the ravages your personal history," "read your mind," or "meet all of your deepest needs."[28] No one can absolve you from the responsibility to heal. No one can serve as a substitute for your deepest dreams. We don't have a right to become upset with people for not saving us, because they were never meant to save us.

And not being saved doesn't mean we aren't worthy, powerful, or limitless. It doesn't mean anything. You may have taken your mistreatment, or the lack of deliverance from it, as a testament of who and what you are, believing you are as you're treated. You're not. *It doesn't define you.* Your acts—*not* the acts of other people—define you. How you permit yourself to be treated, and how you treat others, matters now. Love your imperfect self, and find others who are able to do the same.

If a dopamine rush creates the illusion of connection, how do we determine what connection is? How do we determine what love is when we can't trust our C-PTSD, our wounded narrator, our less than perfect attachment style? We follow the feelings of safety, peace, and respect, of consistently being seen and heard over time. It should feel like low-key coherence. We look at the acts done by the person rather than who we want them to be. We look at the acts we do, and what is built over time. Secure attachment doesn't lie. Acts of love, empathy, and acceptance don't lie. Healthy connections challenge and enrich us. Healthy connections enliven and invigorate. They do not make us feel worried or demoralized, or induce tension. Test all of your connections—the euphoric, the draining, and the comforting.

Relationships, if approached and cultivated in a healthy manner, can be tremendous tools for healing attachment and interfering wounds.[29] The practice of connection is healing; it's not the other person who heals us—it's our relationship, our interaction, the acts we give and allow ourselves to receive. We can't rely on finding the right person to heal us and make us feel whole; we need to practice and heal before and during such relationship.[30] We can only rescue ourselves.

Perform Acts of Love, Empathy, Acceptance, Service, and Creativity

The best way to bring good people into your life is by doing good. You foster intimacy, social belonging, and healthy connections. You also heal, grow, learn, energize your context, and create opportunity by performing acts of love, empathy, acceptance, service, and creativity.

Acts are how you move yourself forward and become the person you want to be. Acts are how those of us with C-PTSD restore our wholeness and eliminate the fear of the void. Acts are how we overwhelm the wounded narrator. Acts are how we break down limits and tap into our power. We're not victims. We're capable of extraordinary empathy, radical acceptance, and unconditional love. We can give our time and resources to help those in need. We can create and build things that bring others meaning and joy.

All of our relationships, and our place in the network, are *defined by* the acts of love, empathy, acceptance, service, and creativity that we do for others—not what those others do for us. These acts are how we show the universe that we believe we and all others are worthy. By caring about others through our actions, we demonstrate that overall well-being (including our own) is something to be cared for, too. For example: Listening to your partner's concerns openly and non-defensively, considering them, and adapting your behavior respects their needs and your own autonomy at the same time. Other examples include creating an artwork and sharing it with the world, volunteering and donating, offering to help a stranger in need, smiling at and thanking the barista at the coffee shop, and inventing and sharing a new recipe or technology. Depending on your personality, some of these may be more challenging than others. All of them, however, will heal and empower you and the other(s) impacted by your acts.

We all have a natural tendency to contribute to the universe, to do and share, that may have been corrupted by our childhood trauma. It wasn't your fault and it may be harder for you than others, but you don't get to be selfish and retreat from the goodness you are capable of giving others. By being brave, by acting in the world, we become as good as the best.

Through repeated acts, this natural tendency to contribute is revitalized and integrated into who we are. Acts of love, empathy, acceptance, service, and creativity open a path to redemption for all of us who, at one time or another, may have felt like we ourselves were the toxic ones. Contributing to the network of connection is our way out. It's our way to take ownership over our destiny.

Acts of Love

Love is an act, not a feeling.

Love is a choice—an intentional practice that demands bravery, self-awareness, and commitment.

As a child, my family convinced me that something was wrong with me and I was incapable of love. One of the most hurtful things my father would say to me as a child was that I didn't know how to love anyone. He said it when I disagreed, didn't give in, or simply tried to disengage, whenever I wasn't completely accommodating to his needs and wants. I didn't stop disagreeing, but I did end up believing he was right. I believed I was selfish, heartless, and maybe even inhuman. I believed this was the trade-off for being my own person.

I was not shown unconditional love, and I was taught that to love my caregivers was to yield to abuse in various forms and then to pretend it never happened. Like many of us, I was born with an inclination to love that was corrupted by trauma. It took me a long time to understand and trust what love really is.

Maybe it's easier to describe an act of love for what it isn't:

Submitting to a narcissist or other person who doesn't value you as a human being is not an act of love. Standing up to them actually is, as it puts them on notice of the reality of boundaries, perhaps reining in their behavior. In any event, if you love someone, you don't let them be abusive to you or anyone else. Letting them be their worst selves is not love.

An act of love is not a fantasy. It's not playing the rescuer or having someone rescue you to avoid the hard work of healing.

Falling in love is not an act of love, although it involves feelings of love. Falling in love is probably too connected to our hormones and deep programming to be a pure choice, but acts of love—and loving—are pure choices. Sometimes, it may even require simply letting go of the person you're in love with, if they desire a different path or don't return your feelings.

At the same time, acts of love don't demand perfection from either person. The perfect partner doesn't exist. The perfect friend doesn't exist. Everyone has unresolved issues.

I believe that an act of love is to will the good of another person. An act of love is deeply altruistic, performed for another person's sake and not for our own. Loving someone is a continuous intentional practice that requires bravery, self-awareness, and commitment.

If you search "acts of love" on the Internet, the top hits relate to the concept of "love languages"—the idea that everyone expresses love in different ways. I don't like the concept of love languages, other than as a mechanism through which to understand patterns of behavior. An act of love can only be an act of altruism. An altruistic act is sometimes defined as an act that is undertaken despite the perception that it involves some loss of one's own well-being. I think it's more accurate to think of it as something undertaken despite the fact that it may not be your inclination. It's doing the thing that's a little bit hard.

This means that giving someone a gift or service they don't want is not an act of love. Narcissists are especially guilty of burdening gifts with the weight and expectation of narcissistic supply. Similarly, physical touch is only an act of love if it is desired by the recipient. Same for quality time—time that is spent with someone out of obligation or possessiveness is not love.

You don't get to choose how someone else defines love based on your own propensity. That doesn't mean there isn't something in it for you; there often is. An act of love is giving someone exactly what they need exactly when they need it, *even if it's hard for you*. Not when you need to feel good about yourself, although an act of love should still feel good to you. Acts of love are for the benefit of someone else while being authentic to us.

To perform an act of love is to walk a fine line, which is why they're the hardest of all of the acts, and ultimately rare. You may feel love in your heart, but what really matters to the network is expressing it in a way that's perceived by the other person. Love is empathy and service, but it goes beyond those things, too. An act of love can soothe, cheer, or even challenge (in a healthy manner) another person. An act of love can save someone's life or simply make them feel seen. An act of love can be a physical act that is welcomed and appropriate (such as a hug), a verbal act that expresses encouragement or how much someone means to you, spending time with someone, sharing material goods, protecting someone, or caring for someone who is ill. It's giving someone the last piece of cake when you both really want it (thank you, *Best Man*), giving your sweater to someone when you're both cold, or donating an organ that you both need (but they need it more).

One of the most profound types of acts of love is forgiveness. Western society places a great emphasis on forgiveness. Many motivational and healing books, even some modern and progressive ones, insist you must forgive to heal. I believe that they're wrong.

It's too much to ask.

It's too much to ask of many of us to forgive our abusers, especially at the beginning of our healing.

You're not required to forgive anyone but yourself. Forgiving yourself is the ultimate act of love. And an inability to forgive others is not a stumbling block to expressing your dreams.

Forgiving yourself should arise somewhat naturally from engaging in the therapies and practices discussed in this book. Your trauma has never been your fault, and it never will be. Be accountable for your healing and for your actions, not your trauma. Be compassionate with yourself. Forgive yourself for doing what it took to survive, for taking an uncomfortably long and circuitous path to healing, for causing others pain before you began your healing journey. Look through your memories for the incidents that you still feel bad about, and forgive yourself. I'm not sure if I've forgiven myself for the way I punched a boy two years younger than me so hard that his tooth was knocked out and he cried and cried, for example. I wanted to be tough, I wanted to be a boy, because boys had power. I wanted to be a winner. I wanted to hit someone else so I could know what it felt like (it didn't feel good to me).

Forgive yourself for loving your abuser, for wanting to make someone who hurt you happy, for wanting to be like them so that you could stop being a victim. Forgive the child, forgive the teen, forgive the person in their twenties. Forgive the person you were yesterday. Forgiveness requires owning the regret and the bad feelings, and not making excuses. Forgiveness requires release.

However, with respect to others who have harmed you, focusing too much on forgiveness during the healing process is a distraction. Forgiveness is a loaded word, with complex and varied connotations. I don't like it, because I was often put in the position of being forced to perform forgiveness to survive—to be quiet and to let go, or pretend to let go, of the anger I had about my abuse. Anger needs to be acknowledged and validated before it can be transformed. Sometimes forgiveness comes with healing, in slow drips. Sometimes forgiveness comes when the person who harmed you meaningfully apologizes and changes their behavior. Sometimes it doesn't come at all, because the anger about the abuse becomes an anger about the lack of accountability. Sometimes forgiveness is impossible, at this moment or ever.

It can't be forced if it doesn't feel *right*.

And it's okay, because you can heal without it. Unearned forgiveness is not a restorative choice, for you or the perpetrator of abuse. In fact, an act of forgiveness given to someone who has not taken accountability simply enables more toxic behavior. I think people advise forgiveness because it carries an air of finality to it, a false promise of closure, and a feeling of resolution. Having residual anger seems open-ended. But having residual anger is reality. Open-ended situations are reality. People who were supposed to love you unconditionally repeatedly harming you and not holding themselves accountable is a reality. If forgiveness doesn't feel right, then it's probably not right (at least right now). Forgiveness will come naturally for the ones who've earned it, and if it doesn't come naturally, it's okay. Empathy is another positive act you may be able to extend to such people.

Acts of Empathy

Acts of empathy are in some ways easier than acts of love, and in other ways they are more difficult, because empathy requires the mind to engage. We only experience our experience, but we can use our minds to *try* to experience someone else's. An act of love can be blind, but an act of empathy must see. To be empathetic is to understand, be aware of, be sensitive to, or try to vicariously experience the feelings, thoughts, and experiences of another. Empathy is *hard*.

We were born inclined to empathize, just as we were born inclined to love. We have mirror neurons, which means that when we watch someone else do something, or share in their experience, our mirror neurons respond as if we too are doing the act or engaged in the experience.

Empathy is corrupted for many of us with C-PTSD because we may have never experienced it from our caregivers, or we may have been expected to inauthentically perform empathy to appease our caregivers. I had to go on a journey to even understand what empathy really is, and what resonated with me most were descriptions of empathy as presence, an openness to exposure and honesty, listening to and being with, without judgment. We don't look away, figuratively (by not focusing or listening) or literally (by ending the conversation and suggesting our disinterest). Not looking away can be excruciatingly painful for those of us who were inappropriately inundated with the emotions of our caregivers as young children.

Empathy requires that we really listen, without projection or self-interest. We listen without rushing to solutions or judgments. We listen without worrying about what the other person thinks of us, or what we'll say next, or our own similar experience. We listen knowing that we're now free, aware, and healing adults who won't drown in the other person's feelings or narrative. We won't be annihilated. We may be terrified, but we are open and curious. We create space for another to be seen the way we want to be seen.

Empathy lives in the mind, and it relies on the mind's ability to affect the body's signals to another—that we are listening, that we care, that we get it. Even though empathy often motivates us toward action (if someone expresses pain, we want to help), empathy isn't about action. Empathy is permitting yourself to sit with someone in their feelings, with appropriate boundaries. Boundaries are particularly important if we choose an act of empathy toward the perpetrator of our trauma, or someone we might be drawn to because they exhibit similar behaviors to them. Some of us with C-PTSD have been programmed to perform empathy to appease others, to dissolve our internal, organic boundaries in service of the feelings of a selfish parent. And so, it can become difficult for us to disengage, to not internalize the feelings of others, and to distinguish our own. Empathy becomes distressing.

Studies have demonstrated that empathy intensifies traumatic bonding of the sort discussed in the previous section. Feeling empathy can create a powerful emotional attachment, which might then be used to rationalize mistreatment. But healthy empathy doesn't make excuses for toxic behavior. If there's someone whose toxic behavior you can't keep from excusing due to your own trauma, empathy is not an appropriate choice with respect to that particular person, or it should be circumscribed (for example, we can have empathy for the traumatized child the person may have been, but not for the abuser they became—because *they knew how it felt and did it anyway*, repeatedly, and didn't apologize). In those situations, acts of acceptance are the only restorative choice.

Acts of Acceptance

Perpetrators of abuse and neglect define their destiny through their decisions to intentionally hurt, and your acts of love or empathy will not change the choices they have made and continue to make. You don't have to forgive an abuser (an act of love). You don't have to empathize with an abuser (an act of empathy). You do have to accept them as they are. Acceptance means accepting the reality of the situation, but not necessarily accepting someone into your life. It means accepting human nature as it is, and our heartbreaking, immutable inability to change it.

They perpetrated trauma and they may do it again, and there's nothing you can do about it. They may or may not change, and it has nothing to do with you. Let go of the rage, and let go of the desire to control, fix, manage, or rescue. Nothing you do will make a difference, but that doesn't make you helpless. It makes you free, strong, and focused on what matters.

It takes profound courage to accept the person who hurt you as they are, to accept that your parent or caregiver was and is deeply flawed. If you can forgive without losing yourself, great. If you can have empathy without losing yourself, great. If not, that's great too. But do accept.

I disagree with the aphorism that forgiveness is required to lose an emotional reaction to someone's presence or their name being mentioned. All that is required is acceptance, and you can accept without forgiving; the two paths should not be conflated. You lose the emotional reaction to another's name or presence by accepting them, as they are, and giving yourself permission to feel all of the feelings that arise, fully and without judgment. Accept that the person is who they are and did what they did, and nothing you do (including even an act of forgiveness) will change their choices.

Acceptance brings freedom. Acceptance led to accelerated returns with respect to healing for me, whereas the misguided emphasis on forgiveness held me back. When we can't authentically forgive, we may feel like there is something wrong with us. We may feel forced into forgiveness, forced to suppress our anger and pain. Forgiveness—authentic or not—will not heal our anger and pain. The only way to handle anger and pain is to turn inward with awareness and outward to release and transform, to regulate and integrate, to engage in the practices, to engage in therapy, over and over and over again. It's not to criticize, judge, or condemn. Those actions are depleting. If the feelings of judgment come from a particular venue, such as social media, remove yourself from it until you feel calmer and more regulated. Avoid your triggers until your command over your thoughts is strong enough to withstand them. The only way to dissipate the anger and pain is to accept what you don't and could never control.

Acceptance is excruciatingly painful when we want to believe it could have been or will be better—especially for us, the dreamers, the optimists, the survivors, the ones who are so sensitive to injustice or disequilibrium. I had to create and keep a physical boundary to carve out the space to heal. Acceptance meant accepting that I can't have a relationship with someone who lies to me about the most painful moments in my life and expects me to accept their lies. I can't have a relationship with someone who takes no responsibility. I can't have a relationship with someone who could randomly erupt and say the cruelest words imaginable to me. I had to grieve the loss of what I thought was possible but never was.

It may feel like you're ignoring them, but an act of acceptance radiates back to the person you're accepting. You have accepted them as they are. It's a beautiful act with an empowering frequency. You're not trying to change them, or control them, or project your ideals on them; you're accepting them, and you're letting go. It is a transcendent act. Only when you stop fighting reality do the residual feelings of anger, sadness, or lack of closure dissipate.

Acts of Service

An act of service is an act of community service or assistance to those in need, large or small. Acts of service can be inspired by acts of empathy, or they can be an act of love for someone you don't know. Acts of service also include simple actions like holding the door for the person after you, helping someone locate a lost item, donating to a cause, or encouraging or teaching someone. Some people have careers that entail everyday service, such as teachers, coaches, firefighters, and therapists. Those of us who don't can find a way to incorporate it into our lives.

Acts of service are a great way to expand your exposure to the network of connection. Volunteering can open up your network and create social belonging. Helping a stranger, running a charitable marathon, or attending a fundraiser provide opportunities for new friendships.

The act must be genuinely helpful to that particular person or community, and not something you think they'd want or you'd like. No acts should be done with expectation, but this point is particularly salient with respect to acts of service. Acts of service should not be done with the expectation of gratitude or attention. Attention doesn't take away from the act necessarily, but it takes away from internal and external attunement. Attunement is ensuring that the act is in harmony or resonance with the needs of another person. Acts of service should not be patronizing. Acts of service should be imbued with respect.

Acts of service can be uncomfortable. We may wish to avoid seeing the reality of others' suffering or poverty. Some manifesting books say we should avoid looking at hardships or even engaging with people experiencing hardships, but difficult realities exist—and you know this, because you've lived in one. You can't run away from truth. It's your obligation to the network to assist others on their path in a way that's not too emotionally draining for yourself.

Balance performance of positive acts and the preservation of your dignity, autonomy, and physical and emotional health. Sacrifice is not conducive to your healing, empowerment, or attainment of your dreams. Self-sacrifice is not a virtue. It not only depletes sacred time and energy, but it also fosters imbalanced, discordant connections. It creates psychological and physical stress; one study found that the wounds of caregivers took nine days longer to heal than those of non-caregivers.[31] We all know stories of those who burned out performing unselfish acts. Those of us who have C-PTSD are looking for mental and/or physical escape and may be especially vulnerable. *Get help*. Anyone who expects self-sacrifice, or accepts it without a loving act in return, won't benefit from the act anyway. They may even become worse.

Acts of Creativity

An act of creativity is the origination and sharing of art, invention, or innovation with the universe. Acts of creativity manifest in many forms, from writing, building, creating (this could be anything from woodworking to soapmaking), inventing something helpful, making music or art, suggesting innovative solutions to problems big and small, or posting content on social media that makes people laugh, think, or feel less alone.

Acts of creativity come from and were discussed in connection with the practice of the imagination. Most people have a sense of the types of creative works in which they find meaning or excellence, but if you don't, go back to the practice of imagination. Acts of creativity are often aligned with our most authentic and reverent dreams—that to which we aspire, but also that to which we're drawn by an invisible force and compelled to bring forth into the world. You have a distinct perspective about life and the power to express it. You have a unique way in which you can contribute to the universe. You have the power to create something tangible through which others will find meaning, understanding, pleasure, or comfort.

CHAPTER 4

PRACTICE BRINGING FORTH

Jesus said, "If you bring forth what is within you, what you bring forth will save you. If you do not bring forth what is within you, what you do not bring forth will destroy you."

Gnostic Gospels, Gospel of Thomas

Ask for what you want and be prepared to get it.
Maya Angelou, Wouldn't Take Nothing for My
Journey Now

Dream big.

Dream huge.

Possibility and opportunity are yours.

Express the dream that is within you, and life will find a way to unfold in alignment.

To practice bringing forth is to acknowledge your dreams, goals, or intentions and to bravely pursue their unfolding with tenacity, detachment, and a conviction in inevitability. Self-awareness, decisiveness, conviction, commitment, and a yielding trust in the universe will bring forth your dreams.

I have chosen to use the term "bringing forth" (which has a rich poetic history) instead of "manifesting" or "goal achievement" for a few different reasons.

First, society has a bias against the law of attraction, the law of assumption, manifesting, scripting, and similar concepts (referred to collectively herein as "manifesting" for the sake of simplicity, although differences exist among them). Manifesting, essentially, entails using the power of belief to turn intentions into reality, although unfortunately, manifesting has become analogous to wishful thinking, the whisper of a whim-like dream, and desire lacking force. I believe, however, that manifesting has the ultimate force behind it—firm and unyielding faith in success, unimpeachably empowering beliefs. And many times, *it works*. People with easy and successful lives manifest all the time.

"Goals" may be more socially acceptable, but a goal is a dream stripped of all magic, an aspiration watered down by a depressing view of reality. Goals and dreams are not as materially different as the biases of our culture and language suggest. A goal is just a socially approved version of an aspiration, aim, dream, or wish. A goal has the patina of hard work, practicality, and control plastered on it. For example, the popular SMART system for goal-setting suggests a goal should be "Specific, Measurable, Achievable, Relevant, and Time-Bound." As comforting as its clarity is, many problems are inherent in such a framework. These include the suggestion that you have all the answers, that it's all under your control, and that you should settle for what you know you can achieve relatively quickly.

Language exerts a powerful force on our perception, and words carry cultural weight. As a result, it may be impossible to conflate terms such as "goal," "dream," and "intention." None of these terms is accurate or inclusive. The law of attraction connotes a magnetic, automatic pull; in reality, the process is gentle, can proceed at a variety of paces, and might meet disparate points of resistance—although it certainly can act like a magnet at times, as well. Manifesting sounds gentle enough, but feels flimsy and modern instead of timeless. Goal-setting lacks an appreciation for the imagination, sense of abundance, and serendipity that leads to luck—the meet-cute, the random encounter that leads to a job interview or investment opportunity—and the fortuitous benefits an event outside of our control can bring us.

Finally, self-empowerment itself has been corrupted through its commercialization. It has turned into something that is either too esoteric or too ambitious, too childish or too Instagrammable. Influencers, writers, speakers, and gurus (often despite good intentions) make people feel like something is wrong with them if they're not 100 percent successful implementing their solution to life, while exploiting the hopes of the very same people with each successive book. Money is made off the back of the cycle of worthlessness and re-traumatization felt by those who are still in the process of healing from childhood trauma (or who haven't even begun but feel drawn to self-empowerment).

As a result of what I view as unfortunate baggage, I'm using "bringing forth," which encompasses both the magical and practical, and recognizes that your dreams—what you most authentically and reverently desire—arise from the deepest, most authentic part of you that also wants to connect, contribute, share, express, and thrive. Your wishes/goals/aspirations spring from your imagination, and your will (your ability to decide to pursue them and to maintain conviction and commitment) turns them into reality.

The practice of bringing forth is hard, whether we have C-PTSD or not, and it materially differs from other theories of manifesting or goal achievement because it harmonizes the intrinsic (and often ignored) challenges of the practice. The practice of bringing forth acknowledges that failure in attracting what you want is *not* entirely your fault. This is its most dramatic divergence from most, if not all, books about the topic. *It's not your fault.* The things that have already happened to you—the traumas, the pain, the suffering—are not your fault. You did not manifest trauma into your childhood. The mistakes you made trying to manifest a goal while feeling a deep unworthiness—they're not your fault. You didn't know enough, and you didn't feel good enough. We can't start to take accountability until we have autonomy and the understanding that what happened to us was wrong.

Once you know enough and are starting to feel good enough, you're responsible for using your will to bring forth your dreams. And yet even then, the residue of trauma can disconcert you. Even then, you'll still live in a complex universe comprised of multiple intentions and wills, collective and individual. It can be overwhelming at times, but as soon as you start participating in the complex system in a powerful way—through your will, and with trust—you have a significant say in how things play out.

You can be accountable to your dreams while not being blamed for your previous missteps, or even a misstep you make tomorrow (as long as you take ownership of it). Accountability and self-empowerment are two sides of the same coin, but many people who have experienced childhood trauma don't see or feel that way. Many people with unresolved trauma experience accountability as blame, so we'll proceed delicately. Blame actually undermines accountability. You're not to blame for your past, but you're accountable for making a difference in your life, starting now. As you proceed, you'll begin to see any actions you took that hurt others or that you otherwise regret in a new light. You'll be able to atone in a way that is natural, healthy, and empowered, instead of twisted and self-flagellating.

In addition to subjecting the reader to a great deal of blame in the name of accountability, much self-empowerment assumes the audience already has the proper foundation, that they're a blank slate and just need this or that fantastic hint or insight to transform their lives. It doesn't address that we've all grown up in a flawed world. It doesn't address the traumas a person may have experienced and the self-protective adaptations they've naturally made in response—naturally, and for their short-term protection, but not to their long-term advantage.

The practice of "bringing forth" is both simpler and deeper than these other versions of manifestation and goal-setting. It encompasses nuance and doesn't assume the absence of challenge, and yet it's even more certain, because it recognizes that your dreams already exist in some form, as *they are you. They are what you were always meant to be.* Your responsibility is to bring them forth, to will them into reality.

***

Many possible explanations exist for why believing—with your mind, body, and subconscious—that you'll attain your dreams will lead to the attainment of those dreams. It might be quantum physics, or that human existence is a simulation, or it might have something to do with us all being God. *It doesn't really matter and is unknowable.* If you're interested in exploring these theories, many books have examined the "why." This book is not one of them. Curiosity is fun, but worrying about having all the answers and explanations puts you in an inherently mechanistic view. You can attain 100 percent comprehension of neither magic nor science. You can have conviction without understanding precisely how it all works.

Bringing forth encompasses both magic and common sense. The convincing, common-sense explanation is this: Your thoughts and beliefs affect your actions and reactions, and your actions and reactions, even at a micro or subconscious level, determine the way others react to you. Your actions and reactions perpetually feed into the network of connection, creating ripples, a sort of butterfly effect. The energy you put out into the universe comes back to you because others are necessarily reacting to it, even when they don't realize it.

For example, if you want a certain job, and you share your intent with everyone you meet with confidence and enthusiasm, eventually you might connect with someone who will sense your confidence and enthusiasm and help you obtain that job. And if you want a partner with certain traits (you absolutely *cannot* bring forth a particular person and make them love you, as we'll discuss later), you may socialize more and share what you're looking for, and be more alert to people with those traits who are open to a relationship. You might take so many chances it becomes inevitable that you'll meet someone amazing.

The magical explanation isn't really an explanation. It can only be felt when you experience the universe seemingly conspiring in your favor. It's a synchronicity that seems inevitable. I can't even come close to explaining the chance encounters I've had that led to my desired opportunities (and I say this as someone who has zero facilitative connections resulting from my family or community of origin). Seemingly random events can change our lives in an extraordinarily positive way. Luck is real, and it blesses those who believe they are lucky and who feel deserving of luck, and therefore look for it.

The fact that you experienced what you did and are somehow here, reading this, is a miracle. Anything and everything is possible, and you can bring forth through the following five steps:

1. Decide what you want.

2. Acknowledge what you want.

3. Be brave.

4. Accept that you have no control, other than not giving up.

5. Accept that you already have what you want.

I like to think of bringing forth as a personal, self-directed form of cognitive behavioral therapy ("CBT"). CBT entails identifying unhelpful patterns of thinking and behaving, determining their underlying causes, and cultivating more beneficial patterns through the development of healthy habits. It's not about the habits themselves, but rather how they restructure the mind; for example, making a list/schedule for the week can help you feel healthier and more in control of your life. Similarly, following the steps above will help you develop thoughts and actions that serve your dreams. You'll feel more ownership; develop empowering thoughts, beliefs, and ideas; and build a structure to lean on when you feel like you're at a loss.

In practice, you can start big or small (or both at the same time). To start small, pick something with low stakes (like a parking spot or a table by the window at a restaurant) or something that is fun and pleasing to you (spotting a yellow convertible, or a dragonfly, or a Keanu Reeves look-alike).

Here's an example of something with low stakes. About a year ago, I started attending classes at a hot gym in my city. I loved these classes, but when I first started driving to the gym, finding parking caused me a lot of stress. I would drive around for up to ten minutes desperately searching for a space. I started to leave home earlier and earlier, anticipating the difficulty of finding parking, anxious the whole time I was driving over. Often, I'd barely manage to find a spot in time to make it to class.

I decided to practice bringing forth to quickly find a parking space close to the gym.

1. I decided what I wanted. I wanted to find a convenient parking spot quickly (within three minutes of entering the area). I didn't let myself view it as a competition, or view finding a spot as taking away a spot from anyone else.

2. I acknowledged what I wanted. I said aloud that I'd find a spot easily. I visualized the open spot, but I tried to do so in a detached way that didn't assume I had any particular spot.

3. I attempted to be brave by putting myself out there. This step took a counterintuitive form—it meant not adding in the extra minutes that assumed finding a spot would be a struggle. I only built in a reasonable amount of time, assuming it would work out. It was uncomfortable.

4. I recognized my anxiety, while also accepting that it was okay if I didn't find a spot. To let the anxiety pass over me, I physically relaxed my shoulders, neck, and even my tongue while thinking about finding the spot. I engaged in breathwork. I "detached" from the outcome, accepting that it was okay if I missed a class (although I would be charged $20). It was only a class.

5. And finally, I eased into the belief that I would find a parking spot easily, that it was more than possible, that it was already mine. Plenty of parking was available, and it would all work out; all I had to do was show up. The emergence of the fifth step from the fourth step can be a bit indistinct.

Almost immediately, finding a great parking space became easy, although occasionally, I had to walk a little farther than I preferred. My luck was so consistent that I started to leave my home later and later, with no fear. The steps gave me a structure that took me out of my anxiety spiral. The times my emotions were a bit frazzled or inconsistent, the practice didn't work, but I could usually point to an error in following the steps as the reason.

Again, we can come up with common-sense reasons why it worked: Perhaps I became more alert and savvier about noticing people leaving spots, or I figured out which spots to check first. Perhaps parking became less crowded due to external factors, and I happened to benefit. Perhaps my release of anxiety helped me see more clearly, or faith in my success sharpened my approach.

It doesn't matter. The practice of bringing forth lives in the space of miracles. Miracles are part common sense, part magic, and mostly inexplicable, yet accessible to each of us.

Decide What You Want

Decide. Decide who you are, what you do, and what you have. Deciding is a powerful commitment. Through deciding, we tell the universe who we are and what we are capable of. We give the universe something to work with, and we shape our reality. By deciding, we celebrate the divine gift of free will.

In the space of the imagination, ask yourself: What would I do if I could do anything? What would I decide without monetary or time limitations? What would I decide without fear or insecurity? Without a desire for recognition, or a desire to hide? Without worry that I'm not good enough? Without the lies that trauma taught me?

Take your time. Your imagination will give you options. Self-awareness will give you the answer. Use fearless, uncompromising honesty and authenticity to settle on a decision. Who are you, and what makes you feel alive? What makes you feel like you? What brings you happiness, inspiration, contentment, or peace? Acknowledge and quiet the wounded narrator, over and over again, until you become aware of what remains in the space left behind. Begin to listen to and trust that clear, compassionate, and calm voice.

Don't be realistic. Don't even worry about figuring out what's realistic, because you don't know. Don't worry about testing your dream for practicality or possibility; your assessment will be extremely biased due to the influence of your wounded narrator. Don't preemptively limit yourself. I disagree with self-empowerment writers who advise people to be aware of trade-offs. The universe will sort out what needs to be sorted, and the universe knows better than you. You shouldn't worry at all, but trade-offs are the last thing you should worry about. Goals are rarely self-contradictory, and even if they are, you aren't unbiased enough to comprehend the contradictions or lack thereof.

Some of us struggle with limiting beliefs that constrict our options, while others of us think expansively but become quickly overwhelmed and struggle to choose. More than one option may feel good or even right. Allow yourself to live in active uncertainty, taking in information and paying attention to your authentic self. Listen to your thoughts and feel your sensations, but be aware of which are tied to your traumatic programming and which ones are your highest self surfacing. Look for signs and messages from the universe—not because they are telling you what to do (a misunderstanding many people have)—but because your awareness of them is really your inner wisdom trying to make itself heard.

Use authenticity and reverence to test your options. Authenticity means the decision is undisputedly true to you, and reverence means the decision is aligned with your highest self. You can neither bring forth from a place of conformity or pretense nor from a place of selfishness, ego, or competitiveness. Reverence means the decision does not attempt to control or spread ill will toward others. Ill will includes taking anything away from someone else or wishing conflict for yourself or another. Control includes attempting to make a specific person fall in love with you (the full implications of this are discussed in Chapter 9).

Ask yourself: *What do you want, and why do you want it?*

Perhaps you desire a luxury jacket. You should ask yourself *why* you want it. Is it to obtain status (in other words, feel "whole")? Is it to feel better than someone else? Is it to be accepted by a social circle? None of these are an authentic reason. The most authentic reason is that you like it, and you'd still like it even if everyone else hated it. You're not materialistic for wanting something beautiful and well-made. Beauty—visual, tactile, and other—brings joy. Beautiful things are examples of craftsmanship, which is one of the most spectacular human achievements.

As long as the dream is authentic and reverent, you're good. Be curious about what your authentic, reverent self is suggesting, but never judgmental. Judgment is toxic; it's almost always the result of external conditioning, and often the internalization of what your parents thought (and therefore what you assume other people's opinions are). *Judgment is the opposite of possibility.* For this reason, when thinking about yourself and your decisions, avoid adjectives. Every adjective is loaded with heavy, limiting, judgment-laden connotations.

For example, you're not greedy for wanting wealth. Wealth facilitates self-actualization. It serves as a tool for positive change and an avenue for liberation. You can do far more good with money than without it, for yourself and for others. Without money, you have to spend too much time trying to survive, which detracts from your own artistic, commercial, and social pursuits. Never feel guilty for desiring wealth when we're all stuck in a capitalist society. Welcome abundance.

Wanting wealth is a significant hang-up for some of us. It's more than acceptable—it's amazing—to want wealth. Say it aloud: It's amazing to want wealth. Some people are totally fine with wanting wealth, but as we discussed in Chapter 1, many grew up believing that they shouldn't aim too high, or that more money causes more problems. No, it doesn't. Money solves a lot of problems and solves them quickly. Money gives you power and freedom, no matter who you are. That power and freedom can be especially empowering as a survivor of trauma, or a woman, or a person of color, or a member of any historically disenfranchised group. As Marcus Garvey stated, "power is the only protection against injustice." We do not live in a just world, and in service of protecting yourself and making it more just, acquire power. You can make your life easier, you can give back, and you'll be given a greater voice through financial contributions. For better or worse, it's one of the most effective ways to positively influence the world.

Authentic also doesn't mean loudly spectacular. You don't have to desire to be super famous or to win an award. Your dream may be for a quiet, everyday miracle, such as finding a partner who treats you well, running a marathon, or selling your craft on Etsy or your food product at the farmer's market. It doesn't matter if someone else (or your wounded narrator) thinks it's too "ordinary." Being a content person with self-worth is absolutely extraordinary in this world.

Your dream can't be for social media photos. It can't be for bragging rights. Making a decision for the wrong reasons—such as money, fame, or attention—takes you down a blind alley. It must be for your own life, your authentic self, which has nothing to do with other people's opinions. Only you have the obligation and privilege of living in your skin every day, and no one's opinions will fundamentally change what that feels like to you. Others' opinions can only provide false paths, never the delineation of a dream. A dream is what you have to be, to express your fullest and most authentic self.

Finally, you can anticipate and accept the possible consequences of our dream. The moment a dream is brought forth is immediately followed by consequences, some amazing and some challenging. Work through them in your mind and ensure you're comfortable with them.

The following is an example of how to perform an inquiry into consequence, using my own dream. I originally decided: *I am a successful writer.* I engaged in the following inquiry.

What does success even mean? That everyone likes my work? Well, that's impossible. That a few people really love it? That it's so polarizing people can't stop talking about it? That it's on a bestseller list? I settle on what success means to me—that it is read by millions of people and makes 85 percent of their lives better, and that leads to a connection with my readership. I also consider other traditional markers of success, such as fame: I don't care that much about being famous, but I also don't think I'm the type of person who would mind some level of fame. I can imagine it allowing me to bring attention to issues I deeply care about, which would be a cool power. And wealth: Wealth is freedom, and I welcome it, but it's not directly attached to this particular dream, other than its power to give me the means to focus on my writing.

After testing my dream many times and working through a few different forms, I changed it to: *This book is a bestseller helping millions of people.* This felt and still feels authentic to me.

After testing your dream with respect to reverence and authenticity, let any uncertainty go. Honor your decision, and its ambition, and the creativity and honesty that brought you there by beginning to take action in line with it. The decision to act brings assurance and vitality in itself, pushing out any lingering doubt because our brains don't enjoy cognitive dissonance. Celebrate your decision, and feel the conviction take root.

Some people find comfort in keeping their options as open as possible, or feigning a decision and then procrastinating. That's perfectly wonderful, but doing so won't propel you forward with the force that conviction brings. It will almost certainly cause delays and confusion in bringing forth a specific dream. If the aim is wishy-washy, or if you don't demonstrate commitment through action, the network of connection will play with you, sending you mixed signals as if asking, "Are you sure?" And maybe you're not sure. That's fine as long as you recognize and appreciate that you're in the stage of delay and that the stage of delay may entail more chaos than ordinary life already does. Keeping options open or procrastinating are simply ways the wounded narrator temporarily alleviates the dread, self-doubt, and fear that it brings to all decisions and actions. But you remain stuck. Decide on a dream so authentic and reverent that it gives you the will to keep pushing through those limiting beliefs.

I decided to write this book, and I'm living this decision every day I place words on a page. You are with me as I perform my decision. I'm ordinary and extraordinary, just like you. I'm wholeheartedly dedicated to reaching you and others through this book, and to learning from you. My creative work is both an expression of my desire and my path to receiving it. I'm not writing to be accepted, or loved, or deemed worthy. I'm writing because I love writing. I'm writing because I love this book, and I already love my readers. I'm writing this book because I want my readers to feel good. Because my dream is authentic, I'm invigorated by it, helping me push through the difficult moments, and they lessen over time, and my conviction grows. I feel like myself, and I feel alive.

Deciding is living, while indifference is death. Or, at least, it's the status quo. I don't think you're reading this book to remain in the status quo.

You are as good as the best.

You can do anything anyone else has done, and you can do what's never been done before.

Decide and do.

Acknowledge What You Want—Consciously, Visually, or in Writing

Acknowledging your dream means communicating to yourself, internally and externally, the decision you've made. State what you want, as definitively as possible. Don't plan the means. At this stage, planning the means circumscribes the avenues to bringing forth your dreams.

Your decision is your future reality, your destiny. Repeat your decision over and over again, until it becomes like breathing. It's not easy to get to the point where you can repeat your decision with absolutely no discomfort and complete ease, in your body and mind, completely owning it. Repeat your dream when cooking, falling asleep, or brushing your teeth. Even better, internally acknowledge your dream while performing a calm, pleasant, or endorphin-inducing activity, such as walking in nature, biking, running, sunbathing, or enjoying good food. Perform activities that make you feel the way realizing your dream will make you feel. By doing this, you connect your dream to a sensory reward, and your mind will begin to associate realizing the dream with rewarding feelings.

The goal is to make your body and mind feel as if your dream has already come to pass. The process works on two levels: First, you're telling the universe what you want. Second, and more importantly, you're telling your subconscious what you want. The unresolved trauma held by your wounded narrator can create conflicts with your decision. You can acknowledge those conflicts, be curious about their origin, and accept them as a part of a wounded narrative.

You're allowed to have thoughts and beliefs without choosing to keep having them, without choosing to act on them. You can listen and determine what still needs healing, but in the meantime, you can use a sleight of hand to align your subconscious with your dream. You can also make your mind and body feel as if your dream has already come to pass through some of the integration practices described in Chapter 6.

Simply acknowledging your decision sends a message to your subconscious and to the universe. Written words add vibrancy, spirit, and positive loving force to the declaration, particularly if they suggest your dream has already been brought forth. Fixing your dream in writing fixes it into your awareness in a way internal acknowledgment can't. Giving your decision form breathes literal life into it.

Here are two of my favorite examples of powerful aspirational writing.

- Octavia E. Butler wanted to be a bestselling writer but was struggling financially and professionally. She wrote in her private journal, in the present tense: "I shall be a bestselling writer. ... This is my life. I write bestselling novels. ... I will find a way to do this. So be it! See to it!" LeGuin commanded the universe with a gorgeous, vibrant statement: "My books will be read by millions of people! So be it! See to it!" Her exclamations added enthusiasm, as did calling what she wanted her "life." Her conviction assured her destiny as a successful and influential science fiction writer.

- Jim Carrey was a struggling stand-up comedian and wanted to be a successful actor. He wrote himself a check for $10 million—a real check—and dated it ten years into the future. He kept it in his wallet. Ten years later, he received a check for $10 million for the movie *Dumb and Dumber*.

Using a physical check that has real meaning and use in the world made Carrey's dream tangible before it was realized (and carrying it around with him showed conviction).

Some people find success acknowledging their dreams in a concrete, no-nonsense manner, and others succeed using emotion. Adding emotions to words can make them feel unequivocal, but only if sincere. You should use what feels most authentic to you.

Be careful with your language, because the words you say create your reality. Never say a negative version of your intent. For example, don't say: "I don't want to fail the exam." Say: "I have passed the exam," or if that makes you uncomfortable, "I will pass the exam soon." *Never* use qualifiers like "but," "if," or "maybe." These words introduce weakness. Only use positive phrasing, and use present or future tense if possible.

You don't need to use language that reflects perfection or 100 percent of anything. Saying "I am perfectly healthy" or "I am in possession of unlimited energy" is counterproductive; it's false and will always be false. No one is perfect with regard to a particular trait; it's impossible. You'll never be perfectly anything, because you're human. *But you don't need to be perfect to be loved and to have your dreams come true.* Being mostly anything is pretty amazing. In fact, these types of statements create pressure to manifest flawlessness, which undermines the whole effort. Not only is perfection unrealistic, but it also saps the energy you need to bring forth. Expectations can be high without being oppressive (see the 85 percent rule discussed in Chapter 2).

If you desire a specific amount of money, writing down the amount over and over again or imagining the amount is a fantastic start. However, it's even better to imagine the actual experiences you desire. It's best for the image not to be static and motionless. Even if it's a material thing you desire—say, a beach house—after you've imagined the tangible details most important to you, imagine yourself experiencing it. Imagine what it would feel like being there, traveling there, waking up there, going to sleep there, and hosting there if that's what you intend to do. Try to make yourself feel the feelings you want to feel there—happiness, peace, companionship, or adventure. As if you're using a paintbrush, apply your feelings onto your image.

You can add dramatically more power by visualizing the bringing forth of your decision. Visualization is directly connected to the imagination. Visualization takes the stream of thought inspired by the imagination and focuses it on something specific. You permitted your imagination to be boundless, and now you are making a decision and concentrating on a specific image or set of words.

Visualization means picturing what you want in your mind, and it works best with a very concrete dream. You can imagine receiving a check, or a phone call, or an award. You can imagine a picture of yourself doing what you dream of doing. You're not imagining the path, but rather the result. Imagine the feelings that moment will bring you. Really try to feel them. Imagining those feelings will eventually make you feel them internally in the present, as if the moment has already happened. Just as your body doesn't know the difference between real and imagined stress, it also doesn't know the difference between real and imagined success. Your body and subconscious will begin to align with your mind in its certainty, because they already feel as if the moment has happened.

Vision boards are a way to get the ball rolling, but I think their benefits have been overstated. First, they're unjustifiably busy—though making a simple, clean one for a particular dream, like what you want your house to look like, might work. They may seem convenient for those of us who have trouble making a vision, and benefit undoubtedly exists in the selection of something specific, but too many people clutter their vision boards with disparate and wide-ranging aspirations. It's overwhelming and confusing. In addition, the static nature of images cut from papers and magazines is less powerful than the visions created by our own minds.

As a part of my visualization of this book's reach, I imagined it on a bestseller list. I looked at the list and saw my book, and I felt a full-circle happiness. That's the only emotion I could think of feeling: happy it had performed well and reached many people.

I had also thought about writing positive reviews of this book myself, as if they were written by others, before I realized I can't control individual reactions without negatively impacting authenticity. I want this book to speak to people and be informed by a shared reality, but I can't let fear of what other people may think dampen my expression. I also want feedback for purposes of learning from it, and how could I possibly learn from something I already anticipated? Instead, I wrote an email to myself asking me to speak at an event. I also wrote the acknowledgments to this book before I was finished, thanking people who had helped me along the way. This incarnated my dream, along with a dash of gratitude for what is and what would be.

You may want to include a specific date by which you'd like your dream realized, but *only* if it doesn't induce anxiety. If it does, eliminate all thought of it. A date keeps you and the universe accountable, but the resulting anxiety can be a limitation.

Repetition is critical. Repeatedly acknowledge your dream, in moments of peace and in moments of activity, in moments when you're working toward the dream and moments when you're thrown off track. Try to weave the acknowledgments into your everyday life. For example, you can make your acknowledgments into passwords you use on a regular basis, such as "Success-is-easy" or "Wellness-is-my-reality" or "my-Art-sells." Or you can place your written or visual acknowledgments in a place where you'll look at them every day, like next to your bathroom mirror or where you place your keys.

At times during your acknowledgment, you may feel a pang of negativity. Embrace the pang, examine the resistance, and let it ebb back out of your body. Don't suppress it with forceful "replacement" thoughts. Acknowledge that it's unwanted, but don't struggle to push it out. Prematurely pushing it out will cause it to reemerge at an even less convenient time. Where is the resistance coming from? What is your worry? Where does that worry come from? Engage with curiosity until it's resolved, knowing it won't overtake you. Ride the emotional wave and take back control during the downward ebb.

Don't waste your time on this internal acknowledgment if you're feeling lousy. It won't work. You must work through the lousy first. Allow yourself to feel the full extent of the lousy for a day or even a week, and then try a physical activity or a change of scenery. Grief may take months to work through, but other forms of lousy shouldn't require nearly as long. Allow the dream to remain present off-stage.

Some wonder if praying counts as acknowledgment. The answer is sometimes. Prayer is problematic if it's desperate, and many people only pray when they're desperate. Acknowledging is not begging, praying, demanding, or bargaining. Begging and demanding are desperate and generate a low frequency. Would you like to be begged? Do you enjoy clear and confident requests with high expectations, or do you prefer a lot of drama? I'm guessing the former. Bargaining, in particular, weakens your chances of reaching your dreams. When bargaining, you will over-promise or compromise and then enter the cycle of worthlessness when your bargain or compromise doesn't work, and you'll feel like you lost something in the process. You don't have to negotiate with God or the universe or the network of connection or your own sense of worth. You don't have to give something up.

Many manifesting books suggest you should not advertise your aims to anyone, for fear of toxic influence, scrutiny, judgment, or the injection of doubt. This avoidance is unnecessary and perhaps even harmful, as it's based on insecurity. Acknowledging what you want means being brave enough to be vulnerable.

You're vulnerable when you acknowledge that you want or need something, whether that's made public or not. But we all want and need, and pretending we don't isn't fooling anyone.

It's okay to be vulnerable. Acknowledge and validate your vulnerability. Living in the process of bringing forth makes the vulnerability dissipate and reemerge as a force that pushes you forward. I felt vulnerable when I first started writing my dreams in a book that will be published. Over time, the vulnerability began to dissipate and re-emerge as a force of will.

Once you've worked through this book and its practices, other people's opinions aren't going to take you down (for long anyway). Your destiny is not fragile. You don't need to advertise your dreams to anyone, or use a lot of specific details, and you certainly shouldn't brag—but sharing has positive benefits. By telling people what you're doing, you're being both brave and vulnerable, a magical combination. It also keeps you accountable. It's possible you'll attract negative energy or jealousy, but thinking that way—fearing the jealousy or even relishing it—is profoundly unhelpful. You cannot fear or control or seek specific reactions from others.

Be Brave and Put Yourself Out There

Be brave. Take actions that align with your dream. Become a dream come true.

Bravery is putting yourself out there, exposing yourself, or making the leap. Even if you're struggling with self-worth, power, and possibility (as we all do at times), being brave pulls you in and through. Being brave tells the universe you believe in yourself and your dream. You are your acts. You are your bravery.

I use the word "bravery" here instead of "courage." Many of my favorite motivational writers espouse "courage" to great effect. I like "bravery" because "bravery" comes from the Italian word for "bravo," which means "bold." Originally, however, it meant "wild, savage," and that original meaning allows the word to retain connotations of spontaneity. Whenever I've been brave, that moment—that actual moment of doing the thing—was *spontaneous*. That moment was *wild*. I knew the action was a step I needed to take, and I prepared for it. I typically procrastinated a bit, and spun my wheels, and subconsciously distracted myself with whatever I could because I was scared to jump off the cliff into the cool blue water below. But the brave moment is the jump. It's not sullied by thought or feeling; it's pure action that changes your life forever. I was ready, but I didn't plan the very moment of action. I simply did it, without thought. That's how bravery works.

At some point, you decide to do it and you do it. Think back to the brave acts you've performed: sticking up to a bully, walking up to someone and introducing yourself, moving to a new place, or committing to your partner. If these moments were full of thoughts and planning, you would have been immobilized. Bravery lives in the space of pure action.

Bravery is harder work in that one moment of pure action than "working hard and believing." Many people who have achieved great success emphasize all of the hard work they performed. It's an empty (and dangerous) platitude that you can achieve anything if you work hard. It's a deceptive cliché promoted for many reasons, including because people feel guilty for being successful (always at least in part) due to their lucky breaks (privileges) and their practice of much of what is in this book (which give birth to luck, confidence, unreserved commitment, self-worth, resilience, and synchronicity); because hard work is the engine of our capitalist society, and therefore we're all conditioned from a young age to valorize it; and because, due to childhood trauma and/or cultural conditioning, we believe we must prove our worth constantly through accomplishment.

Many people work very hard, and most people are doing "something" almost all the time, to the extent they exhaust themselves mentally and physically. People who never work hard are incredibly rare and such long-term listlessness is often the result of a mental or physical health issue. Most of us are doing, doing, and doing. Working hard is such a foundational aspect of our society that, for many people, working hard is excessively safe mentally and emotionally—too safe to lead to results. Hard work pegs people into a reality that is pre-structured for them. It's dull and safe being a cog, and it can even feel cozy. Work is comfortable because it's familiar and a distraction from anxiety, authenticity, vulnerability, and the imagination. Productivity is a palliative for many people because it's designed to be one. It makes us feel less powerless, all while keeping us mostly powerless.

It's dangerous and limiting to emphasize hard work over bravery. Look around you at all the people working incredibly hard at menial, low-paying jobs. I drove through central California last summer and saw hundreds of people picking strawberries in 100-degree heat. These people were (and are) working unfathomably hard. Their work has tremendous value for our society; they are literally making food available to us (how many of us would survive if we couldn't rely on others to pick and process our food?). They're working as hard or harder than famous billionaires, and they're just as worthy of the life of their dreams. If you're currently working a menial, physically or mentally taxing job, it's not a reflection of your power or possibilities. You could work very hard at such a job or not work hard at all, and it wouldn't change your fundamental worth and what you're capable of. Your job doesn't make you better or worse than anyone else. We all deserve self-actualizing work—*work that doesn't feel like work but feels like finding ourselves.*

You may work the job you work to provide for yourself and your family, but to go beyond survival you need bravery. I want to be clear that I'm not shaming or blaming anyone for not leaving a menial job, least of all those hard-working agricultural workers. And for some people—especially those who escaped oppressive environments, who feel blessed to just be in the States working—the monotony *may* be the dream, at least for a while. I'm saying that the only way any of us can break out of monotony is by taking a risk. Those of us who don't have family wealth or connections need bravery to go beyond, to expand our luck surface and increase the chances we'll experience the opportunity that leads us closer to our dreams. The wild, spontaneous leap into that beyond is bravery.

The wild, spontaneous leap is how we learn, become free, and intentionally choose our dreams over perceived safety. The brain likes to feel in control and safe, even if it's wrong. Our brains associate familiarity with safety, even if familiarity doesn't align with what we truly want. If your dreams are to lead a familiar existence, that's acceptable. But otherwise, safe will not express your dreams, no matter how hard you're "working." The only way to break out of safety is through acts of bravery. Acts of embracing uncertainty, emotional exposure, authenticity, creativity, and opportunity—yes, whether you're picking strawberries or serving time in a prison cell, whether you're a cleaning lady or a bus driver, or an underpaid or overpaid attorney. While bravery involves effort, in the sense that it entails action, being brave will save you a lot of pointless work. Things will flow out of those beautiful moments of bravery. Luck. Shortcuts. Connections. Synchronicity. People who succeed excel at putting themselves out there and connecting to the network. Network effects and social reputation strongly influence success in fields where performance is hard to measure (like art).[32]

What you believe about the universe is true. So, if you believe you need blood, sweat, tears, or decades to attain some small amount of success, so it shall be. If you believe that you can protect or prove yourself with hard work, so it too shall be.

Being brave is how you reinforce to the universe what you want, and how you actually prove yourself. The universe can't misinterpret bravery—it's too strong a message. It's brave to insist on our dreams. And it's through brave acts that we bring forth our dreams and become our best selves.

YOU ARE CAPABLE OF BRAVE ACTS.

If you feel resistance to the brave act, let yourself feel the full weight of the doubts, insecurities, and uncertainties. The resistance is real, and it can't simply be replaced by positive thoughts.[33] Resistance will find a way to make itself heard unless it's worked through, emotionally and intellectually. Be aware that the resistance arises from limiting beliefs, and the limiting beliefs are a lie. They were meant to protect a child from danger, and now they are preventing an adult's self-actualization.

The nervous system can be acutely involved in the resistance to bravery; the body wants minimization of uncertainty and a balanced state of homeostasis. The nervous system simply acts in service of our safety, without consideration for meaning or motivation. It's adaptive. Honor the survival actions—move from self-criticism and blame to curiosity and compassion for the wounded narrator. By doing so, we permit our authentic self to direct the narrative. The authentic self can give the resistance space to expand and be seen without letting it control our actions.

Being aware that your wounded narrator is shaping your current reality is much of the battle. Ask yourself where their limiting beliefs come from. Perhaps journal about it. Perhaps cry about it. Allow yourself to feel the weight of resistance and call it what it is: a vestige of the past. It's not a referendum on your worth. It's not a sign as to what you should or shouldn't do. *It's just resistance.* You're resisting the bravery—and you're trying to get rid of resistance—so don't resist the fear. Let the fear move through you and allow it to lose its power and meaning.

Imagine yourself doing the brave act, and work through the resistance with your mind and your body. Move into the resistance (don't worry, it won't overpower you). While feeling it, relax your shoulders and then your neck, and then each part of your body. Allow the resistance a gentle expression. The resistance is not negative. It just is. Gentle expression allows you to dilute the resistance, to break it into a thousand small pieces that dissipate. The feeling will be brief but intense. Focus on your breath—1-2-3-4 in, 5-6-7-8 out—or other exercises. You are safe.

Breathe into the positive and inspiring thoughts. The resistance is moving on. Feelings are ephemeral. Our physical experience of our feelings only lasts ninety seconds, meaning our feelings only last ninety seconds if we don't allow our thoughts to continuously reactivate them. Feelings are not you, and you are not your feelings. Giving your feelings gentle expression, even in the briefest moments, depletes their power and solidifies yours. Tell yourself: *It is safe to let go. It is safe to release. I am releasing.*

This practice may need to be repeated many times to work through resistance. When resistance is sticky, when the thoughts won't depart or you find yourself acting in a manner inconsistent with what you desire, acknowledge to yourself: "I gently reject this thought/belief. It is an unwelcome vestige of the past."

And then take an opposing action. Act differently from how you feel. Choose to act in alignment with your goals while allowing yourself to feel your feelings. Behave as your aspirational self. The intentions that align with your dreams should drive your life. You are what you repeatedly do. Both healing and dreams are accomplished by movement and energy. To be self-actualized is to be in an active state, a dynamic balance.

You can also work through resistance by dipping your face in cold water for thirty to sixty seconds, which activates the vagus nerve. Activating the vagus nerve slows the heart rate and redistributes blood flow to the brain, dampening intense feelings and disrupting thought patterns.

You will never eliminate all of the resistance. That's what makes bravery so special. At some point, you'll know you're ready. You'll still be scared, and you'll do what you need to do anyway, and it will feel extraordinary.

Channel Detached Tenacity (or Tenacious Detachment)

Be persistent. Accept that your dreams will be brought forth and keep going until they are.

But always understand:

You can't control how your dreams are brought forth.

You can't control the timing or manner or route or level of precision.

Most importantly, you can't control other people.

Trust me, I've tried in my naïve days.

Give no thought to how or when things will happen for you. If you start contemplating, ruminating upon, or worrying about the means to an end or a precise timeline, you severely limit the power of your dreams. You obscure and complicate paths to success. You may become so attached to a particular path that you can't see an opportunity right in front of you, or you can't take advantage of a fortuitous coincidence. If you have a clear idea of the sequence of steps that will lead you to your dreams and you become rigidly attached to it, you shut out a whole range of possibilities. A lack of specificity with respect to the means gives you the strongest chance of success.

People like to make plans because they imply that security is possible through control. Use plans as a way to structure the way you spend your time (something you control), but understand you don't control the unfolding of your dreams. Thinking you do seems to promise security—the state of feeling safe, stable, and free from fear or anxiety. Security through control, however, is an illusion, because control itself is an illusion. Control is impossible, but the illusion of control is seductive. We tell ourselves that if only we could control the process, we'd feel okay. We'd feel secure and safe, and we'd believe.

That's not how it works.

The brain likes to think it's in control and safe, even when it's wrong. Our brains associate familiarity with safety, even if familiarity misaligns with what we want. The search for security is an attachment to what is already known, which is the past. Attachment to the past is based on fear and insecurity. Our fear makes us so desperate to control that we live in the past, but the past doesn't contain our dreams. The past doesn't contain possibilities, opportunities, or greater knowledge. Those all lie in the unknown, in what is not directly under our control.

If you don't want the future to look like the past, you can embrace the unknown, the space for imagination and miracles. You can embrace security in the only things you can: your authentic self and the power of your beliefs, thoughts, and actions. That's where true security lives.

A compulsion to control can also arise as an unintended consequence of healing your imagination. You may spend excessive effort imagining too precisely how things will play out for you, creating limiting expectations and restraints on possibilities, obscuring your perception of resources and opportunities. Instead, keep an open mind, because the universe knows better than you. The universe can see behind the scenes and balance multiple goings-on while bringing your dreams forth.

Strangely, the more we let go of (always illusory) control, the more power we actually have, and the more our success is assured. We let go of control and are rewarded with a more relaxed certainty. To acquire anything in the physical universe, we must give up attachment to its acquisition. Attachment is a form of control, whereas detachment demonstrates conviction—and the universe loves conviction. The universe loves being told what to do, but not how to do it.

One way to detach is to create a "give up" moment, where you say aloud that this or that may not happen and you'll be fine. This is detachment. You want the thing, but you're not attached or desperate to have the thing. You're not giving up on the thing, but you're not obsessed with it, either. Getting what you want is about surrender, not sacrifice. You are still you, and you still want it, but you're letting go.

Another aspect of letting go of control is accepting that you can't control other people. Part of owning your life and your thoughts, beliefs, and ideas is understanding that everyone else owns their own, as well. You can't control—and therefore you're not responsible for—anyone else's decisions or opinions, dreams or aspirations. You'll never be able to project a sense of yourself curated for other people's reactions, because you can't control their reactions. The more you try to, the more everything goes awry and the further you disconnect from your authentic self. Don't squander your time on someone else's perceptions. People are not chess pieces to be moved around, and thinking in such a manner undermines the integrity of your dreams.

You also can't change people. You can inspire them, and you may even be able to influence them, but you cannot change them.

Accept others as they are, and stop being mad at them for being themselves. It's wasted energy. The only things you can control are your perception and your actions—and, to an extent, the types of people with whom you surround yourself. Make your thoughts, beliefs, and ideas work for you within this context, and materialize them.

Just as you can't control or change others, no one can control or change you either. Excluding violations of the mind and body that occur during traumatic events, no one can control an adult without their consent. The mind is always free. If it feels as if you're being controlled, it's an illusion. A person may even experience a sense of comfort in believing they're controlled, as it abrogates their own responsibility. Responsibility can feel as heavy as it can feel liberating, depending on one's perception.

One way to dilute a compulsion to control is to accept and release what annoys you. Even finding people annoying or rude simply demonstrates that you believe you have a right to control others. You don't. People are triggering. They can hurt your feelings and complicate your life. Everyone can be difficult at times, and it's usually not personal. Maintain boundaries, but accept and release others' words and actions as a reflection of their own inner being, not yours. Choose not to remain upset about something that has nothing to do with you. Often, you will be released from the offending behavior's effects on you quickly.

I was at a pool at a wellness resort when a group of women started talking loudly and crudely. I tried to ignore them and flow through my meditations, but it was too much for me. I accepted my lack of control over them. I accepted that they were just people having a good time together. I also accepted my own frustration and that I was no Zen Buddha able to comfortably tolerate them (instead of berating myself for being imperfect and impatient).

I then went to the spa in another area of the grounds and meditated. I removed myself from a loop of negativity. Sometimes, when the annoyance or anger or frustration is too high—when you can't reach your positive thoughts—you can only snap out of them by removing yourself physically.

While I meditated, I accepted that I couldn't control timing.

When I returned to the pool area about twenty minutes later, the women were gone.

I let go of control. I let go of attachment. I willed a better outcome while accepting it could go either way.

I also didn't give up. I went back.

Maybe it would have happened anyway, or maybe not. But handling it the way I did certainly felt better than annoyance, desperation, or direct conflict.

Believe that the universe is working with you for perfect timing. Let go, but don't give up. Give commitment room to breathe.

Tenacity makes us extraordinary. We don't give up on our dreams, and we don't give up on our healing. If you believe you're worthy of your dreams, you won't give up until they are attained, and you won't try to control the means of attainment. Detached tenacity will be like breathing. It will feel like coming home.

Accept Inevitability

Cultivate a yielding trust in yourself, your dream, and the universe. Know that if it's been done, you can do it too, and that if it hasn't been done, you can and will be the first. Know that someone always succeeds, and that someone is just as likely to be you.

Nurture the conviction that your dreams are inevitable.

Accepting inevitability is extraordinarily difficult and often rife with limiting beliefs. As we discussed throughout this chapter, we can note these discomforts and barriers, like fear and shame, and accept them, examine them, and remain curious about them. We can separate from them. They don't get to be in charge. By accepting the reality of these limiting beliefs without letting them overpower us or make our decisions for us, we put them in their place.

Believing you will have what you want—that it's inevitable—is not the same thing as controlling its receipt. Trying to control receipt will undermine the belief in inevitability. Faith does not equal control. In fact, faith is equivalent to zero control. Faith is letting go of control completely, because if your faith is strong, you don't need to desperately cling to the illusion of control. When you have faith in something or someone, you have no need or desire to control them. You trust them. You don't doubt them. When you lack doubt, you have complete faith.

Don't worry about timing. Accept the wait. What you perceive as a delay may happen for many reasons, including your uncertainty, a misstep, limiting beliefs, or the seeming randomness of the universe. Sometimes you can do everything right and still experience an unwelcome delay. Perhaps your aspirations confronted the complexity of the universe in a manner that caused delay, but will ultimately be in your favor. Sometimes a dream deferred is a blessing.

A famous Chinese parable is included in many self-empowerment books for different purposes:

Once upon a time, there was a Chinese farmer whose horse ran away. That evening, all of his neighbors came around to commiserate.

They said, "We are so sorry to hear your horse has run away. This is most unfortunate."

The farmer said, "Maybe."

The next day, the horse came back, bringing seven wild horses with it.

In the evening, everybody came back and said, "Oh, isn't that lucky. What a great turn of events. You now have eight horses!"

The farmer again said, "Maybe."

The following day, the farmer's son tried to break one of the horses, and while riding it, was thrown and broke his leg.

The neighbors then said, "Oh dear, that's too bad!"

The farmer responded, "Maybe."

The next day, the conscription officers came around to conscript people into the army, and they rejected his son because he had a broken leg.

Again, all the neighbors came around and said, "Isn't that great?"

Again, the farmer said, "Maybe."

Some interpret the parable as being about good arising from bad or bad arising from good. I like the parable's deemphasis of closure or an ending. All kinds of things happen, and we never know how each event will shake out, but we can have such a strong conviction in eventually realizing our dreams that we are relatively unfazed by the uncertainty stirred up by day-to-day occurrences.

Waiting for our dreams to come true can cause impatience and anxiety, which can make the wait feel even longer or otherwise undermine our certainty. Impatience arises from the illusion that time is scarce. The more time you spend on a goal, the more vibrant and fulsome its ultimate product will be. And time is also relative (as we'll discuss in more detail in Chapter 10). Think about times in the past when you were impatient or anxious, and how meaningless those feelings are now that the events evoking those feelings have passed. Your future self will look back and not remember those moments as viscerally as your current experience may suggest.

If you've engaged in the practices and followed the steps shared here, allow yourself to trust the timing of inevitability. The dream is already yours. Tell yourself (and others, if they ask) that it will happen "soon." Or, if appropriate, that it's already happening. When you think about your dream, think of it as happening or having already occurred.

One way to handle any unwelcome anxiety related to the wait is to work on being ready, so that when an opportunity appears, you can see it and seize it. This is something we can control. Often, we think we're ready when we're not. Anticipate the consequences of realizing your dreams and ensure you're comfortable with them. Notice worries, fears, and hang-ups while becoming comfortable with the consequences that will naturally occur as a result of your dreams coming true. For example, winning an Academy Award means having some level of fame. It may not mean excessive fame, but winning inevitably comes with fame. Owning a home comes with additional responsibilities, although they can be minimized. Having a partner means giving up personal space. Are these natural consequences acceptable to you? Are they part of what you want your life to look like?

Not being ready for the consequences that will flow out of our realized dreams can be a significant blocker to realizing those dreams. We may think we want something badly, but we haven't thought out everything that will flow from it. Circle back one more time and ensure you are comfortable with wanting what you want and receiving what you want. If your dream came true tomorrow, would you be all in? If not, you have more to do.

For example, when I first started writing this book, I was practically paralyzed with the shame of being disloyal to my family and a fear of judgment from people in my community with whom I'm not even close. Rationally, upon listening to and being curious about these fears, I could understand that they were the result of my injury. They might have made sense when I was young and had to survive, but they don't make sense anymore. I considered what would happen if I were thought to have betrayed family loyalty, or if people in my community started speaking ill of me, and I realized it wouldn't matter in the slightest. I'm okay with those consequences, as well as those I haven't even been able to think of.

The limiting beliefs don't make sense. I make sense. My dream makes sense. My dream is the deepest part of me, so it's inevitable. It wants to blossom. This cohesion between self and dream takes us through the hard parts, when despair threatens. The wounded narrator may tremble in the wake of the unfolding of the dream, but it's not their dream. The authentic self is all in.

Once you're all in, declare that you are ready. At this stage of the five-step process, you should be ready, and you should be at ease receiving what you want at any moment. Sometimes, simply declaring your readiness over and over again makes you ready. For those who struggle to feel ready, practice affirmations like: "I'm ready for success" or "I'm ready for opportunity."

My dream is my destiny. Your dream is yours. Fractures and judgments will not destroy us, if they happen at all. We can't control others. Nor do their thoughts, beliefs, and ideas affect us unless we choose to allow them to. I don't permit my wounded narrator's thoughts to overwhelm me—I choose, with all of the power I can generate, to give them space and then release them. I continue to decide to let the fear, shame, guilt, and self-doubt go, over and over again, until I eventually let go completely. I make that choice with every word I place on this page and every step I take to heal my wounding, in tandem, always.

The moment in which a dream is brought forth is full of sparks, but it's not what will sustainably fill our spirits, or heal our wounds, or give us self-worth. It's this journey to creative expression, connection, and authenticity that will. The journey will heal you, and healing—by strengthening, regulating, and integrating your body and mind—will support the bringing forth of your dreams.

Chapter 5

Practice Perpetual Healing

The moment you know how your suffering came to be, you are already on the path of release from it.
Buddhist teaching

Know Thyself
Oracle of Delphi inscription

Do you remember the moment you started believing you were limited? The moment someone conveyed to you (with words or actions) that you weren't good enough or worthy enough? That you weren't going to get love, safety, and stability? That you were ridiculous for even considering the possibility?

That was the moment your wholeness was ruptured. The moment your natural inclination to be authentic, connect, imagine, and believe anything is possible was ruptured. It was an assault, whether you or others recognized it as such. It was the moment that severed you from all that you could be. That moment—or series of moments—inflicted your interfering wound.

To practice perpetual healing is to recognize your interfering wound and to heal over time within a dynamic state, while trusting the process to progress.

I use "interfering wound" to refer to a wound caused by a trauma that imposed false limits on all that you can be, and created limiting beliefs that made you feel insecure and fearful. Your interfering wound is the wound that undermined your self-worth and chilled your imagination. It might have made you scared or hopeless or pessimistic, or too realistic, too prone to settle, too passive, too self-sacrificing. Your interfering wound interferes with you living in alignment with your highest self.

I remember mine, but for some, it's hard to access. For some, it's a series of instances. For some, it's lost in a sea of pain. Children can be wounded by events, but also by omissions—the experience of not having been seen, accepted, or supported, even by ostensibly loving parents or caregivers. The experience of being judged harshly, held to unrealistic expectations or no expectations at all by a teacher. The experience of being ignored or being rewarded for all of the wrong things by a peer group. The experience of having an identity defined by someone else and feeling powerless to do anything about it.

Your interfering wound distorted your perception (and therefore your reality) by teaching you limiting beliefs about yourself and the universe.

Let yourself consider this wound. Call it a wound. Let the tears, or anger, or desire to disassociate come.

The limiting beliefs that arose from your wounding protected you, when you were a child without options—a child lacking love, security, attunement, comfort, or encouragement. They prevented cognitive dissonance, helped you work through grief, and prevented you from behaving in a way that could invite danger. Now, they are blocking your ability to heal and to bring forth the life of your dreams. We allow our wound to shape us to the extent only the most severe physical wounds ever could, because living with them feels deeply comfortable and safe. If we permitted our physical wounds to shape us to such an extent, we'd lose all sense of balance and our bodies would be unable to function normally. Similarly, our interfering wound creates imbalance in the relationship between our mind and body, and imbalance in our relationship with the universe. Our interfering wound distorts our perception, making our progress awkward and stumbling and our interactions with other people fraught with its imprint.

You are not your interfering wound. Your interfering wound is not you. You are not your injury. Someone else's repeated assaults on your integrity don't define you. Someone else's imagination does not define you. You are *your* thoughts, ideas, actions, and reactions. And therefore, you define yourself in every moment, with every choice you make, whether conscious or subconscious.

You are your present. Your present is you.

In your present, you can heal. In your present, a life as good as the best is available to you.

The only way to develop the robust self-worth and belief in power and possibility conducive to a life as good as the best is through perpetual healing of your interfering wounds. The healing is perpetual because it's a process to progress. Healing is not a ladder. Nor is it chaos. Rather, it's a sinuous, shifting river, with drop-offs, currents, swirls, streams, and waves. At some point, you reach relatively calm waters, but you're never promised perpetual tranquility. The payoff of reaching the relatively calm waters, however, is enormous. The payoff is no longer being scared, knowing how to navigate, and trusting that you'll get through the occasional rough patch.

Your healing is your responsibility. Only you can disarm your demons, find your meaning, and love yourself. And it's hard. It takes time, but you have time. All of life is time.

***

I don't like thinking about my interfering wounds, I don't like talking about them, and I certainly don't like writing about them. If there was any way I could have written this book without sharing them with you, I would have. For a long time, I wanted to find a shortcut to evade engaging with my own story. I thought, that's brilliant—a shortcut to transcendent positive thinking. Why hadn't anyone thought of it?

Part of my insight was correct—getting stuck in the muck of the past is not healthy. It contradicts the fundamental philosophy of this book, which is to sit with the present (and therefore the future). For many of us, the past is truly muck, foul and repulsive, and it sticks to us when we engage with it. It's deeply unpleasant. And it can be so easy to become stuck and create a negative feedback loop, replaying moments of trauma, feeling consciously vindicated and subconsciously worthless, or vice versa. At least that's how I felt when I thought about the past.

I also really hate the idea of people deriving cheap titillation from my trauma, as they do from so many books about trauma and as my mom did from Lifetime movies.

I didn't want people to know what happened to me. Would people I know see me as less worthy because I had a traumatic childhood? I thought they would look down on me—and by projecting those thoughts, it's clear to me now that I was looking down on myself. The thoughts themselves elucidated my interfering wound. Despite all the work I had done, all the confidence I thought I had, I allowed myself to think of myself as uniquely damaged and pathetic. My limiting belief was (but thankfully no longer is): Someone who came from what I did could never escape their demons and liberate themselves.

You can only live a life as good as your subconscious—the part of your mind refusing to give your interfering wound space to heal because it's so desperately holding onto limiting beliefs—allows you to be. What you believe about yourself, whether you say it aloud or not, will be true. I allowed my interfering wound to define me. My trauma had taught me that I didn't deserve ease or comfort or security. It taught me that I deserved to suffer. And so I had to disabuse myself of the notion that life had to be hard and then transcend the limiting beliefs holding me back.

It was only after engaging in mind-body integration therapies (I'll share them with you in detail in Chapter 6) that I realized shoehorning the practices in the book on top of unhealed wounds is a form of suppression—and suppression is toxic for the body and mind. Although short-term wins are possible, it doesn't work long-term.

In addition, I had to write from the truth, from the deep, authentic core of me that learned tough lessons. I had to acknowledge the rain cloud that I've imagined having to beat back my entire life because of the feelings of darkness, despair, and chaos my childhood engendered. I realized I had to demonstrate what I ask you to do, to live my book, even the hardest part. I couldn't merely describe how to heal and overcome the wounded narrator; I had to sever my story from my sense of worth first. I had to accept my greatest fear: the risk that my readers would define me by my trauma. By letting my fear control, I was committing that very mistake *myself*.

As a child, I felt trapped and demoralized, overwhelmed with a deep feeling of injustice. My first memory is being in a crib drinking thick formula out of a bottle and listening to my parents fight in the other room. I was frightened and I was powerless and I was alone. My second memory is being on a bed being hit by my father, smacked across the face and body repeatedly. [34] I was crying furiously, confused, scared, alone, vulnerable. I was in physical, emotional, and spiritual pain. When it was over, no one comforted me—not that time or after the many times that followed. Looking back, and having addressed that moment in therapy, I know it was a turning point that broke my trust in the world, myself, my family, and my community. I felt utterly unsafe and unworthy.

Although not as physically painful as other forms of physical abuse, and accepted as of minimal import in some cultures (like mine) when it's done to older children, someone staring you in the face and then repeatedly slapping you across it, when you are a tiny child in need of love, who barely understands language or the world, is deeply traumatizing. It's a dark and soulless act; it's something only a person who feels deeply unworthy themselves can do. It sends a palpable, crushing message of worthlessness that lodges itself in every part of your physical and spiritual being.

The abuse took place in an environment of poverty, addiction and narcissism. I grew up in the industrial Midwest with my parents and two younger siblings. Although my parents were immigrants who spoke poor English and didn't go to college, extended family helped them when they arrived to the United States. My father was a skilled tradesman who quickly found a well-paying blue-collar job through family connections. But he allowed his unresolved trauma to sabotage his life, and he dragged us down with it. He was an alcoholic—he would drink and drive, get into accidents (thankfully, no one was seriously injured), and spend nights in jail repeatedly. He was a gambling addict; he would spend his entire paycheck at the horse tracks the day he received it, leaving no money for food or rent. He was angry. He would get in fights with his bosses and quit his job, and he would abuse his family.

My father was also a narcissist. He was to be the center of the universe. Our family life revolved around appeasing him so that by some miracle he wouldn't erupt (he always erupted anyway). No one could ever outshine him. When I received good grades, I was "smart like him." Despite such success at school, I was the scapegoat of the family and the target of my father's narcissistic rage. When something I did or didn't do upset him—a look, a word, or anything else he could project onto—he demeaned me as worthless and/or hit me. His rage was always "my fault." Now I understand it was my fault only because I was desperately holding onto all that was authentic, human, honest, and brave. Those were unacceptable qualities in my family. My mother was terrified by and also rapturously in love with my father even though he treated her terribly. She didn't stand up for her children and perpetually made excuses for him and his behavior. My mother projected onto me all the anger and blame she couldn't project onto my father (perhaps for fear of triggering his rage or fear he would leave her), and she also manipulated me at times to play the "adult" and fix things in the household. Both of my parents saw the world as unfair and against them. Their comfort zone was chaos and confusion, uncertainty and insecurity, scarcity and worthlessness, victimhood and martyrdom.

When I was six, lenders foreclosed on our house. We moved and rented another home for a year, during which time my father's gambling addiction worsened. My youngest sibling was born, and my father continued to spend his entire paycheck at the horse races. Our extended family would bring over diapers and formula. At some point, my father also lost his job, we started receiving diapers and formula through the WIC program, and we were evicted from the rental home. We then spent the next seven years in the home I previously described, in the poorest neighborhood of a lower-middle-class town. Our extended family also stopped speaking to us at this time.

I could tell many disturbing anecdotes about my childhood, so absurdly heartbreaking that they're hard to believe unless you've experienced something similar. I won't. Instead, I'll tell you the result: I grew up on high alert, invariably expecting the worst to happen. I especially expected the worst to happen during a rare happy moment, because it usually did. I didn't know how to feel my feelings or make sense of the world, other than to feel responsible for everything. I didn't have physical, mental, or emotional space; I felt like I couldn't breathe, like I couldn't *be*. I never felt safe. My only escapes were school, books, and outdoor play, either alone or with neighborhood children going through their own difficult circumstances. Yet even those were not true escapes. At school, I had to follow the rules and hide my secrets; in books, I was only a visitor to someone else's story; and in my neighborhood—well, the culture of trauma was ever-present.

It was dark and stifling. In my experience, abuse, both physical and emotional, becomes suffocating in small spaces. The lack of escape becomes overwhelming. For a long time, I had claustrophobia in small, enclosed spaces like elevators, quickly feeling overcome by panic and a sense of entrapment.

We spent seven years living in that duplex (a fact my father would deny once I was an adult, claiming we only lived there for a year) until my mother saved money and built up her credit by cleaning hospital rooms, enabling her to make a down payment on a small house a few blocks away. It had been her obsession all of those seven years, the achievement that might somehow make her feel whole, worthy, real. The house was small and not very nice, but it was a house, without a landlord and with a fenced yard. It was a house, but it didn't make the abuse stop.

I remember very clearly the last time my father hit me. I was around fourteen, and we had moved to this new home. I have no memory of my supposed transgression, but I remember trying to walk away and being followed and smacked across the face. I said, "Do it again; it doesn't hurt." I had numbed myself to the physical and mental pain by then, and I truly felt no pain. My courage—for a long time, I looked back at it as courage—came from a deadening, the death of positive expectation. He walked away from me, and he never raised a hand to me again, although his emotional abuse worsened. He said unimaginably cruel things to me in his rages, but to me the most painful were the ones that disparaged how I defined myself and the only things that gave me hope—for example, deriding my reading as "brainwashing."

Once I realized college was my out, I committed to doing everything I could to get there. I joined every nonathletic team, club, or group at my high school and obtained my first part-time job at fifteen (as a server at Pizza Hut)—anything to stay away from the chaos, gain freedom, and make college more likely. College was the destination, the everything.

I shut out my father's insistence that I attend a nearby community college and continue living at home. I received generous financial assistance (scholarships, loans, and work-study) from a small liberal arts college I was excited to attend. I arranged for my parents to pay only $200/month, which I knew based on my review of their finances was realistic for them. When I returned to school for my second semester, I was informed none of it had ever been paid. They had never bothered to tell me.[35]

When I returned home, even for short visits, my father's rage and hurtful words were far more severe. My pursuit of education and my growing confidence seemed to trigger something dark and vicious in him. He screamed at me and told me I was nothing. The contrast between college and the dysfunction of what was supposed to be "home" was unbearable. I returned home less and less frequently; I spoke to my parents less and less frequently. But even as an adult, even once I graduated college and worked, even once I was in law school, even once I graduated law school and took a prestigious, high-pressure job, even once I was married, even once I had a child, it continued. It continued and continued and continued. Nothing I said or did, and none of the breaks I took from it, stopped anything. I would forgive and give countless chances, I would help out in myriad ways. All the while, my father told outright lies about the past consistently, which we were supposed to go along with in silence, until the toxicity, narcissism, chaos, and lies reached an unprecedented level—or perhaps it was my recognition of them that reached an unprecedented level. As I shared in Chapter 3, I gradually ended contact, first by going low contact, and then going no contact.

Through my healing journey, I learned that the dynamic of my family required a scapegoat, and I was it.[36] The scapegoat, by definition, receives immensely wounding blame and pain rather than the unconditional love they deserve. The scapegoated child's inherent worth, goodness, and lovability are ignored. Instead, parents decide that insults, bullying, neglect, abuse, and gaslighting are appropriate for the scapegoat. Often, the child who radiates the most light is turned into the scapegoat. For example, a child who is sensitive and inquisitive may be perceived as a threat and scapegoated by a parent who lacks these qualities. Often, the truth teller of the family—who refuses to accept the lies and illusions—is turned into a scapegoat.

Putting all the blame on the scapegoat maintains equilibrium in family life, and by displacing blame, the perpetrator of trauma never has to be personally accountable for their own actions. The scapegoat's ability to feel emotional safety and trust is sacrificed at the altar of this deeply dysfunctional equilibrium. The gaslighting wielded by the perpetrator creates a blurry muddled mess for the scapegoat, who struggles to set boundaries, recognize toxic behavior, and know within that the way they are being treated has nothing to do with them. The scapegoat may treat all relationships as conditional or transactional, because that's all they've known.

No one deserves to be a scapegoat. No one can remain in touch with their authentic self being treated that way. No one can break free of their limiting beliefs when they're being inundated with them.

Trauma itself can cause us to make ourselves our own scapegoats. We blame ourselves, because if we don't—if it's not all our fault—we have to admit that our parents, who we relied on completely for many years, are malicious or mentally ill. We have to admit that we were all alone, with no power and no way out, and that they did that to us. We have to let the weight of devastating deprivation and injury wash over us, which is harder for our wounded narrator to accept than the coping mechanism of blaming ourselves. Because the idea that if we just work hard enough, one day we will finally be worthy and lovable, still contains within it hope—hope of an unconditional love we didn't receive, of redemption, and of it all making sense.[37]

**

I wrote this section at 5:30 a.m. one morning before my kids woke up, and I felt so uncomfortable in my body afterward. I felt strain in my back, and my movements were awkward. The healing is not over; it's still in process, and engaging with it is painful. I try to notice its effect on me, to recognize it and imagine it passing through my body, being flooded out through a bright light I'm shining on it. Later, I felt an itchy spot on my neck where my lymph nodes had previously been swollen.

Each time I reviewed my draft, I felt fewer physical symptoms. And each time that ease made me feel more whole.

This is a book about realizing the miracle of your dreams—and I will tell you, my life is full of love, abundance, security, and peace. If you had told that little girl I once was, or that teenager, that her life would one day be this way, she wouldn't have believed you. The fact that I am writing this in a comfortable home with a wonderful family sleeping upstairs is an extraordinary everyday miracle.

How do you accomplish something as extraordinary as finding peace after trauma? How do you believe you can be and do anything, and accept the gifts of the universe with gratitude and humility?

I know you have a story, too. A story that contains multitudes of beauty and horror.

You may have experienced different types of abuse than I have, or been even more limited in your opportunities. Or you may not have been physically or emotionally abused, but still been a part of a toxic family dynamic that limited you somehow. Sometimes, parents with good intentions fumble dramatically because of their own interfering wounds and a lack of self-reflection or understanding of the gravity of their role. For example, perhaps your parents were inattentive to the extent you didn't feel seen, supported, and able to show the real you. This type of trauma can make you doubt and limit yourself, and fail to connect to your authentic self. Or perhaps your parents denied, minimized, or ignored your emotional pain, whether the result of everyday conflict with other children or emotional or physical assault.

Trauma is trauma, and it can and will distort your thoughts and beliefs. Unless you take the time and effort to heal your interfering wound, you are likely to continue the cycle through not only your children, but all your relationships.

The first step to perpetual healing is to take power over your story and own your perpetual healing, while ceasing to align your sense of self with the trauma. Your trauma impacts you, but your trauma is *not you*. The abuse perpetrated against you was a reflection of someone else's pain, not you as a person. And the way others react to your trauma has nothing to do with you. You're not a bad person because you had trauma that interfered with you accessing power and possibility. It was never your fault.

The way you break free isn't by looking backward. It isn't through repression, suppression, or running away. It's by allowing yourself to feel the full weight of the awful feelings. It's by calling the trauma out for what it is. It's by choosing the thoughts, ideas, actions, and reactions that align with your authentic self and your dreams. The healing of the wound is an ongoing process, but even partway through, it starts to feel like peace. It starts to feel like ease. It starts to feel like rest.

CHAPTER 6

PRACTICE MIND–BODY INTEGRATION

Neuroscience research shows that the only we can change the way we feel is by becoming aware of our inner experiences and learning to befriend what is going on inside ourselves.

Bessel A. Vander Kolk, The Body Keeps Score

Health is the first of all liberties; preserve it, and the mind is free.

Henry David Thoreau, Walden

The mind and body should be as healthy as possible individually, and integrated and balanced with one another, to clear the way for the possibility of a life as good as the best. Poor physical or emotional health is so draining that it crowds out opportunity. Moreover, the way you treat your body and mind is one way you tell the universe how you believe you deserve to be treated. You deserve a body and mind that you're aware of, and that are as healthy as possible. I'm not a therapist, nutritionist, or expert in anything in this chapter, and my treatment of each section is cursory by necessity, but I wrote this chapter based on what has worked for me and what I believe can serve as a springboard for further exploration.

Practicing mind-body integration starts with recognizing that your interfering wound likely wired your body, your mind, and their relationship with each other in a counterproductive manner, and that all three can be healed, regulated, and restored.

I first felt the power of the mind-body connection when I started running. Prior to beginning my running routine, I had a mushy, untoned body from which I was completely disconnected. I engaged in very little physical activity for many reasons. I had convinced myself I was a failure at sports at a young age. I was invariably one of the last picked for sports teams; I stood against the wall during dodgeball, afraid of throwing the ball and afraid of being hit (undoubtedly a trauma response). Prior to college, my physical activity was limited (at various points) to folklore dancing, marching band, and waitressing. At times during physical exertion, including during the first week of marching band every year, I would grow dizzy and come close to passing out. My health dramatically improved in college, as my migraines and allergies disappeared, but I didn't exercise (unless walking to class or dancing at parties counts). My body felt better, but I didn't think much about the way my body felt at all.

I can't remember exactly why I started running. I was in Washington, D.C. during the fall semester of my junior year of college for an internship. I spent my days serving subpoenas in neighborhoods with high crime rates, and my nights and weekends adapting to city life. I met many new people, had a lot of fun, and was relentlessly challenged. It was inspiring, stimulating, and sublime. It was also overwhelming, destabilizing, and dysregulating. Maybe I was searching for something regulating and private, an anodyne for emotional chaos. I remember running being brutally difficult when I started; I could only slowly jog for a few minutes before needing to walk it out. I questioned what I was doing. Fortunately, I discovered that music and beautiful sights were tremendously motivating, and I hit my stride running the National Mall while listening to hip-hop. Gradually, I built up my speed and endurance. I realized my body could change, could become stronger. I experienced endorphin rushes, catharsis, and the movement of my body transforming my mindset. Creating a flood of euphoria solely through the movement of my body felt like a superpower. I felt a sense of agency and empowerment, and I was better able to handle the stresses of my new life. *I felt saved.* My body began healing and regulating my mind, and my mind in turn began healing and regulating my body through an exquisite, barely perceptible feedback loop.

This feedback loop is inescapable. Consider it on the most basic level: It's hard to accomplish much with low energy; debilitating physical ailments are an enormous distraction; focusing on pain makes it worse. We don't have complete control over this feedback loop, but we have substantial power over it. We can use this feedback loop to our advantage to facilitate integration between our mind and body while strengthening both, giving birth to a wholeness that we should have always had.

Wholeness is bringing our body and mind into an integrated relationship that's consistent with the best of us and all we aspire to have and to be. Wholeness is the intent of healing, and wholeness is healing in itself. Wholeness feels good, right, and like what should have been true all along. Our trauma caused us to disintegrate, to fall apart and put ourselves back together on the fragile frames of limiting beliefs. Now, we can integrate our mind and body on the foundation of empowering beliefs.

A mind-body relationship is a relatively new idea in the West, where the body and mind were traditionally considered split. Early

Christian teachings propagated that the primary purpose of one's life was preparation for the afterlife; thus, the body was perceived as sinful (as something that could undermine the soul's purpose with its base desires and needs) and a person's soul was all that mattered. The body was not important to one's life in and of itself. The Church controlled the limited education available, and that education focused on cultivating the mind rather than the body. In the seventeenth century, Descartes's dismissal of the idea that the mind influences the physical character of the body precluded, for the most part, further examination of the relationship between the two.

The resulting culture has conditioned most of us to view the mind and body as separate, to view the body's sensations at best as an inconvenience and at worst as something to be suppressed, and to ignore the subconscious so intimately connected to the body. Once we lose active awareness of our subconscious and the limiting beliefs it may hold, we permit it to rule our bodies. When we take control of our bodies, we speak to and influence our subconscious, breaking down our limiting beliefs.

C-PTSD is a natural but dysfunctional reaction to repeated trauma that ruptures the integration of the mind and body, and depletes and harms each, creating pain, discontent, and limiting beliefs. Many of us with C-PTSD spend the majority of our lives avoiding certain bodily sensations, thoughts, or emotions that remind us of past distress, even if they're harmless presently. Our trauma damages our prefrontal cortex and hippocampus while increasing activity in our amygdala (home of the fight-flight-freeze-fawn response, which we'll refer to as fight-or-flight for simplicity).[38] Our dysregulated body may become perpetually stuck in fight-or-flight, causing emotional dysregulation, heightened levels of stress, anxiety, and even panic in response to mild stressors, and difficulty controlling our responses.

These reactions further feed a state of constant arousal, which can become such a part of how we experience life that we don't even notice it as something distinct from our authentic selves.

We can't heal in a state of hyperarousal. We can't heal if we don't even realize we're in a state of hyperarousal, if the trauma remains lodged in the amygdala where we have no agency over it. We end up in a state where feelings we aren't aware of permeate our bodies and cause us to behave in ways that seem out of our control. We end up in a state where these feelings dictate our thoughts, beliefs, actions, and reactions. We exit hyperarousal by bringing traumatic bodily sensations, memories, and feelings to the surface—physically or consciously—to be released or transformed. Over time, we begin to master them.

The body is a reflection of our subconscious—including our wounded narrator—as well as a channel to subvert it. Until we address our subconscious, we'll keep shifting our limiting beliefs only in our conscious mind and wonder why we still can't connect, imagine, or bring forth. It's easier to feel and believe in your surface-level, conscious mind, because you can lie to it. You can't lie to your subconscious, and the subconscious can weaken, undermine, and sabotage the efforts of your conscious mind unless it's brought into alignment with it.

Your entire history lives in your subconscious and permeates your body and mind, until it's recognized and released or transformed. Your body continuously interacts with other bodies in space and time, revealing *everything* and influencing others' reactions to you. You can use your body as a superpower, or it can be your undoing—there isn't any in-between. Unless you become aware of it, your body will reveal your subconscious beliefs, which is why body language is so revealing in other people, and why we react to others' gestures, posture, facial expressions, eye gaze, and movement (we'll discuss the implications of this in Chapter 9).

Rewiring the subconscious is enormously difficult. Perhaps counterintuitively, data supports that one of the most effective ways to rewire the subconscious is *without letting the conscious mind know*.[39] For example, in one study, a team found that implicit interventions in an elderly study group—those interventions that participants were not aware of—significantly strengthened conscious positive self-perceptions of age, much more so than explicit interventions or a combination of implicit and explicit interventions.[40] The implicit intervention took the form of words such as "spry" and "creative" being flashed on a computer screen too quickly for the conscious mind to process.[41] These elderly participants developed positive stereotypes about aging (overriding common negative ones), which led to improved self-perceptions and even improved physicality.

While other forms of therapy are supportive,[42] I believe mind-body integration practices are one of the most effective way to rewire the subconscious, override the wounded narrator, and move beyond C-PTSD, for many reasons: The body was often the locus of the abuse; the way you treat your body is a reflection of how you feel about yourself overall; to feel worthy, you honor each and every part of yourself, including your body; the pain has to go somewhere, and given its inconvenience to the conscious mind, that somewhere is often the body; you can only make this pain go away by letting it go or turning it into something else, and once it's gone, you learn to relax into a new sense of self that does not carry it; if your body and mind are not in sync, your efforts towards achieving what you want will be undermined, including due to others' reactions to you; and a healthy body makes way for clarity, energy, and optimism.[43]

Traumatic energy that fuels limiting beliefs—and controls our life experiences—remains in the body until we engage in mind-body integration therapies. Through these therapies, we can feel the trapped sensations, memories, and feelings in a safe (or at least safer) way by not necessarily being hyper-focused on them. We can acknowledge and reject the unwelcome thoughts of the wounded narrator from a state in which our body feels calm, cherished, or distracted.

I believe you can transform your body and mind and thereby transform your thoughts and beliefs. I believe this so much that I don't discuss all of the ill effects of early life adversity on physical health (which might be real and damaging but can be undone), because we can't change our past, only our present through our beliefs. And beliefs are enough to change *everything*. One of my favorite studies involved researchers telling half the cleaning staff at seven hotels that they were burning enough calories in their daily work to meet national recommendations for an active lifestyle; the other half of the cleaning staff was told nothing. The cleaning staff didn't change their behavior, and yet four weeks after the intervention, the informed group not only perceived themselves to be getting significantly more exercise than before, but actually lost weight and lowered their blood pressure, body fat, waist-hip ratio, and body mass index.[44]

This chapter highlights practices and nontraditional therapies that honor and take advantage of the mind-body connection as a conduit for healing C-PTSD and transforming limiting beliefs. It's not meant to be an exhaustive description of these therapies or others that might be available to you. Other books have done it far better.

The Building Blocks of Bodily Health

The foundational elements of bodily health are sleep, nutrition, and exercise. You can't optimize the function of your mind and body without optimizing these three areas. Sleep, nutrition, and exercise reduce inflammation (higher inflammation is not only associated with physical disease, but also depression, anxiety, brain fog and sleep disorders), mute autoimmune reactions (those of us with C-PTSD are more likely to experience autoimmune dysfunction and disease—I have grappled with several), and facilitate emotional regulation, among other benefits that support healing and repair. This brief section is intended to orient you toward a curiosity and commitment to bodily health and an awareness of your body and how different things might make it feel.

Nutrition

Different diets work differently for different people. We all have different genetics (and epigenetics), live in different environments, and hold different personal histories. Some people thrive on a vegetable-forward diet, while others may need meat. I won't go as far as to say you should eat mostly plants, because I know some people who thrive not doing so. Provide your body with the baseline nutrients in one way or another, even if in supplement form (and the requirements commonly cited are far too low). Being low in vitamins and minerals absolutely affects your energy levels, your ability to resist disease, and your moods. Key vitamins and minerals include Vitamin A, Vitamin B12, Vitamin D (+K2) (if you don't react poorly to it; if you do, try adding exposure to natural sunlight), Magnesium, and Selenium. Herbal supplements, such as turmeric and black seed oil, and herbal teas, such as dandelion and chamomile, can also reduce inflammation and provide essential minerals. CoQ10 strengthens mitochondria (the powerhouses of our cells), which are often worn down by trauma.

Avoid the following, which create inflammation in the body and brain:

- Processed foods (this includes anything packaged; I like the rule that if you buy something packaged, it should have no more than five ingredients)

- Excessive sugar (use fruit, honey, and maple syrup as sweeteners to the extent possible)

- Seed oils (these include corn oil, safflower oil, cottonseed oil, soybean oil, canola oil, and sunflower oil)

Alcohol and coffee consumption are two subjects of ongoing debate. I don't think either of them, in moderation and to the extent they're high-quality, is a problem for most of us. It's important to watch our body and mind for signs, no matter what we're consuming. If we feel bad during or after eating or drinking something, we shouldn't continue to have it. We're adults, and we're worthy of our own trust. Some people thrive when drinking coffee; other people thrive when having a glass of red wine or a cocktail every night. The data is mixed precisely because it's such an individual experience.

Try to include the following in your diet:

- Healthy fats. Fats are critical for optimal brain function. These include olive oil, coconut oil, egg yolks, butter, ghee, and tallow. My favorite is olive oil, but I don't cook with it because with high heat it potentially oxidizes, producing harmful byproducts. I also consume eggs often and find they greatly improve my mood. Omega-3s, a type of polyunsaturated fat found in fatty fish such as mackerel, reduce inflammation in the brain and improve overall mental health.

- Protein such as meat, seafood, nuts, and beans. Protein provides amino acids necessary to produce neurotransmitters, and insufficient intake can lead to emotional dysregulation. I've found that at times when my mood has been off, consuming pure protein has given me clarity and energy.

- Fruits and vegetables—organic, to the extent possible. Eat a variety, so your body can pull from them what it needs.

- Healthy, whole starches. Although some people have great success on low-carb/keto diets, many people (especially women, and including me) need some carbs for mood balance. I like potatoes and bananas but react negatively to rice. Find what works for you.

Other foods, such as probiotics or cold-pressed juices, may serve your body well. Most importantly, pay attention to your body. Notice the way different things you consume affect you, and respond accordingly.

Sleep

Try to get at least seven hours of sleep a night (even if you're convinced you don't need as much), and if you need a nap, find a way to take one. Inadequate sleep leads to mental distress, an inability to think quickly and accurately (which impacts our judgment and behavior), and an impaired immune system. Chronic lack of sleep leads to anxiety, depression, and irritability. The amygdala becomes more sensitive to negative stimuli, something those of us who are healing can't afford. Sleep helps the brain grow, reorganize, restructure, and make neural connections, leading to better problem-solving and decision-making, and better emotional regulation and control.

Those of us with C-PTSD often struggle with sleep and unlocking the incomparable restoration it provides. We may stay up late and wake up early, claiming we don't need much sleep when really our traumatic programming is driving us to be doing, doing, and doing more; we may believe that we don't deserve the deep and healing restoration of sleep, or that sleep is for the weak or needy, or that only lazy people sleep for seven to nine hours. We may have adrenaline or cortisol swings that prevent us from sleeping. Some of us may have been woken up regularly by our parents or caregivers as children—by their screaming, violence, or neediness; I often was. I remember my drunk father waking me up in the middle of the night as a small child and asking me to tell him that I loved him. I didn't love him in that moment, but I was consumed by fear, so I had to lie. Sleep didn't feel safe.

It's hard to let go and trust sleep after these types of experiences. It's hard to be comfortable simply being in our bodies in the pre-sleep relaxed state, hearing our breath, noting our heartbeats, and trusting our bodies. For a long time (and even sometimes now, unless I engage in breathwork), I couldn't fall asleep unless I was reading a book. I would become so tired that the book would slip out of my hands, and only then was I able to let go. I have a friend who can only fall asleep listening to podcasts. These are signs that our relationship with sleep is impaired.

A lack of sleep will wear you down and prevent you from making the most of your capacity to heal. You may struggle to regulate your moods and emotions, to focus, and to be patient with yourself and others, leading to more adrenaline and cortisol swings and further impaired sleep. The only way out of the feedback loop is to prioritize sleep.

I know it can be hard, practically, to sleep (none of my children slept through the night until they were close to four years old). Do your best. Examine any traumas that touched on your sleep at all, on any level, and determine your limiting beliefs about sleep. Create a peaceful sleep environment, a place of comfort with no or low lights and no screens. Many natural supplements, including black seed oil and magnesium glycinate, can facilitate sleep for some of us. And then sleep, whenever you can, in a manner that makes you feel good the next day.

Exercise

Find a way to move your body. Exercise is an extraordinarily effective way to heal the body and mind, and to open the lines of communication between them. It can also augment traditional and nontraditional therapy. For example, trauma-focused therapy in combination with a few half-hour exercise sessions per week and some walking has been found to lead to greater symptom reduction than trauma-focused therapy alone.[45] The ideal (and found by at least one study to be most effective at healing PTSD) is a combination of cardio, weight-training, and flexibility/agility practices such as yoga.

Exercise is profoundly regulating for those of us with C-PTSD, through several mechanisms. Data indicates that exercise:

- stimulates a supportive and steady stream of blood flow to the brain;

- enhances brain oxygenation and delivery of nutrients to neurons;

- supports the development of synaptic connections and neuronal networks, which enhance neuroplasticity (the nervous system's ability to change its own structure, functions, and connections), thereby influencing our responses to intrinsic and extrinsic stimuli;

- is associated with a significant increase in gray matter volume, especially in the hippocampus and prefrontal cortex;

- burns off the adrenaline so many of us with C-PTSD have an excess of, which calms us and improves communication between the mind and body, taking us out of high alert;

- releases endorphins, which serve as a natural painkiller and also increase energy, stamina, and a positive mood;

- serves as a temporary distraction from our busy minds, giving us the opportunity to take a break from our thoughts and focus on our body and sensations instead (although we should remain aware of our thoughts so that we aren't using exercise as a compulsive way to remain on high alert in our bodies instead);

- gives us a safe way to develop presence within our bodies while focusing on our sensations, to really live in our bodies (for example, the external stimulus of something like weightlifting can connect you to your body so you feel your muscles and joints again);

- facilitates sleep by pushing our body and making it unavoidably tired;

- improves posture (a critical form of body language, which we'll discuss in Chapter 9); and

- potentially rewires the brain of those with C-PTSD (mice who exhibited PTSD-type behaviors and had access to an exercise wheel experienced a significantly greater reduction in symptoms than those who instead had cells replaced and the hippocampus rewired).[46]

While exercise, like nutrition and sleep, supports and nourishes the body and mind, exercise is also a form of somatic therapy (a form of therapy we'll discuss in the following section) because it encourages focus on physical sensations. This focus is critical. We should try to remain aware of our bodies during exercise, rather than exercising with the intention to *not* feel our bodies (which is a common desire for those of us with C-PTSD). Some of us may seek the overwhelming feelings exercise gives us, and the resulting dissociation, as it can be evocative of our childhood experience. We may enjoy feeling as if we're fighting, or even the sensation that we're beating up our bodies because we deserve to feel pain.

Instead, we can pay attention to the sensations in our body and place boundaries, deciding when to stop and when to breathe, and when to say "no." The pain of training increases strength, speed, and flexibility, but training should never hurt too much, and it's always up to us when to pause. Through the experience of choosing to pause, we reconnect to an agency that our trauma crushed. We honor and trust our freedom. Our mind learns to trust our body, and our body learns to trust our mind. We widen our "window of tolerance," the space in which we can comfortably handle stressors (or even simple feelings), a space often constricted by trauma. We are better able to regulate, and better able to believe that we'll be okay.

You are strong. You can do hard things and move your body in ways you never thought possible. Your body is beautiful and powerful—*all of it, even the traumatized parts*. All of it can be transformed from a source of struggle to a source of strength.

Never give up on your body. In my mid-forties, I was finally able to straighten my legs in a yoga class, something I previously thought impossible.

The Building Blocks of Integration

A strong body that we are fully aware of is a huge step toward integration. The next step is repair. People with PTSD and/or

C-PTSD often experience alexithymia (an inability to identify what's going on in the body). Many of us with C-PTSD have minds that severed us from our bodily experience to protect us from pain, storing our trauma deep into our subconscious and deep into our bodies. We wanted to survive, so we buried memories, sensations, and feelings without even realizing it. The trauma became invisible, which made life bearable. But as a result, the integrity of the mind and body connection was ruptured.

We may be so disconnected from our bodies that *not* feeling feels more normal than anything, and certainly feels better than physical sensations, which remind us of how inundated we were at the time of injury. This tendency to disconnect saves us from being overwhelmed, but it destroys us eventually. When we don't allow ourselves to be aware of our sensations, we unknowingly take on destructive physical habits such as shallow breathing, tight muscles, or the bracing of our bodies. We may react, physically or emotionally, based on a memory being triggered. A part or parts of our body may be frozen in time, out of alignment with the rest of us, and out of alignment with our conscious intentions. We have tension to be relieved, uncomfortable thoughts and feelings to bring to the surface, and subconscious inclinations to transform.

This makes it very difficult to heal through traditional means. "Integration therapies" encompass exercises, therapies, and movements that bring our body and mind to a vibrant, regulated, integrated, imaginative, and focused state. They heal the distorted relationship with our bodies that so many of us have, typically by supporting greater awareness of our body's sensations, signals, and reactions (such as pain, discomfort, or dysregulation) and balancing and calming our nervous system.

Through integration therapies that are somatic in nature, we learn how we hold thoughts, feelings, sensations, memories, beliefs, and experiences within our bodies. In his remarkable book *The Body*

Remembers, Van Der Kolk notes that "simply noticing what you feel fosters emotional regulation, and it helps you to stop trying to ignore what is going on inside of you." Awareness is profoundly liberating, bringing us to a centered wholeness, a place of unlimited potential, beyond reason and practicality—where we were always supposed to be. Body awareness transforms us, from the inside out and from the outside in.

Talk therapies can also be tremendously helpful, especially CBT, but they often aren't enough. Our traumatic programming has wired us with limiting and deeply rooted beliefs that are not always accessible by cognitive approaches, nor by all the mantras and affirmations in the world. The wounded narrator preserves these beliefs to protect us from anticipated heartbreak, imprinting them on our nervous and other bodily systems. The trauma is enmeshed in us, and sometimes the only way we can convince our minds that these beliefs are wrong is through the conduit of the body. If we recognize and heal the body, it can lead the mind to a better place. For example, according to Dr. Herbert Benson, Mind/Body Medical Institute Professor of Medicine at Harvard Medical School, a "relaxation response" (the opposite of fight-or-flight, and activated by many of the therapies discussed in this chapter) alleviates symptoms of anxiety and improves heart rate, blood pressure, oxygen consumption, and brain activity.

One of the most fascinating aspects of somatic therapies is that they can augment the placebo effect (an effect instrumental to the practice of bringing forth). Focusing on physical experiences while expecting a positive outcome tends to lead to us *aligning* our physical experiences with beliefs about a positive outcome, resulting in an even stronger perceived effect. Put simply, what you believe about your body is even more likely to come true when you bring awareness to your physical experience.

All integration practices should be trauma-informed, imbued with a sense of safety and connection to your senses and the present moment. Unlocking buried trauma and the accompanying limiting beliefs—that can themselves be so severe and deflating—can be extremely uncomfortable and distressing. Remain present and aware, and go as slowly as you need to. Be patient and compassionate with yourself. No method helps everyone, for many reasons. Discomfort can be healthy and lead to new synaptic connections, but if you notice yourself disconnected, not fully present, or engaged in other types of reactions that suggest re-traumatization, take a break, ask your practitioner for a modification, or switch to another therapy or practitioner. We can't allow ourselves to be re-traumatized by a poor approach to therapy. For example, I don't like closing my eyes in certain therapeutic contexts, as it can elicit flashbacks and hyper-arousal for me. Nothing is wrong with me, or you. We're figuring out how to heal and reawaken our agency and integrity.

Meditation

Meditation refers to powerful practices that focus, clear, and calm the mind, bringing it into a neutral state. Meditation (and other inner practices that use discipline to transform consciousness) have a long history in many different cultures around the world. Meditation asks you to nonjudgmentally observe your thoughts, emotions, and physical sensations, always recognizing their transient nature and allowing them to rise to the surface and float on without becoming attached to them. Every feeling and thought is as impermanent as every breath; they are each simply a moment in time. Recognizing this impermanence allows clarity, optimism, and freedom from trauma-related distortions to unfold.

Consistent meditation can regulate the overactive stress response so common to those of us with C-PTSD, reducing arousal and fostering composure, which helps soften intense emotions and physical sensations. Meditation counteracts the structural damage to the brain caused by traumatic stress by strengthening activity and increasing gray matter in the prefrontal cortex and hippocampus while dampening activity in and reducing the size of the amygdala (traumatic stress does the opposite in each case).[47] This, in turn, improves neural functioning (including learning and memory) and enhances emotional regulation.

Meditation can be guided (involving a teacher, either in person or via a recording leading you through) or unguided (independent). For many of us with C-PTSD, a guided, nonaggressive, trauma-informed approach provides us with a steadying structure. We should also ensure that we meditate in a comfortable space that is as free from triggers as possible; something as simple as a smell or texture can trigger a traumatic memory and its related thoughts.

For some of us with C-PTSD who struggle to keep our bodies still, mindful meditation can be the easiest initial practice. In mindful meditation, we focus on a particular object or thought exclusively while observing any bodily sensations, thoughts, or feelings. We might drink a cup of coffee while completely focusing our attention on it and nothing else. We can notice the sensations of temperature, smell, and tactile experience. We might focus on a natural object, such as a tree we're leaning up against or a rock we're holding in our hands. We can also focus on relaxing music (ideally with no or few words in it). Whenever our mind wanders, we gently redirect to the object of focus.

Mindfulness can be performed while sitting down in a traditional meditative pose (a seated position with an upright spine, with crossed legs and each foot placed on the opposite thigh) or while engaging the body in a mundane task (such as doing the dishes or folding laundry, or anything that doesn't require thought). This latter form of mindfulness can be extremely freeing for those of us with C-PTSD, who at the beginning of our journeys may not be comfortable sitting in silence and observing. We may have been conditioned to be perpetually on high alert or busy, but we can compromise by allowing our body to remain at work while our mind rests. Moving meditation is an analogous practice that involves engaging in mindfulness while walking, gardening, or practicing yoga, qi gong, or tai chi. The focus on movement (rather than an object or thought) fosters a deep connection to the body and the present moment.

Many other forms of meditation are available for experimentation, including body scan meditation, where focus is slowly drawn to the relaxation of one muscle group at a time throughout the body (especially beneficial right before bedtime); Zen meditation, an ancient Buddhist practice that involves sitting upright and paying attention to the way the breath moves in and out of the belly, while letting the mind rest (helpful for fostering a sense of presence and alertness); and Vipassana meditation, which involves focusing on the internal experience in a non-reactive manner to facilitate insights into the nature of reality.

By focusing on the present through meditation, we can learn to recognize trauma-related feelings, sensations, and memories as discrete from our present moment. They are remnants of the past, intrusions that only have meaning if we decide to give them meaning. We can shift our focus to them, or we can notice them while remaining in our present state, and then watch them recede. We decide. We don't have to react to them, and we don't have to suffer because of them. We are not our injury, nor are we our feelings, sensations, and memories, or the thoughts they may give rise to.

Yoga

Yoga is the most well-known and popular form of mind-body integration practice and perhaps the most accessible for most of us, given that it's a modality commonly guided in person. Yoga evolved from practices in ancient India focused on liberating the self by stilling the fluctuations of the mind. Yoga incorporates a variety of regulating and integrating mechanisms for the mind and body, including movement, postures, breathwork (discussed below), and meditation (discussed above), which in combination are immensely healing.[48] For those of us with C-PTSD who crave structure, yoga classes provide it. Yoga was the first integration practice I tried, and it was only through yoga that I began to notice my breath and become able to engage in breathwork and active meditation.

Types of yoga include: vinyasa yoga/vinyasa flow (most common), which is active and syncs breath to movement in a continuous rhythmic flow, calming the nervous system while providing a workout; yin yoga, a slower form in which poses are held for several minutes, sometimes with props like bolsters, blankets, and blocks, which increases circulation and improves flexibility (in my experience, the longer holds lend themselves to reaching progressively more meditative states and teach me to honor the practice of being still); hot yoga, which consists of a series of poses always performed in the same order, with strict rules, in a hot and humid room, facilitating deeper postures, improved circulation, and detoxification; and restorative yoga/yoga nidra, which aims for complete down-regulation of the nervous system and sometimes includes a guided meditation (one hour of yoga nidra is equivalent to a few hours of sleep).

In addition to the physical benefits and relaxation response quickly gained by its poses, yoga reduces stress, anxiety, depression, and chronic pain, improves sleep patterns and cognitive health, and enhances overall well-being and quality of life.[49] Other data suggests that yoga leads to an increased sense of self-compassion, a sense of being grounded, healthier coping skills, a stronger mind-body relationship, and better relationships with others.

Yoga requires us to take notice of our bodies, of our breath, of which muscles are activated by different yoga poses, in the present moment, which can reduce dissociation and repair a disrupted connection to physical sensation. As we become aware of the natural limits of certain poses (whether we're pushing past a previous boundary or placing a new one), we slowly begin to trust our bodies and our own agency. Being present with our bodies also leads to a temporary (but non-avoidant and helpful) detachment from the interfering wound and other trauma symptoms (such as fear or shame). This temporary detachment gives the body a chance to enter a calmer state, a state of deeper breaths and looser muscles, and the body stops bracing out of fear, opening up space in the mind-body feedback loop for healing.

For those of us with C-PTSD, yoga calms our tendency toward hyperarousal and extreme reactions to triggers and intrusive memories. Yoga does this not only by easing our muscles and improving our confidence, but also by improving heart rate variation (HRV), which is a measure of the variation of time between each heartbeat. HRV tends to reflect the balance between the parasympathetic and sympathetic nervous systems, which together make up the autonomic nervous system. Low HRV is more common in people who have high resting heart rates and the accompanying adrenaline surges (like many of us with C-PTSD), because when the heart beats fast, less time is left between beats, reducing the opportunity for variability. The variation of time will remain short and consistent. The sympathetic nervous system believes stress and danger are imminent, and it takes control to protect us. Healing is suppressed when we live in a state of sympathetic nervous system control. Balanced HRV tends to be higher, demonstrating a variability that reflects a calmer state and an ability to adapt to real conditions. The body understands it doesn't need to focus on survival and can shift to healing.

Studies suggest that yoga is at least as beneficial as medications—and possibly more beneficial than medications—at alleviating traumatic stress symptoms.[50] After yoga practice, the areas of the brain involved in self-awareness show activation in neuroimaging studies (these same areas tend to be deactivated by trauma). In my experience, yoga's multifaceted approach can open up emotional blockages, causing tears, anger, or other emotional responses during or after a session. Sometimes this deluge feels like an emotionally painful detox; other times, it feels like absolute exhilaration.

Breathwork

Breathwork can be practiced on its own or in connection with any of the other integration practices. Breathwork entails focusing on the breath, including through deep or controlled breathing or meditation techniques that bring attention to the breath. For most people, noticing and controlling the pace and depth of breathing activates the parasympathetic nervous system and almost immediately reduces stress, relieves anxiety, and relaxes the body and mind. For people with C-PTSD, the situation is more complex, and these practices can have the opposite effect, stirring up feelings of anxiety, panic, or even terror. Breathwork—too much too soon, or practiced without awareness—can bring back trauma-related memories or feelings and seem like a prison rather than an escape. I didn't realize the extent of my interfering wound until I realized how uncomfortable I was with exercises that seemed so simple for other people. Paying attention to my breath was so scary that I never wanted to try again.

But I did, and I'm glad I did. Trauma-informed breathwork has turned out to be the best tool I've found to ease the tensions of my mind and body, integrating each and bringing me into equilibrium. I get to decide how to breathe. It's not outside of my control. I can align my body and subconscious with everything my conscious mind aspires to, through my breath. Breathwork is an almost magical conduit to reach your subconscious with your conscious, to bring it into peace, regulation, and alignment. Yes, even for us, the traumatized so afraid of lost breaths, of suffocation, of devastation.

Our body (usually without our knowledge) is uniquely focused on breathing, and signals from our respiratory system have priority over other signals in our body. When we change our pattern of breathing, we change *everything*. We reset signaling, and we reset our frequency to neutral and centered. This is why sighing—a long and deep breath, typically audible, that resets the respiratory system—is the fastest way to deliberately calm down.

Most people, whether they have C-PTSD or not, take too many breaths per minute. When we overbreathe, we tell the nervous system that we're stressed, which further disrupts our breathing rhythm. And then our disrupted breathing signals more stress to our nervous system, over and over again, in a negative feedback loop. According to James Nestor in *Breath* (the best book on the topic), the perfect number of breaths is 5.5 per minute.[51] I'm not quite there yet, although I've finally been able to extend my four-second inhales and exhales to five seconds.

As an initial step, breathwork advocates typically suggest sitting with your spine straight and then "simply" observing the natural inhale and exhale of your breath. They ask you to pay attention to the gaps—the spaces between your inhales and exhales—and to start to notice them expanding (I found this particularly alarming). You are asked to keep your body still, and if you notice your mind wandering, to bring attention back to your breath.

A gentler approach is starting breathwork in combination with a natural partner, such as yoga. Many different types of breathwork practices are incorporated into various yoga practices, including Pranayama, a traditional yogic breathing technique that involves slowing down the pace of breathing, elongating the breath, and holding the breath for extended periods of time. In Vinyasa, instructors will often align breath to movement—moving while breathing, while having a marker to help align where your breath should be, is protective of those of us who are otherwise anxious that if we change the way we breathe we won't know how to do it anymore.

Holding your breath—knowing you can hold it and being confident that you can make the choice to breathe again—can be particularly healing for those of us who are dysregulated. Box breathing can be tremendously helpful in moments when stress takes over physically and we need to immediately relax our mind and body. Box breathing stimulates the vagus nerve, which helps to lower the heart rate and bring the body out of fight-or-flight: Inhale for four seconds/hold the breath for four seconds/exhale for four seconds/hold for four seconds. The pauses between inhalations and exhalations cue the nervous system to relax.

I find counting my breath tremendously stabilizing. The numbers—1-2-3-4—are a support, something to hold onto instead of getting swept away into the abyss (or living in so much fear of getting swept away into the abyss that I can't breathe). Counting my extended inhales and exhales is the first tool I've found (besides reading) that calms me enough to fall asleep when worries preoccupy my mind. I hope one day I won't need to count anymore and can make my breaths longer. It's okay either way, though. As long as we're noticing and elongating our breaths, we're regulating, integrating, and healing.

Craniosacral Therapy

Craniosacral therapy is a gentle form of bodywork (performed by a practitioner) that focuses on the craniosacral system, which includes the brain, spinal cord, and surrounding membranes and cerebrospinal fluid. The intent is to give release to or transform areas of tension, imbalance, and restriction in the body, through light touch that may include gently holding or manipulating different body parts, such as the head, spine, or sacrum (a practitioner I used to see would even put her finger in my ear). Craniosacral therapy is based on the idea that the body has an innate ability to heal itself: to purge energy, emotions, and blockages; to release stored tensions; and to move the nervous system out of fight-or-flight so it can focus on receiving nutrients, support, and relaxation instead.

Involving an outside practitioner can be fraught for those of us with C-PTSD. Human touch holds tremendous power, and some of the most effective therapies in this chapter are forms of "bodywork" that involve a practitioner placing hands on you. For those of us who are healing from trauma inflicted by others, it can be extraordinarily difficult to trust someone placing their hands on us. We should look for practitioners who make us feel safe (this may mean different things to different people—for example, someone who talks a lot, talks little, or has a certain gender, appearance, or energy) while allowing us to approach the edges of a breakthrough. We may realize right away that we aren't comfortable with a certain practitioner, for whatever reason. It doesn't have to make sense, and we don't have to keep seeing that person, no matter how great their reviews or recommendations are. We can consider what questions to ask and what boundaries to place in service of our safety. These days, many practitioners ask for consent initially or at various points in the session, and we should use those opportunities to consent only if we mean it. Then, we can take a leap and trust someone who has made this their job, who wants to heal others, and see what happens.

I rarely enjoyed traditional massage, as much as the world told me I was supposed to. I felt somehow primed to fight back, or as if every touch came with a demand to relax. I was even once admonished by a massage therapist that I was making their job difficult by not relaxing. Craniosacral massage is much gentler and far less demanding. Parts of you are held, for extended periods of time, conveying a type of nurturing patience that is deeply reassuring and restorative. After a session, I've felt a sense of lightness in my body, as if a boulder had been lifted from my chest. I've felt more present and connected to my body. Practicing breathwork during a craniosacral session reinforced the positive effects.

I'm not sure how or why craniosacral therapy works, and little scientific evidence exists for its efficacy. But I know it works for me and others. Craniosacral therapy is the only integration practice that has made an impact on my tendency to brace my muscles in response to random triggers or casual touch. It may, as its originator contends, restore balance in the rhythm of the cerebrospinal fluid to enhance the function of the central nervous system. It may, through touch, ease restrictions in the connective tissue (fascia) that surrounds the craniosacral system and thereby activate the parasympathetic system (reducing stress and inflammation and allowing the body to shift to healing mode). Some practitioners claim that they access and release deeply held emotional trauma stored in the tissues through somato-emotional release. Maybe all of that is true, or maybe it's about learning to trust that we are safe and cared for in someone else's hands.

Somatic Therapy

Somatic therapy is also a body-centric therapy, but unlike craniosacral, it explicitly treats the experiences, feelings, memories, and sensations trapped within the body that many of us are eager to heal, guiding their release and dissipation. Somatic therapy aims to reawaken the internal resources that regulate our emotions, move us out of fight-or-flight, and—through our bodies—revisit past trauma to bring about a redeeming or even transcendent outcome. This is done through a combination of psychotherapy ("talk therapy"); movement, motion, or other physical acts ("bodywork"); and physical therapy/massage/light touch ("tablework").

Somatic therapy allows us to viscerally experience our emotions flowing out of us and dissipating. It involves the unburdening of our deepest feelings, sensations, and memories, leading to the realization that now, as adults, we have the resources to handle them. To accomplish this, we maintain awareness of physical sensations and communicate this awareness. If you're distressed, your therapist might ask where you feel the distress in your body. It might be tightness in your belly, a weight on your chest, heat in your face, or any number of sensations. Your therapist might note gestures and postures you're making without awareness, such as leaning forward or crossing your arms. They might help you identify movements you wish you could have made during a difficult time in the far or recent past. A therapist might identify areas of constriction, tension, and overwhelm, as well as thoughts, feelings, and actions that promote a feeling of calm and safety, and call your attention to them. They might help you find ways to expand these nurturing thoughts, feelings, and actions. As a result, it becomes easier to identify physical sensations in general. Over time, this leads to "centering," the development of a calm home base within the body.

We develop grounding tools to help calm and regulate our nervous system when we are feeling overly activated or triggered.

Elements of somatic therapy include:

- co-regulation, where a therapist engages with us in a regulated (warm and composed) manner, making it easier for us to regulate;

- self-regulation, which provides tools to regulate on our own;

- titration, which allows the body to experience small levels of distress in order to release and discharge tension, expanding the window of tolerance;

- pendulation, which is moving focus from painful memories to calming thoughts (and tends to work with titration to reach a point where the body and mind can tolerate discomfort and release the emotions that need to be released);

- sequencing, which entails tracking a thought, feeling, or memory through the body to a point of release, while observing it move and shift as we describe attendant physical sensations (with words such as *warm, cold, sharp, numb, heavy*); and

- the goal, an "act of triumph."

An act of triumph releases trauma from an injury by engaging the body to act out the defense or resistance that was impossible at the time, perhaps because we didn't have the strength or it was dangerous to do so. Because we wanted to act and couldn't, we were left without agency and closure. Now, we can shout "no," run away, or push someone away (the therapist may stand up and hold a pillow for you to push up against, or you might use a wall). The action might not be aggressive—it could be hiding behind a couch or looking away, or even crying, when we couldn't do it at the time because it would show weakness our abuser might exploit. This time, we stay with our urges. These crushed intentions are easier to access, process, and release when combined with movement, and the body experiences a deep relief it can't experience by simply talking about the injury. Afterward, we may feel lighter, capable of a wider range of movement, or markedly more present.

My favorite thing about somatic therapy is that it's rare to be asked to work through memories. Somatic therapy doesn't dive headfirst into rehashing your injuries. Going too quickly in therapy can make those of us with C-PTSD feel panicked, on edge, trapped, numb, disconnected, or at a loss, leaving us re-traumatized and breaking down any potential trust in our therapist or the process. Sometimes we don't want to share all of the painful details, *and that's okay*. We can still unlock trauma and free ourselves.

Another healing aspect of somatic therapy is the experience of setting boundaries by giving or not giving the therapist consent for different approaches, verbally and nonverbally, allowing us to become comfortable saying "yes," "no," "stop," or "okay," or even "maybe" and "let's see how it goes." Some people with C-PTSD are uncomfortable with any of those words, but for me, "let's see" is the hardest. As a child, "let's see" wasn't permissible to me. Saying "let's see" is still communicating and still setting a boundary. Setting boundaries helps us feel safe and comfortable in our bodies.

Our interfering wounds were so devastating because we were children who needed someone to help us process the consuming emotional and physical abuse our nervous system couldn't handle independently. This time, we have someone to support us throughout the revisitation of our injury, so we can transcend it and deplete it of its power over us. Through release, we can exit the patterns built by our interfering wound and limiting beliefs and begin to consistently engage in more regulated and integrated emotional patterns, as well as thoughts, beliefs, and actions aligned with our highest self.

EMDR

EMDR (Eye Movement Desensitization and Reprocessing) is a psychotherapy that processes, resolves, and integrates traumatic memories by removing blockages to healing the original injury. The memory is brought to the surface and then rewired so that natural healing can resume. It's less about the body and more about sensory perception and working memory.

An EMDR therapist might ask you to hold different aspects of a traumatic memory in your mind, along with new positive beliefs (including a new, happier, or more supportive ending, which may be fantastical or realistic), while using a form of bilateral stimulation. Bilateral stimulation can be accessed via vision (such as using your eyes to track the therapist's hand or a light in their hand as it moves back and forth across your field of vision), sound (where speakers on either side of your body play tones), or touch (by tapping on your hands, arms or thighs, or holding a device that pulses in your hands), among other forms. It's unclear exactly why EMDR works, but one theory is that actively engaging in two sensory acts simultaneously (such as visual imagery and eye movements) leads to competition between the two sensory acts for limited working memory resources. This results in the emotions related to a memory becoming less intense. With less intensity, we can create distance from a traumatic memory, opening up space to reevaluate it without being overwhelmed by our emotional response.

EMDR assumes the mind naturally wants to heal injury. The gravity and intensity of a traumatic injury serious enough to cause

C-PTSD impedes the mind's natural inclination to heal, in part because it's faster to bury it, and in part because it truly wasn't possible for us to heal while we were alone and subjected to trauma we couldn't prevent. We were left with our interfering wound submerged in our subconscious, an indelible part of us. Our memories are stored in an unhealthy, obstructive manner. As a result, we become imbalanced, dysregulated, and at constant risk of undermining our dreams. Our body and mind are left in deep conflict, always partially living in the past instead of the present, while simultaneously resisting revisiting the injury and anything we saw, heard, felt, or smelled during it because it's so distressing. It doesn't work. We're still triggered by sights, sounds, and smells, a look, a manner of dress, or a holiday because they remind us of our trauma. We may feel fear, anxiety, anger, panic, or sadness and be overwhelmed by it, and not understand why. This may occur in an uncontrolled, distorted, and overpowering way during a flashback. The danger is over, but we have allowed the past to become present.

EMDR helps us transcend this self-protective, damaging repression (or suppression, to the extent it's conscious). To me, EMDR feels almost like time travel because of the new imagined outcome. You access the tangible details of a memory and rewrite the ending, a reprocessing that repairs the injury from that particular memory. After reprocessing a particular memory, remembering what happened may no longer feel like reliving it (in other words, like terror), and the related feelings become manageable. My reprocessed memory would feel profoundly different after a session, lighter and less intense, and connected with more positive beliefs. Feelings of powerlessness became feelings of agency, feelings of degradation became feelings of dignity, and feelings of constriction became feelings of possibility. The transformation is so deep it can feel magical.

EMDR is strongly backed by data. More than thirty randomized controlled studies demonstrate EMDR's effectiveness and speed of results for PTSD recovery. One study found that 100 percent of single-trauma victims and 77 percent of multiple-trauma victims no longer were diagnosed with PTSD after only six fifty-minute sessions.[52] In another study, 77 percent of combat veterans were free of PTSD in twelve sessions (with significantly less intrusive thoughts, avoidance behaviors, hyperarousal, and depressive episodes).[53] While EMDR is likely to bring accelerated recovery for C-PTSD as well, given C-PTSD's complexity, more sessions than described above would likely be required for results.

Although EMDR doesn't typically require talking in depth about memories, it does require an assessment and discussion to determine which memories to target. EMDR may sound easy and pleasant, but I found it difficult, although ultimately extraordinarily healing. EMDR doesn't require clinical interpretation; our own emotional processes heal us. This is empowering, but it also requires a great deal of initial energy. I always felt absolutely awful during the sessions (when I had to remember the painful memory) and amazing after reprocessing the memory and leaving the office. After reprocessing a good chunk of memories, and despite my success, I stopped going because I just didn't want to summon the energy it took to travel to those memories, despite how transformative the experience was.

***

Your mind and body are redeemable and recoverable, no matter what was done to them. Your mind and body, and a healthy relationship between them, can be used to heal and undo what you may have thought could never be undone. They can be used to reach depths and heights of flourishing you may never have thought possible. They are your superpowers. Never give up on them.

CHAPTER 7

PRACTICE AUTHENTICITY

If your success is not on your own terms, if it looks good to the world but does not feel good in your heart, it is not success at all.

attributed to Maggie Lena Walker

Disobedience, in the eyes of anyone who has read history, is man's original virtue.

Oscar Wilde, The Soul of Man under Socialism

The practice of authenticity requires us to act in accordance with the deepest, truest, and most inviolable part of ourselves.

This part of ourselves has many names: our inner nature, true self, uniqueness, or spirit. I'll refer to it as the authentic self. It's the truth already within us. It's our intuition as to how life ought to be lived and how its truths ought to be expressed. It's the part of us that refuses to yield to limiting beliefs and is committed to expressing our destiny.

The expression of our authentic self is required to both determine and bring forth our dreams. Our authentic self centers us, and by knowing it, we know our dreams are not simply internationalizations of norms and ideals with which we've been inculcated. By exposing our authentic self (which is often a frightening experience at first), we demonstrate trust in ourselves and trust in the universe. By refusing our authentic self, we invite struggle. The authentic self is the touchstone against which our dreams are tested and validated.

As we discussed in Chapter 4, social belonging is meaningful. Social belonging ensured the survival of the human race. Unfortunately, like everything good in life, social belonging also has trade-offs, the most insidious of which is conformity. Conformity is acting in accordance with socially accepted conventions because we think it's necessary for belonging. Conformity promises a shortcut to belonging, but it's a cheap and unsustainable illusion. It's neither necessary nor sufficient for belonging; true belonging comes from the gathering of multiple authentic individuals who see each other as they are. Agreeing with people is not a problem if it's natural, but often, it's not. Society frequently demands a sacrifice of authenticity at conformity's altar, and it takes heroic resolve to resist.

Conformity has a long history. Some theorize that it protected the tribe, which sought to survive and thrive as a group when priorities such as securing food and evading predators dominated. The tribe came first, not the individual, and if an individual wasn't subscribing to the way things "should" be, they might be left to die. In such a context, nonconformity was truly dangerous. The conventions at the time were limited and grounded in survival. Later, small communities such as villages took on a similar role of enforcing norms, although over time such norms became less a matter of life and death. Conventions became more centered around protecting a way of life, because that way of life was all that was known, and anything novel felt threatening. Gossip drew the lines of what constituted acceptable minor nonconformity and what deserved physical or social ostracism. Although nonconformists might not be left to die, ostracism caused suffering for them and their families. Meanwhile, through the enforcement of these social norms and conventions, the community curated, reaffirmed, and imbued with meaning its own identity. It created a dogma that made people within the community feel safe, protected, and valued (albeit in a hollow way).

Yet, even in the face of these serious long-ago threats, nonconformity persevered. We know this because our history, myths, and fairy tales focus on rebels, mavericks, and disruptors—those who very publicly stood out from the crowd. These individuals typically do something spectacular: They defeat a villain, save lives, find freedom, introduce an invention or innovation, or otherwise self-actualize while disrupting conventional paradigms. Think about Achilles, Boudica, Martin Luther, Toussaint Louverture, Sitting Bull, Harriet Tubman, Albert Einstein, W.E.B DuBois, Henry Ford, Louis Armstrong, Marie Curie, Jackson Pollock, Nikola Tesla, Frank Lloyd Wright, Walt Whitman, Cinderella, Galileo, Jesus, Joan of Arc, and Robin Hood. They all practiced authenticity. They were courageous enough to be themselves in a world that urged them to submit, and they were at times met with anger, violence, or other punishment.

People can become angry and lash out when the beliefs that make them feel safe are challenged. Yet those beliefs that make them feel safe are so often limiting beliefs, learned and passed down over time to protect against the worst, or the unknown. And limiting beliefs should always be questioned. It's hard, if not impossible, to do interesting things without questioning them. Stories of those who follow along, blend in, don't rock the boat, and always follow the rules *don't exist*. They don't exist because they'd be boring and meaningless. They don't exist because they don't teach us anything.

They don't exist because we all admire the courage of authenticity, whether we are comfortable admitting it or not.

Life has changed dramatically, but conformist impulses bred through millions of years of social evolution live on. In some ways, we're freer: We may be punished for our nonconformity, but given the porosity of nations, communities, and groups, our punishment tends not to be ruinous, because we can always move. We no longer need to conform to survive, but the virulent pressure to conform continues to find expression, including in media of all kinds. We're inundated with messages about how we should be doing what someone else is doing, wearing what someone else is wearing, and accomplishing the goals someone else is accomplishing. We live in a world where inauthenticity, mirage, groupthink, and manipulation are easy to find if we look for them. If we allow ourselves to be swept up in their current, we'll be lost. We won't know what we want or what we're capable of.

You don't have to become a story. You don't have to sacrifice your life to save the world. You just have to find, listen to, and see your authentic self, and then be brave enough to expose your authentic self in service of your dream. You just have to live for your own imagination, not the imagination of others.

And as an aside, we don't have to practice authenticity perfectly. The universe is nuanced and complicated. Rare situations may present themselves in which authenticity is superficially and temporarily sacrificed. For example, you don't have to go around shouting your political views at work if it makes you a target and prevents you from succeeding, but you also shouldn't lie about your opinions or remain with a company long-term whose values you don't support. Inauthenticity will lead you away from your sense of worth, your dreams, and your highest self, so use it only sparingly, as needed to protect yourself in a complex world.

It's not unusual to become alienated from the truest part of ourselves. Those of us with C-PTSD may be programmed by our trauma to such an extent that it's hard to differentiate what's us and what's our injury speaking through our wounded narrator. "Listening to your heart" doesn't always make sense for those whose hearts have been shattered by abuse, whose intuition has had to withstand efforts to dominate or warp it, whose spontaneity was crushed, or whose inner nature was treated by contempt by those closest to them. Our gut feelings may be corrupted to the extent that we can't reliably trust them, at least not early in the healing process.

We can take time to ensure our limiting beliefs aren't wresting control from our authentic self. It's difficult and confusing at first, but we can engage with and question our inclinations and urges. Ask yourself the following questions: What are your gifts? Where do you excel, and what do you like to do? What have you always been drawn to? What do you feel compelled to learn? What truths have you tended to perceive? What sparks a curiosity in you? What do you tend to think about? Your thoughts hold tremendous clues; they will tend to revolve around what you value most.

We can stop pretending and listen and see what comes into the empty space that pretending leaves behind. We pretend because the wounded narrator tells us it's required for a crumb of affection or approval. What speaks, what answers these questions when you quiet the performance of the wounded narrator is "you." What exposes itself when you look away from everyone else is "you." What couldn't be broken is "you." Separate your authentic self—the beautiful, sacred core—from your trauma,[54] and then listen. You are not your trauma. Your sense of what ought to be, of what is true and real, seeks to express itself. Let it. Your authentic self is messy, radiant, torn, and gifted. It's still the perfect expression of you.

Find you.

Be you.

Stop pretending.
Start being.

Time and patience help. Compassion for yourself helps. Therapy helps. The practices help.

Society will engulf you with the most conformist trends, ideals, and aspirations. Society's inundation is based on fear and control. People will bombard you with their opinions, judgments, and advice. It's a waste of time wondering why people do the things they do, or whether they like you or not. People's thoughts about us and resulting behavior is, in large part, a reflection of how they feel about themselves. We'll never find purpose, contentment, or happiness contorting ourselves to appease a particular person's, community's, or society's ideals.

If the "you" that feels natural, coherent, and true doesn't quite "fit in," whatever that means in your context, forget fitting in. You need to be you first, whether that's someone who fits in or not. Fitting in for the sake of fitting in brings nothing but superficial, performative belonging and surface-level friendships. If you sacrifice your authenticity to do so, the cracks will invariably show. Fitting in will not make you a hero, nor will it make you a successful entrepreneur or artist, nor will it make you wealthy. Fitting in will lead to some (not even all) people in your community thinking you fit in and support their values, and *are not a threat*. It will make those people feel better about their conventions and values. It will prop up their superficial confidence. That's all it will do. Is that worth giving up your dream?

Don't worry about appeasing the horde.[55]

Society will try to get you to be like everyone else. *Resist.*

Society will try to flatten your spirit. *Resist.*

Society will nudge you into being a cog, consumer, and predictable piece of data. *Resist.*

You are an unrepeatable miracle. It's your destiny to express your uniqueness. Focus on your gifts—all of your gifts deserve your tending. If something makes you "different," pay attention to it. Nurture it and see what grows. Let yourself shine and see what happens. See what new knowledge of yourself arises.

Be bold. It may seem natural to fall back on doing nothing, letting passivity wash over you, and fading into the background. It may seem comforting to avoid any possibility of failure. Avoiding any possibility of failure *is* failure. If you numb yourself by retreating, you'll destroy your spirit, your light, and the possibility of your dreams. The numbing—the deadening—of passivity may provide the illusion of control and certainty so tempting to those of us recovering from C-PTSD. Conformity will promise certainty. It's a lie. As we've discussed, certainty is an illusion.

Dreams, by their nature, are uncertain. And closure is unreachable. We only have open endings in life. Realizing a dream is just one moment in time. It happens, and a new moment and potential journey begin. Accepting the uncertainty and open-endedness of our journey takes us to the land of plenty. It gives us space to be authentic, in our messy complexity. When we insist on certainty and closure, our connection to our authentic self atrophies. Our dreams stagnate and eventually die. If you give up on your authentic self, at some point you'll feel like you're drowning and you won't be able to remember why.

When you practice authenticity and swim against the current of conformity, you'll be noticed. You may not be popular. You may be envied. You might inspire rage.

You'll be okay.

You will also be seen. You'll set an example of what's possible. You may be admired. You may inspire others to live their best life, even if they don't realize they're being inspired.

As we heal and connect to our authentic selves, and as we live and express our lives in a way that feels right to us, our intuition—knowing what we know without knowing how we know it—will grow stronger. Through practice (and mistakes), we can refine our intuition, and enhanced intuition will further feed our courage to explore and experiment, generating luck. Luck is events, people, ideas, and bold authenticity colliding. Luck is resources and opportunities perfectly aligned with your dreams. If you live in the universe as your authentic self, emanating who you are and what you want, and surrendering to the flow, luck will find you and you'll recognize it. Your dreams will unfold.

Practicing authenticity also fosters an appreciation or even a celebration of the authenticity of others. Voices outside of the mainstream often provide critical insights into health, wealth, healing, and motivation. We won't find the hidden paths to our dreams by listening to mainstream opinions, financial advice, or health recommendations. The mainstream doesn't teach entrepreneurship, self-love, how to game the stock market, or how to write a book. Most people are not living their dreams. Look outside of the mainstream to find those who are.

But don't be different solely for the sake of being different (which usually means trying to fit into a sub-community that is "different"), as that's another road to conformity. Social conventions vary by gender,[56] and they exist even within nonconformist subcultures. Sometimes, it seems as though as soon as you find an identifier that feels authentic, you're subject to strictures and prescriptions based on it. It doesn't matter that the identifier is ostensibly nonconforming, as it all ends up defeating the purpose. Once again, you're burdened by the need to fit in or adhere to a paradigm. Remain connected to your authentic self. *We can be different within difference.* We can own our complexity, and still belong.

One of the most deeply inauthentic things you can do is settle too soon for a fragment, illusion, or substitute for your dream. "Settling" means to become too comfortable in a situation inferior to what we really want, typically due to a limiting belief that it's the best we can do. Settling leads to other undermining, low-frequency states, including a lack of ambition, a lack of imagination, and a lack of enthusiasm. It's tempting for all of us, but settling is lying to yourself. We may tell ourselves that we're tired or that the situation isn't as bad as it could be, but fear is typically underlying this rationalization.

Settling is different from recognizing that the process of bringing forth your dreams can look like a ladder. You may buy a certain house, live in it for a few years, and move into your dream house a few years later. You may have never dated and start dating someone to see what it feels like. You may buy the most expensive sushi you can currently afford, while dreaming of dining somewhere more high-end. The key distinction is that you don't permanently stop on a rung if your dream is higher up. Taking breaks is great, but carry on toward your dreams when you're ready (unless your dreams have legitimately changed). You are as worthy of your authentic and reverent dreams as anyone else. Don't lower your standards because you think that's the best you can do. The best you can do is as good as the best.

Settling too soon comes up often in relationships and careers. Existing in the unknown can feel so scary that we rush to a premature choice so that we can experience the beautiful illusion of closure or being done. For example, I know (and I'm sure you do, too) people who chose partners they don't like very much. They have settled. Perhaps they were and are afraid of the unknown. Perhaps they believed the image of attainment was more important than their own authenticity. An image will promise happiness, and may bring brief external validation, but it's not bringing forth—the experience of an authentic dream coming true.

Never settle for the image of attainment. By staying in a situation that isn't a match for your authentic self, you're telling the network of connection that's what you think you deserve. And the network that so enjoys unequivocal messages will hear you clearly. Settling tells the universe that you don't think you are worthy of contentment, healing, or a life as good as the best. Never permanently settle for a relationship, job, or other situation that doesn't align with your authentic self.

Settling can even feel comfortable for some of us. For many of us with C-PTSD, contentment—or an insistence on it—feels awkward. We think we deserve "not good enough." The strategy I've found most effective to subvert these thoughts is remembering that death is inescapable. The only certainty in our journey is death. Instead of treating this as frightening, we can treat it as our motivation to *do things*, and to *do them as best we can*. To really live. Death is the end of the unrepeatable miracle that we are (at least on this earth, and in this body). This life is our only chance to live a life aligned with our highest self.

A life as good as the best emerges from the practice of authenticity. When we know who we are and act in alignment, expressing our dreams is like the unfolding of nature itself. Our connection to our authentic self sustains us on our journey, which may entail occasional missteps, failures, or struggle. Authenticity feeds the tenacity we need to push through the hard times.

Be you. Be the truth. Be relentlessly real. Do what you know ought to be done. And through your practice of authenticity, begin to shape your reality toward a life as good as the best.

CHAPTER 8

PRACTICE RECONTEXTUALIZING

We would rather be ruined than changed / We would rather die in our dread / Than climb the cross of the present / And let our illusions die.

W.H. Auden, The Age of Anxiety

Our context is our environment, the conditions or circumstances of our existence. As children, we had no control over our context. As adults, we may not be able to fully control our context, but we can optimize it for healing and living a life as good as the best. **The practice of recontextualizing means intentionally structuring our context to align with what we aspire to be, to thoughtfully create circumstances conducive to our flourishing.**

We have been wounded, and our wound programmed us without our permission at a young age, before we could possibly know our sovereignty. If our programming is left ignored, we will continue to take actions based on it, and despair will overtake us. The wounded narrator will overtake us. Our wound gains power the longer we let it fester. As Hollis writes in *The Eden Project*, such a wound can "usurp consciousness, warp perspective, contaminate choice, and seek its own replication." For example, some of us with C-PTSD may find ourselves unknowingly fostering environments of conflict, chaos, and drama, so that our hearts will beat faster and we'll feel alive. It's what we've always known, and what we've been taught to believe we deserve. Over time, these decisions as to what to welcome in and what to reject add up and influence our lives negatively, making it much harder for us to live a life as good as the best.

Our programming is not us. Our wounded narrator continuously seeks to control our context, but *we* are the ones with the ultimate power. We have the power—and obligation—to make best efforts to construct our context in every moment of our lives, with every intention, choice, and act. We bear the full weight of this freedom and responsibility to shape a nurturing context in alignment with our dreams and the life to which we aspire. Doing "nothing" and letting our programming control us is still a choice, a surrender of our power. Letting our programming control us feeds our residual trauma, our wounded narrator, the version of us that isn't really us. If we don't do "something," our wounded narrator will overtake us, submerging us in fear, constraint, and profound inferiority. It's a sacrifice whose only reward is familiarity.

We can only use best efforts to shape our context. We don't get to avoid all pain, frustration, heartbreak, and inconvenience. We will, from time to time, run smack into difficult experiences we'd rather avoid. We can't allow ourselves to get lost in their well-worn current. Not all struggle can be mitigated by the therapies or practices described in this book, but all struggle can be mitigated by taking each moment as it is, as a transitory experience. Moments, memories, feelings, and thoughts are not conditions but transitory experiences. Every feeling passes just as every moment passes. This also means that every moment is an opportunity, a chance to learn something and then to shift or pivot. To decide what to repeat, and what to never do again. We can note our patterns, intend the best, and do better. We can override our wounded narrator and intentionally create a supportive environment for ourselves, which will, in turn, continue to weaken all wounded narration.

You have more freedom, power, and responsibility than you realize. You have tremendous influence over who and what is in your environment. By choosing the good, the aspirational, the authentic, the pleasing, and the inspiring, you cultivate a context in which your dreams can take root. Through the power we wield over our context, we can *feed* our possibilities and *starve* our trauma. We can *feed* our authentic self and *starve* our wounded narrator.

Feed what you want to see grow.

Starve what you want to see die.

Escape Poverty

I've never seen a manifesting or motivational book address the dark and overwhelming distress that defines living in poverty. None of those books speak to the poor. I believe the poor are perpetually ignored and perpetually unseen.

The poor are not the middle class with whom politicians are so eager to identify. The poor lack access to education and opportunity. The poor are on public assistance, miss paying their rent for months in a row and pray they won't be evicted, buy everything used, rely on public or other unreliable transportation, can't buy their children braces or even Christmas presents, and are one emergency away from going completely broke and potentially homeless (or already are). There is absolutely no beauty in poverty. Poverty is not a rural farmer who enjoys a minimalist lifestyle. Poverty is not hippies who grow their own food in the backyard. Poverty is struggling to put food on the table. Poverty is being terrified of that one extra bill—whether it's a doctor's visit or a plumber's visit—because it could cause everything to unravel. Poverty is growing up never flying in an airplane, and maybe never even leaving your neighborhood.

Poverty is not the middle class or even the lower middle class. Poverty is the acute struggle to survive in our unapologetically capitalist system.[57] Poverty is ugly.

Being poor is overwhelming because it means every single part of your day is full of the stress of not having enough money for essentials and emergencies. Being poor is overwhelming because you're typically surrounded by other poor people who also feel stressed, ashamed, demoralized, and powerless. Being poor is overwhelming because you can't find anyone to inspire you, because everyone you know is just getting by, and often vulnerable to violence and addiction. Being poor is overwhelming because you don't receive the benefit of the doubt once consequences such as evictions, arrests, and penalties hit. Being poor dramatically limits your engagement with the best of the universe. If you're fortunate, people only look down on you and feel sorry for you. If you're not, they take advantage of your desperation.

I grew up in poverty, and it was miserable. No beauty existed in any of it. The perpetual struggle was depleting and demoralizing. And when I grew up, I felt I had to hide my struggle. I felt like I had to pass as middle class, just to earn the right not to be thrown back into poverty's terrifying torrent.

The hard and painful truth is: It's hard to follow much of the advice in this book when you're stuck in poverty. It's hard to follow the advice in *any* book when you're stuck in poverty. And I'm tired of everyone being grouped together with respect to motivation as if we were all born with the same privileges. We weren't. Life is brutally unfair. Children are born into poverty due to none of their own doing and are depleted of spirit on a daily basis. And people all across society, across the spectrum of political affiliation, consciously and subconsciously, project worthlessness onto them in one way or another, in part to assuage their own capitalist anxieties.[58]

If you're currently living in poverty, your first step is to escape. We can make strides in an impoverished context, but the process is incredibly difficult and slow-moving. We expend so much energy on surviving that everything else receives short shrift. Poverty can swallow everything whole, taking down with it your physical health and ability to dream, connect, believe in abundance, and be authentic.

And in case you think I think escaping poverty is easy, I don't believe pulling yourself up entirely by your bootstraps is even possible. It's a myth. *Some people don't even have bootstraps.* Despite the rags-to-riches stories American culture exalts, escaping poverty is extraordinarily difficult. The exit rate after one year in poverty is only 56 percent. The exit rate drops to 13 percent after seven years in poverty. It becomes harder to escape each succeeding year.[59]

I believe in dreams, but I don't believe in the simplistic "American Dream," which emphasizes the possibility of upward social mobility and prosperity for individuals who work hard and play by the rules. It's not nearly that digestible. Impoverished people can't escape alone, and it's not poor decision-making alone that leads to poverty. At the same time, poverty is not inescapable, and social programs are not the only source of hope or help. Yes, it's possible to make it out of poverty without public assistance, but there's no escape without help and lucky breaks. Hard work alone will never be enough when you start at the bottom. I know people who claim to have started at the bottom and made it out alone, but it's an insidious lie. They sought and embraced help and luck, as we all should. That's okay. Acknowledging the truth that it's a harder journey for some of us than others doesn't take away from everyone being worthy, and it being a possibility for all of us.

Escape is not rigid or linear. The formula of working hard and playing by the rules to escape poverty works sometimes, but it often isn't enough. Working hard works to the extent it leads to real learning, creativity, business/art/brand/career development, access to successful people/customers/an audience, or prestige. Playing by the rules works to the extent it's necessary to gain the aforementioned benefits. Playing by the rules can bring you to a rung secure enough that you *can* break the rules without being mercilessly punished (and bringing forth your dreams almost always entails breaking a few rules).

People in poverty must often look outside of their own community for ideas for how to escape. I didn't grow up with inspiration around me. No one in my family or immediate community had attended college. The only people I knew who graduated from college were my teachers and a handful of my friends' parents, the most elite of whom was a dentist. I found inspiration in my first-grade teacher (who gave me my own spelling word to learn every day and introduced me to books she thought I'd enjoy, waking up my brain and changing my life); my English, journalism, and history teachers in high school (who truly saw me and encouraged writing and critical thought); hip-hop songs; and young adult novels. The latter two were a lifeline that taught me stories of escape. Other people, who had lives that sounded incredibly tough, had escaped, and so could I. So can you.

I can't tell you exactly how. Everyone's circumstances are different, and escaping is brutally hard. *Hard doesn't mean impossible*. If you're living in poverty, search for inspiration wherever you can—in others, in the arts, in the tangible and the imaginary. Use every social program available to you and your family to your advantage. You should not only accept help but also look for it wherever you can—in nonprofits, churches, and support groups. Build relationships with mentors, teachers, investors, clergy, or others. Talk to people. Share your dream. Focus on escape, and use every resource you can. Help and luck are more abundant in some contexts than others. If you're living in poverty, you can't afford to wait for these contexts to show up but should rather seek to place yourself within such a context. For me, that was high school extracurriculars and college. For you, it could be a new community, a different school, the sporting field, or a workplace full of energy and opportunity.

Focusing on escape from poverty means bigger dreams may at times be subsumed to this one aim. I'm only able to see this with respect to my own life in hindsight. In high school, I dreamed of being a writer. Once I arrived at college, I realized writing was a privileged profession, providing only a precarious income. The law was interesting to me, so I eventually obtained a law degree, thinking I would take a job in the public sector. When I continued to struggle financially, I made the decision to take jobs that paid well. At the time, none of it felt like a sacrifice. I loved many of my law school classes. I lived in my dream city and in my dream neighborhood (as subsidized by law school loans). I made incredible friends and met my husband. I only have the privilege of writing these words today because I took that path. While it's possible to write while living in poverty (J.K. Rowling did it), it's also extraordinarily difficult.

If you can work on achieving baseline stability while healing and pursuing your dreams, work on both in tandem. If not, get to baseline first. Baseline will be richer in possibility and freer from worry and stress. If you struggle to use your imagination, believe in abundance, or connect to others because of the pressures of poverty, get to baseline. If you can't remember or know your dreams because of the pressures of poverty, get to baseline. Escape first, and give yourself the small luxury of time and space to connect to your authentic self and figure it out.

Poverty doesn't reflect your worth, power or possibilities. Create a context that does reflect them. People who make it out of poverty somehow implicitly understand that this is possible, even though it's purposely hidden by a system requiring submission to capitalism.

They know they're meant for more. They can see and feel their dreams. They are brave, they take risks, and they take and use help with gratitude when it's offered. They are extraordinarily patient and extraordinarily persistent.

You're not alone. It's not fair that you may have to put in so much more effort than others do, but you're not alone and you have never been alone. We aren't that common, but we're also everywhere. Many of us are "passing." You can easily search a list of the numerous historical figures and successful present-day individuals who escaped poverty (I can't know who you'd find motivating or dissuasive, so I haven't included a list here). I honor you by choosing to believe it's just as possible for you.

Reject Pain and Suffering

Pain is an indelible part of life. Suffering doesn't have to be.

The bad news: We all experience painful events from time to time. Like the poverty that some of us are born into, those events don't happen to us because of something we did or didn't do or believe. Those painful events don't reflect our fundamental worth, our power, or our possibilities. We have the responsibility to direct our lives, but we don't control the unfolding of the universe, or illness, death, catastrophes, violence, heartbreak,[60] or other events that cause pain.

For a long time, I thought that healing would rid my context of severe emotional pain—that I would never be triggered again, never be hurt again, never feel awful. I wanted so very much to never feel pain again. And although experiences of severe emotional pain decreased in frequency, when they hit, the pain was still unwieldy and my responses still debilitating. I felt destroyed, as I always had. My programming—my wounded narrator—frequently wanted to resort to its old, damaging, supposedly protective mechanisms: to lash out, to degrade others and myself, or to numb myself in any way available to me.

Ah, to feel numb. It works in the short-term and may be all right in limited doses, but we should eventually confront and work through the pain. Confronting the pain means accepting the truth of our original injury and its influence on every other injury since. For me, it included acknowledging that I was afraid of pain and afraid of being exposed as vulnerable to pain. Pain and vulnerability (I couldn't separate them) felt like utter and complete destruction, rendering me shattered, submerged, erased. It was a replay of what I had experienced as a child. I had to learn to ride the waves of pain, knowing the pain was *not* destroying me. *I was not destroyed.* I couldn't lie to the pain, suppress it, or ask it to rush through. I had to feel it and know I could handle it. I had to notice my feelings and the sensations in my body and mind. I had to remember my breath, that I existed, that I was whole. I was *not* destroyed.

We breathe through the waves that feel like destruction. We give the feelings space to expand and release. It can be terrifying, but eventually they pass, leaving a life even better than the one before in their wake. We can cry, scream, punch something. We can find comfort in talking to or simply being in the presence of someone who loves us, or at least likes us. We remember that feelings only last ninety seconds if we let them. We don't rely on damaging short-term fixes, such as making excuses, leaning on victimhood or arrogance, taking it out on others, or numbing ourselves.

Pain is a part of life for everyone. We're not promised a life without bumps and turns, loss and heartbreak. We can fully accept that we don't live forever, we can't control other people, and we have imperfect knowledge and make mistakes, even with the best of intentions. To allow a life as good as the best to unfold, we accept the inevitability of a degree of challenge (and resultant pain) in life while having faith in our ability to minimize such challenges (and resultant pain). We remain in our power while yielding to the universe, feeding possibility.

While pain is not a choice, the experience of suffering is mediated by choice once we're adults. I think of suffering as the ongoing experience of pain, a sort of perpetual trauma environment, beyond a point at which the pain should have passed through emotional release or a change of circumstances. Suffering happens when we're either dominated by our circumstances or when we cling to the circumstances creating pain. Suffering can result from distressing circumstances like poverty, war, emotionally or physically abusive relationships, and literal and figurative prison. When someone is experiencing these ongoing traumas, they are often stuck. Not only will they rarely read a self-help book, but those self-help books don't speak to them.

Here are the broad categories I place suffering within:

- Suffering arising from grief: from loving someone who leaves, either by dying or ending the relationship. There's no cure for such suffering other than time and healing practices.

- Suffering resulting from physical illness. There's no cure for such suffering other than time and healing practices, including physical healing practices (typically, the more innovative, the better).

- Suffering from relationships or environments (including macro-environments) that wreak ongoing pain. In these situations, rejection and escape are the only cures (with healing practices to follow).

Reject suffering. Never endure suffering without a plan for exit. Under no circumstances do you deserve to be treated poorly. Don't sacrifice your dreams. Don't sacrifice your worth. Not for loyalty, or guilt, or a fear of the unknown. Not for anything. If the people in your life, your community, or your environment are perpetuating abuse, danger, instability, or other harms—in other words, if you're immersed in present-day trauma—get out, or work towards change, or carve a path through. Getting out first is best. It will be hard, sometimes unbearably so. Do it anyway. It's the only way to speak to the universe and change it, for you and for others.

Suffering, and its frequent partner victimhood, are seductive. I grew up in a family where no one seemed able to imagine a life of ease and wholeness. Suffering was accepted as a natural state, even clung to like a life raft. Suffering can give life meaning and excitement. Suffering can give someone who feels like they have nothing a story to tell to evoke attention and sympathy. It can give a traumatized person an identity when they don't feel they have one. Being a victim can feel empowering to people who lack confidence. And suffering's perverse predictability can feel safer than trying anything new.

Although embracing suffering can be tempting for those of us who have never known anything different, suffering only begets suffering, never healing—and never possibilities. Our possibilities emerge in the leap we take away from suffering. If you believe suffering has value, or if you believe you deserve suffering, or it's an ineradicable component of your life, it will never leave your life.

You don't deserve to suffer. You never have.

YOU ARE WORTHY OF A LIFE AS GOOD AS THE BEST.

If you're experiencing present-day trauma and you've somehow found the time and means to open this book, I see you. Conventional motivational books may ignore you, assuming privilege of all readers, but I know you're here. If you're in extreme poverty, in prison, in an abusive relationship, living in a crime-ridden neighborhood, or struggling with a debilitating illness—I see you. I'm hoping I can help, but even if I fail, I want you to know *I see you*. You are not overlooked. I believe in you, and I believe you have the power to recontextualize your life. I will not give up on you.

If you live in a toxic environment (and toxic environments may be shaped by particular toxic people, as discussed in Chapter 3), diligently plan to leave in the safest and most effective way possible. And then leave. You may fear the unknown. The known—even if toxic—can be comfortable. Freedom and ownership can feel terrifying at first. Many of us with C-PTSD have been conditioned to see things wrong side up, to see safety in pain and struggle. Many of us lack the self-worth to completely free ourselves, and yet we can't attain the self-worth we need in a context of perpetual trauma.

I'm not underselling evil and its power to cause pain and suffering, nor how difficult it can be to evade or escape. Evil is real and includes slavery, rape, torture, genocide, murder, inequality, and other traumas inflicted by one individual or group upon another individual or group. I understand why motivational books typically don't mention these; it's simpler, neater, and sends the empowering message that it's all up to you. But we notice the omission, either consciously or subconsciously, and it hinders our motivation. With the omission, we are forced to believe that the evil done to us must be our fault. *It's not*.

I can't solve for evil, and I don't believe any philosopher has ever done so effectively. The way I reconcile evil with this book is to recognize that a dark side of human power and imagination exists. The imagination can be used to build dreams of beauty, and it can be used to destroy. Evil is real, and evil has neither excuse nor deeper meaning. There's no point in determining the source. It's impossible to wring reason or value out of something that has none.

We can't change the past, or the fact that cruelty created nations and wealth that live on today. We can recognize it as brutally unfair, and allow our feelings space. We can recognize that it had nothing to do with us and isn't a reflection on our worth, power or possibility.

This is a forward-looking philosophy, with no entrapment by the past. We're not that history, and we're not even our own history. Every day is a new day to take action toward your dreams. Every day is a day to make the world better. Every moment is a chance to diminish evil's power and shape our context in a manner that protects ourselves and others from it.

I have never been satisfied with the explanations for suffering offered by religion and philosophy. To me, suffering is not a punishment or test, per the Christian view, nor is it an ultimately positive experience, something to transform into personal growth, spiritual development, and liberation, as per the Buddhist view. Perhaps some insight is gained by working through pain, but pain is not necessary or sufficient to gain insight. Suffering is simply suffering, and any spiritual growth is a side effect. Although suffering may be a fundamental aspect of human existence, life with as little suffering as possible is a beautiful thing and will not lack spiritual growth or liberation due to its absence. You are allowed to hate suffering. You are permitted to hate evil. You should hate poverty.

Some extol suffering in the form of "self-sacrifice," for a cause or for their family. These people will wear themselves out committing laudable acts of love and service. Perhaps they work in public service, or care for an ill relative and make little time for their own healing. If these individuals don't take care of themselves while performing these important acts, they will begin to struggle in their bodies and minds, and they will begin to sacrifice their well-being. Never permit yourself to be completely worn out or in a state of physical or emotional suffering on an ongoing basis, even for an ostensibly good reason. Step back. Ask for extra help. Don't abandon others, but don't think martyrdom will eliminate your own pain. You can't help others if you're self-immolated.

You may face personal challenges arising from events and experiences that crush the heart and flood the brain—family tragedies or health problems, or macro events like economic downturns. An event that seems relatively minor on its face may gut you, like social rejection. Sometimes, you'll need to put everything on pause and immerse yourself in overcoming these painful events in the healthiest manner possible. Sometimes you'll struggle to maintain the practices in this book while overcoming the pain of these events. *That's okay*. Have compassion for yourself. You can't avoid, suppress, ignore, or drown the pain, or avoid working through it. Over the years, I had perfected the art of all those stopgaps. My favorite way to avoid working through pain was to find new drama, whether it was running for student government office in college, becoming romantically involved with unsuitable men, or applying for new jobs as if they would fix everything. My avoidant-inspired ventures worked temporarily and superficially. The pain was always left churning beneath. The pain always found a way to seep out and corrupt everything it touched.

Avoiding or suppressing pain doesn't work—it creates suffering in pain's place. Allowing it to work through you, and then merging, dispelling, or transforming the pain through the therapies and practices described in this book, does.

You are powerful and limitless, and you can cultivate a context worthy of you.

Even if you are barely surviving.

Even if you are oppressed by your environment, community, or family.

The oppression is external to you.

Your dreams are waiting for a garden in which to bloom.

Brighten Your Environment

What you look at day-to-day becomes your reality. What you choose to observe will saturate your perception, influence your decisions, and become your context. Observation is existence, and the absence of observation can become erasure. Once you've removed yourself from poverty and suffering, or in tandem, make your everyday environment as free from the negative and as full of the positive, energizing, mindful, regulating, and inspiring as possible. It's tremendously difficult for those of us with C-PTSD to find consistent peace—don't make it harder on yourself by choosing the unpleasant, chaotic, or disturbing.

Avoid or limit the following:

- Pessimistic/angry people. They're everywhere and quickly identifiable. Their stories are often about others who have wronged them. They complain. They speak ill of others. They're rude to service people. Emotions are contagious; according to studies by Harvard Medical School professor Nicholas Christakis, emotions can pulse through social networks. This contagion is as present (if not more present) on social media as it is in real life. Pessimism and anger create negative frequencies that crowd out the positive ones. Avoid those who continuously choose them.[61]

- Depressing/violent/sad shows. I've heard it said that media is a vortex of rubbish: it's true, and it has been ever since media became a mass phenomenon. Media tends to reflect the shallow and base. Within that vortex, choose wisely and with intention. The types of movies and shows you watch and the types of content you read shape your view of the world. Watching violent movies may make you see the world as more violent than it really is; watching Hallmark romances may impart just as much of an unrealistic view. Be aware of media's impact on you. Only consume media with a purpose (even if that purpose is entertainment), and know your limits—never consume media that makes you feel icky, or causes stress or anxiety, or gives you nightmares.

What's depressing is ultimately an individual assessment. I can watch the occasional sad and serious documentary, but I can't watch violent thrillers or horror movies. Also, know your limits with respect to time. Spending an inordinate amount of time in front of a screen can dull and distort your perception.

• Sad news. Many of us who like to think of ourselves as worldly enjoy tracking national and international events, but too much information quickly becomes toxic. It's also deeply jarring from an evolutionary perspective. Never before were we able to become aware of a tragedy that occurred across the world within seconds of its occurrence—bad news is always available to us. News consumption becomes overwhelming and will skew your view of the world in a way that doesn't match your daily reality. Unlike books, movies, and shows, the news will *always* trend negative. The local news talks constantly about crime but rarely mentions good deeds or achievements unless as part of an obituary. The WSJ has never once told me how great the economy is, except in retrospect. It's the business model: Bad news sells because it generates anxiety, leading to more consumption in a subconscious pursuit of alleviating the anxiety through certainty, keeping people addicted. Drama generates clicks. I still read the news, but I don't read ten articles discussing war in a day, and I skim local news rather than watching a local broadcast. When I go on vacation, I avoid news as much as possible. When I return, I often find that nothing has fundamentally changed, which is both sad and liberating.

- Social media. The Internet and social media are full of rabbit holes that are designed to narrow your thinking, show you increasingly extreme versions of what you just viewed, and sustain communities that are wholly dedicated to one way of thinking (where any nuance is immediately rejected). Algorithms feed the most primitive part of your brain, so disengage as much as possible. Exceptions always exist. Social media has opened up the exact surprise opportunities on which bringing forth depends. Some people will find a venue for their creativity and a path to riches through social media. The more technology connects us, the more opportunities arise to connect with an audience and find an unusual path to showcase your gifts. In addition, social media can help those of us who feel different in our real-life communities feel less alone. And yet, these very same benefits are quickly flattened due to the algorithms—the copying, the repetition, the tendency toward extremes, and the insularity that quickly develops. If you choose to remain on social media, find a way to create boundaries and manage the emotions it evokes. It's tempting for many of us to pursue validation through the performative status-seeking, voyeuristic resentment, and profound loneliness so inexhaustible on social media. Pay attention to your feelings, both in your body and your mind. Ask whether social media is taking you farther away from or closer to your dreams. Absolutely limit or even eliminate social media engagement if you're triggered by it. I used to tell myself that the snarky celebrity website I frequented was only a release valve, a way to shut my mind off to more serious and pressing matters and to engage with a community. It wasn't true. Snark is toxic, no matter the circumstances. Again, awareness and boundaries are critical. I still indulge in a bit of celebrity gossip, but with time limits, and I'm aware of how it shapes my context negatively.

- Other forms of technology. Too much of any technology is not a good thing. Chats, email, AI, and other forms of technology can have effects as insidious as social media. For example, the soothing, immediate responses and stimulation provided by AI disarms us, engendering a combination of certainty and comfort, dopamine and stimulation. For some of us, this can lead to addiction and anxiety. Take breaks from engagement with technology, whether by going into nature, working out, opening a physical book, or cooking a meal. Use your senses to reconnect to reality. Your senses—your physicality—are the only mechanisms powerful enough to overcome the tunnel vision and anxiety spirals provoked by technology. Try sitting in a room without clocks (or the outdoors without a watch or your phone). You will survive. Christopher Walken doesn't own a cellphone or have email, and he does all right.

- Anything else that triggers you. Anything that evokes negative vibrations without a meaningful purpose should be avoided as much as possible, especially during the healing phase. Triggers are deeply personal, and they are *not* a sign of weakness or a desire to be coddled. Those of us with C-PTSD can have particularly overwhelming (and inane) ones. Things that remind us of our abusers, such as a clothing print or a mannerism, can cause rage, sadness, or just a sense of being overwhelmed, even though it doesn't make any sense. You can't rationalize a trigger (although CBT can be effective at neutralizing them). No matter how ridiculous they seem, avoid your triggers until they stop triggering you, or until the trigger is significantly weakened. Healing will eventually deplete the triggers of power, but not always entirely. Balance avoiding triggers with their transformation. The first step is awareness: notice signs of hyperarousal in your body and mind. Then question where it's coming from: What are you being reminded of? Awareness of what and why you're triggered has an extraordinarily disarming effect. Have a relaxation technique ready, such as breathwork or going on a walk. If you're trapped in the situation—for example, at a meeting at work—excuse yourself and go to the bathroom and splash cold water on your face. It's almost like a mini cold-water plunge; the cold shock response will loosen the debilitation. Have an affirmation ready, such as "I have the power to handle whatever happens" or simply, "I trust myself". Practice the affirmation while engaged in breathwork.

As you're rooting out negativity, intentionally and relentlessly surround yourself with the positive, beautiful, and aspirational. It's everywhere, if you choose to observe it and integrate it into your context. Soak up its energy. Let yourself feel good. Encourage and introduce the following:

- The best people. Surround yourself with authentic, optimistic, energetic, and supportive people. Surround yourself with people who are trying and who are putting themselves out there in one way or another—people who are proactive, people who have passions or at least hobbies. People who are ostensibly successful, and people who are quietly flourishing. People who practice empathy and acceptance rather than judgment. And generally, people who are doing things and living a life you admire, for whatever reason. Again, people become similar to those they surround themselves with, whether they like it or not. Multiple studies indicate that we become similar to our friends—with exposure, interaction, and shared experiences, we tend to adopt the same lifestyle habits, such as exercise, diet, and substance abuse. The people we get to know outside of our immediate family have a significant impact on us from our youngest days; strong evidence exists that adult role models other than parents can nurture, empower, and buffer the lives of children in traumatic circumstances.[62] The imperative to surround yourself with the best people applies to social media as well: Fill your social media with people and organizations making a positive impact (not people you enjoy hating or feeling better than).

- People who have what you want. Turn competitive energy into collaborative and creative energy. If you want to be wealthy, instead of hating wealthy people and/or avoiding them, surround yourself with them. It can be painful and intimidating to integrate yourself. Some may think being a big fish in a small pond will make them feel better (it will to some extent, but avoidance will not generate wealth energy). Associating with the wealthy is not "liberal" or "conservative." Wealth has no politics, because it can be used to support any politics. If you want to be wealthy, you can't hide. Be in the mix while keeping a cool head, learning (both from the successes and mistakes of others), collaborating, and contributing your own energy and creativity. Much of the reason to do this is intensely practical, as opportunity arises from the network effects of being in a community of excellence: client opportunities, business opportunities, collaboration, funding, access to information, and other gifts. The energy of success is also contagious.

- Activities you find fun, engaging, or motivating. Make time for things that make you happy. Whatever gives you peace, whatever makes you smile, whatever helps you regulate should be incorporated into your life as much as possible—sunshine, rain, nature, dancing, great food, art, knitting ... anything. This includes activities that give you a sense of adventure or purpose and expand your outlook, as well as activities that are calming. Regulation and calm bring us closer to our authentic selves, where we can access intrinsic motivation and purpose.

- An aspirational, nurturing, and warm physical environment. Consider how your environment supports your flourishing. You don't have to keep your space super clean if it saps your energy to do so; it doesn't matter unless you believe it does (and if you believe it does, it most definitely does). Generally, extremely chaotic and untidy environments are not supportive. Some of us with C-PTSD are actually more comfortable in chaos, but we should ask ourselves why. For a long time, I used the neglect of my physical environment as a form of control, a form of resistance. It was a hard habit to break. Consider creating scenic ambiance in your environment, through plants, fresh flowers, artworks, stones/rocks/gems, objects from foreign travel, soft ambient lighting, and your favorite colors.

- Art, beauty, and sensory delights. We are evolutionarily designed for aesthetic experiences, and they facilitate our flourishing. Nomadic peoples with few material possessions adorned themselves and decorated objects. Enjoy fashion, home décor, and other personal vehicles for visual and tactile expression. Your style—your authentic expression of truth and beauty—is a gift to a universe that can tend toward the bland otherwise. Have fun with it. It's all art, and art heals. Art lowers cortisol levels and increases dopamine.[63] Art stimulates our emotions, senses, and intellect. Art is also a source of awe and inspiration, encouraging our imaginations. When we place beautiful items on our body or fill our environment with beautiful objects (per our own authentic view), we create a pure, luminous, supportive vibration. We create a gentle dopamine kick. Consciously mold a physical appearance authentic to you that galvanizes, delights, or regulates you (or potentially others). People will judge you based on your appearance, because we're visual beings. By owning that appearance (and having fun with it), you'll accelerate the bringing forth of dreams in alignment with it.

- Music to regulate mood. Music is accessible magic. Music has tremendous emotional power and has been used across cultures over time as a powerful mood regulator. Music can be used to improve your context in a multitude of ways: fueling energy and focus, reducing boredom and stress, providing competing stimulus to pain signals, lessening the perceived intensity of pain, and boosting physical performance and increasing endurance during workouts. Music allows blood to flow more easily, reduces heart rate, lowers blood pressure, triggers the release of dopamine, decreases cortisol, and increases serotonin and endorphin levels.[64] Upbeat music can give us a happier and more flexible outlook (particularly if we intend to be happier).[65] Sad music has benefits as well. I love sad music.

I find tremendous visceral empathy in listening to certain songs. I feel heard when I hear others give voice to my buried feelings or share what resonates with my personal experiences. Listening to music can feel like being with a friend, but more sublime and less intrusive (less intrusive is often easier to tolerate for those of us with C-PTSD). Sad music triggers comforting neurochemical responses, including the release of the hormone prolactin (associated with crying), a chemical that curbs grief and produces feelings of calmness.[66]

- Music and other activities as a form of distraction. By focusing on music's beauty, we can disconnect from painful events. While we're healing, sometimes we need to wrest control from a negative thought by using distraction.[67] Distractions can take us away from unsupportive or triggering thoughts long enough to promote a better path. UCLA research psychiatrist Jeffrey Schwartz has devised a protocol to treat OCD by encouraging patients to immediately substitute something in the place of an intrusive thought, thereby physically rewiring the brain. The displacing thought or activity should be compelling, physical, and sensory, such as listening to music, jogging, or another activity. I have found that this approach also works well for non-OCD thoughts.

***

We are not our programming. We are not our wounded narrators. We shape our lives and our possibilities with every decision we make, including with what we encourage in our context and what we refuse to accept in our context. Over time, through the practice of recontextualizing, you'll create an environment that heightens feelings of warmth, authenticity, clarity, motivation, and regulation. An environment that encourages power and possibility to unfold.

CHAPTER 9

PRACTICE PRETENDING WHAT YOU INTEND

We are what we pretend to be, so we must be careful about what we pretend to be.
　　　　　　　　　　　Kurt Vonnegut, Mother Night

If you have good thoughts they will shine out of your face like sunbeams and you will always look lovely.
　　　　　　　　　　　Roald Dahl, The Minpins

R oald Dahl was right—thoughts are reflected in our outer presentation. The relationship doesn't merely work in one direction, though; we can also brighten our outer presentation with the aim of brightening our thoughts. We can pretend to be what we want to be—and end up being it.

Practicing self-possession means harnessing the power of outer presentation to elevate our thoughts and unlock connection and possibility.

Not every thought is a choice, but the way we react to every thought is. At times, you may have unintentional thoughts that are not aligned with all you aspire to be. Your wounded narrator may erupt. These intrusions are not an emergency, nor will they necessarily undermine the bringing forth of your dreams. These thoughts only control you if you fail to note them, question their source and purpose, and release them. You can't ignore or beat those thoughts into submission. The more desperately you try to do so, the more dangerously hidden and intractable they become. Excavate and examine, and then merge, transform, or dispel them through the practices in this book.

It will be an ongoing process. Healing is perpetual, but your outer presentation—the way you show up physically and energetically in the universe—is *right now*. Because of the mind-body connection, thoughts can elevate, neutralize, or risk corrupting your outer presentation. The mind can drag the body to a place it doesn't want to be, but on the positive side, *the body can drag the mind to a place it needs to be*. Even while we're working on resolving and integrating our complex and nuanced thoughts, even while we're deep in the healing process, we can choose to conform our outer presentation (what people see and experience) to one that is in alignment with our dreams and our highest self.

The body must be healed, but the body is by no means a burden. The body is one of the most powerful tools those of us with C-PTSD can use to cut through blockages we encounter. Simply holding and moving our bodies with intention creates extraordinary vibrations. By pushing your body forward towards your intentions, you'll transform your thoughts and you'll transform the way others react to you. You can cosplay someone who has self-worth and positive, regulated, and integrated energy. You can emanate the confidence and ease of a person who gets what they want. You can dress for the job you want, not the one you have. You can fake it until you make it—or, more meaningfully in the context of this book, *pretend what you intend*.

Pretending what we intend is necessary because many of us with C-PTSD may subconsciously wear "body armor." Body armor is made up of unconscious muscular tension and patterns that develop in response to stress, trauma, and difficult feelings. Some of us have experienced so much ongoing trauma that our body armor is chronic—permanently turned on, inseparably meshed into our bodies. We carry and emanate tension, even more so in response to a particular event or interaction that triggers memories of trauma. Chronic patterns of involuntary tension in the body can dampen or block emotional expression, distort our perception, diminish kinesthetic awareness, and create resistance to a range of motion and movement in our bodies.[68]

Body armor leads to expressions, language, and body language that are rooted in the past and no longer make sense for the person we currently are or want to be. Examples of body armor include:

- physically guarding through a tense, alert posture or crossed arms or legs to create a sense of safety, avoiding eye contact to avoid conflict or emotional exposure, or repeating an action to manage anxiety or avoid being too still, which can feel vulnerable;

- hypervigilance, through monitoring the environment or overreacting to sudden movements or sounds, often due to a perpetual sense of danger;

- emotional disengagement or avoidance, which can also manifest as avoiding eye contact;

- disassociation, by going blank/disconnecting to escape traumatic memories or intense emotions, which can look like zoning out; and

- somatic manifestations, such as persistent muscle tightness, caused by the body's demand to remain alert.

Several of these body armor manifestations have felt like a part of me for as long as I can remember, and writing the foregoing list was painful for me. For a long time, I thought these physical presentations were me, just the way I was.[69] I thought they were defining traits of my personality, but *they are not me*. They are not my authentic self, or my natural way of being, or my personality. They are protective mechanisms rooted in my injuries and in an environment of trauma in which I no longer live, imprinted on me without my permission. They are reflections of my wounded narrator, *not me*.

We can't let our interfering wound determine how we show up in the universe. Instead, we can use our body to convince our subconscious mind to serve our dreams and highest self.

Body armor is eroded by mind-body integration therapies, which take time. You don't have the time to wait and risk allowing your outer presentation to impact your ability to heal, connect to others, and bring forth your dreams. If we allow the body armor to take control of our outer presentation, we relinquish ownership of an indelible part of ourselves. Our outer presentation (voice, language, posture, and other ways we present) can (and should) serve our highest thoughts. We should use our outer presentation to convey our authentic self and high expectations to the universe.

People pick up on the tension we carry, consciously or subconsciously, and react in kind, making eliciting the benefits of the network of connection much more difficult than it needs to be. If we convey insecurity, negativity, lack of care or warmth, disinterest, or desperation, we are less likely to attract friends, mentors, lucky breaks, or serendipity. We are less likely to garner trust or faith. We are less likely to elicit information or connections that could advance our dreams.

We can't control other people. We can't control *anything*. However, we can exercise tremendous influence through our outer presentation. People react to others—consciously and subconsciously—as soon as they perceive them. Some of those reactions are biased, and any biased reactions are *never* our responsibility. Bias of all kinds is undoubtedly real, so perhaps I'm too generously giving the benefit of the doubt when I say most people are reacting to the vibes we're giving out: the tension we hold in our body and face, and our ease, confidence, energy, expressions, manners, and interest in others, among other characteristics that are conveyed through physical cues. This is an unavoidable and unconscious assessment we all make as a result of millions of years of human evolution in social environments. This tendency to assess is too deeply embedded in our DNA to change, and it's deeply embedded because it has advantaged our species. Humans learned to read each other's social cues to survive and thrive. For example, we tend to think someone avoiding eye contact is conveying dishonesty and/or insecurity, that someone with bad posture is conveying poor physical health and/or a lack of confidence, and that someone wearing a scowl is conveying displeasure and/or that they should be avoided.

And much of the time, they are.[70]

Use your body and face to materialize an unformed reality. If people like being around you, if people believe in you, if people trust you, your life will be easier and more pleasant, and you'll have more opportunity. In addition, by pretending what you intend—by pretending you believe you have self-worth, confidence, and ease, that anything is possible, and that bringing forth your dreams is only a matter of time—you take dramatic strides toward making it true. By pretending what you intend, you're imposing the future on the present. You're pushing your dreams into your present day. You're giving the universe—the network of human connection—something to work with, to react to, and to gift. Presentation becomes reality.[71]

The inextricable link between thought and presentation is backed by data. According to one study, increasing awareness of one's posture and movements may help a person make specific changes in their body language that reduce unwanted emotions and promote embodied awareness and more positive emotions.[72] I believe this, in turn, facilitates luck. People who experience luck tend to be more relaxed and open, notice chance opportunities and listen to intuition, and have positive expectations and a resilient attitude.

For a long time, while I thought I was "keeping it real" and not being "fake," I was allowing my interfering wound—my wounded narrator—to dominate my outer presentation and steer my life. While believing I was protecting myself and doing what I had to do, I was emitting woundedness, insecurity, and negative energy to which others, consciously or subconsciously, reacted. This outer presentation *wasn't me,* and yet it was the "me" others experienced. The real me—the me I wanted to nurture and grow—was (and is) confident, positive, warm, and friendly. The real me wanted to connect. I let my authentic self be held hostage by my trauma, I let my interfering wound bury the best of me until I began to pretend what I intend. My outer presentation was a matter of physical survival when I was a child, and it's a matter of spiritual survival now.

The relationship between the body and mind is bidirectional. By pretending what we intend, we're not really faking it until we make it, but rather performing as the truest version of ourselves: the version that aligns with our authentic and reverent dreams. We're using our body to remind the mind of what is true and real. It's one of the most honest acts we can perform for ourselves.

If you want to be a confident and poised person, acting as one is honest and true. If you want to have a ton of friends, being friendly is honest and true. If you want to be fashionable, acting fashionable makes you fashionable. If you want to be confident, behaving confidently will eventually make you confident. By presenting yourself as confident, positive, open, composed, calm, and friendly (and not insecure, negative, needy, closed-off, anxious, or rude), you'll reap tremendous benefits from the network of connection.

In my experience, experimenting with this practice can be fun: smiling at strangers, throwing out compliments, assisting others or giving them the right of way, and directing positive thoughts toward them (such as *I send you peace* or *I hope you have a great day*). I experimented with walking with confidence even when I didn't feel confident and smiling even when I wasn't that happy. I focused on my posture in small group settings. I paid attention to my shoulders; when I was on a run, walking, or writing this book, I would relax them and feel tension release. I'd release my tongue from the roof of my mouth. It could be challenging—I had to patiently expand my window of tolerance for relaxation, for engagement, and even for directing positive thoughts. *But it worked.* As time went on, I had fewer negative interactions with strangers and more positive ones. People said kind words to me and performed kind acts for me. I received information from others in what seemed like a fortuitous manner. Moving through the universe, although never perfect, felt easier and more pleasant.

I'm still keeping it real. There are still people and situations I try to avoid because it's too hard to be my best self with them. But by cultivating an aspirational outer presentation, even when it's not 100 percent organic or instinctual, I'm placing my wounded narrator in the backseat (for some much needed rest). I'm allowing the person I aspire to be to steer. And it feels good.

We live in a universe of others. We are deeply embedded in the network of connection, and we can't ever completely escape it. When we appeal to the universe, we appeal to the network of connection. Other people are always a part of our story, our path to a life as good as the best—we need them on our side. All the network of connection can see of us is what we put out there—our body, face, and words—and that's all to which it can react. When you want to look away, cower in a corner, not reach out, and not pay mind to your posture or facial expressions, remember that it all matters. It's all a language through which we tell the universe (and ourselves) what we think we deserve, every single day, whether we're integrated or not. We're obligated to be aware of the way our subconscious, automatic responses manifest, and to choose to be intentional. We choose to perform our intentions. Nothing is as compelling as integrated energy, but until you get there, pretend what you intend.

Cultivate a Sense of Ease (the Absence of Tension)

Tension arises from feelings such as anxiety, unease, discomfort, worry, and agitation that are held in the body unaddressed. We may not have been able to express such feelings as children for fear of further abuse or neglect, and so we're used to keeping them suppressed. Unfortunately, the tension we hold and radiate spreads from our bodies out into the universe like a virus, stirring up an inevitable instability. It produces awkwardness, missed signs, miscommunications, unpredictable interactions, and problems with technology and machinery (due to our own micro-movements).

Tension demands embodiment, so it should always be relieved and transformed into its opposite, ease. A sense of ease facilitates self-possession, while tension ruptures it. Tension leaves us undone. Tension can't simply be removed, and it can't be suppressed. Trying to suppress tension consolidates its pressure and volatility. It will find its way out in one way or another, and by suppressing, we risk delaying, blocking, or sabotaging our healing and the bringing forth of our dreams.

When my husband, children, and I were still relatively new to our state (and I wasn't accustomed to noticing and working through tension), I had to take a law ethics exam to obtain my new state bar certification. The test happened to be on a weekend when my husband was out of town, which meant I needed a babysitter—the first time we'd have a babysitter for our infant. I was incredibly tense leading up to that Saturday: nervous about passing the exam, nervous about leaving my children with a new babysitter and being unable to respond to them for several hours, and nervous about not having any backup plan in case of an emergency. I worried about every possible thing that could go wrong. I planned the hell out of that day. Or so I thought.

My husband left on Friday evening. Saturday morning, two hours before I was to leave for the exam, a pipe burst in our home. Water gushed through the basement.

I hadn't thought of that. And I can't imagine a more literal representation of the way I felt inside.

All of the tension I'd been struggling to contain found its embodiment. It found its release.

My fight response that followed was intense, but it was also a release. As in childhood, having a concrete problem to address—to focus my thoughts upon—stabilized the chaotic tension of my mind. Everything proceeded smoothly once I jumped back into problem-solving (a tactic that I frequently used as a child to ease internal and external tension). Luckily, my husband was able to quickly arrange for plumbers and a mitigation team to arrive. The babysitter was fantastic and handled the teams and my children with a calm and positive attitude. I passed the ethics exam.

Everything turned out okay, but I learned to be aware of the dangers of escalating tension, which tends to occur before or after triggering events. I could have acknowledged the tension and taken steps to relieve or transform it. I could have journaled about my concerns. I could have focused on my breath and made sure I was obtaining enough sleep (tough to do with young children). I could have done yoga or worked out more. I could have reframed the day as not a day to be dreaded and overcome, but as a day full of exciting firsts.

I've had similar discombobulating tension arise before major events, coming through like a familiar friend, and I've been able to recognize and manage that tension better. In our family, we even acknowledge it by joking about tension finding its release, which seems to lessen its impact. I've learned that it only pours when it rains if you believe it does.

Although I've accepted the tension that arises and permeates my body in a way that feels like it's coming from outside of myself, I still don't embrace it as normal. Some might rationalize away tension as arising from justifiable concerns, as I often did. I don't believe tension is ever rational or solvable, nor that we can ever anticipate every possible thing that could go wrong. For me, tension is the traumatized hope that if I addressed everything possible, if I anticipated it all, everything would (finally) be okay. It's impossible to anticipate everything, and regardless, anticipation only gives an illusion of control. Don't relinquish your ease for an illusion.

Many of us with C-PTSD are conditioned to find tension comfortable. Tension may be so much a part of us that we may feel scared to feel its lack. As we've discussed, if you've experienced trauma or have otherwise been conditioned to expect drama, stress, or chaos, being calm or content can feel empty, emotionally and physically. Being worry-free can feel deeply uncomfortable. *Shouldn't you always be worried about something*? your wounded narrator might shout (mine does). When big events have often carried trauma with them, when they have at times (or even regularly) descended into chaos or horror, to lack tension may feel like letting our guard down and risking reinjury. Any feeling at all—guilt, anger, sadness—is more acceptable than the absence of tension, the experience of peace, because peace feels like emptiness, and emptiness feels like erasure. It's one of the many ways our C-PTSD holds us captive.

It takes practice, but we can stop unwittingly chasing the extreme emotions, racing heart, and borderline nausea that make us feel alive. We can become more accustomed to ease.

- Note what triggers high levels of tension for you. Examples include travel, exams, parties, seeing extended family, or a deadline at work. Knowing our triggers before we're triggered grounds us in reality and in the now. It can be hard to be aware of the escalating tension when it's actually happening; we can become flooded or overwhelmed unless we know what to look for.

- Acknowledge the tension. Make yourself see it, even if you don't want to. Allow yourself to feel the weighty discomfort of it. Although you can't spend time mired in it, you also can't just push past it until it explodes. Note the tension-caused incidents—dropping a bowl, dropping your phone in the toilet. Realizing their cause makes them feel less dramatic and makes them less likely to precipitate a negative tension spiral.

- Be reasonably prepared—not for everything that could go wrong, but for the tension itself. Come up with a plan for dealing with it. For example, try going to bed early for the three days leading up to a trip, going to a yoga class the day before an exam, or seeing friends before visiting extended family. Find what works for you.

- Acknowledge that tension is neither helpful nor productive. Carrying the burden of tension doesn't make you smart, responsible, or safe. Tension is an anachronism, an obfuscation of your reality. It is unwelcome. Your wounded narrator thinks it's your job to be a perpetual problem-solver or rescuer. Your wounded narrator is wrong.

- Once you've acknowledged that the tension is unhelpful, you can reframe and release it. Tension is simply energy that needs to find another path through your body.

- Let go by accepting that it's possible (and likely) for things to go smoothly. Accept that things can unfold easily. Accept the emptiness of peace.

- Speak about the tension aloud to another person. If the tension has anything to do with the way someone is treating you, tell them about it. If they respond openly and empathetically, great. But even if they don't, you're still easing the tension.

- Focus on and ground into your breath. Use the breathwork exercises in Chapter 6.

- Journal about your tension. Question its origin. Follow your stream of thoughts and feelings to expose gaps, follies, and assumptions. What is making you uncomfortable or anxious? Writing is release.

- Physically ease your tension through integration practices and hacks like removing your tongue from the roof of your mouth, relaxing and breathing into your shoulders, exercising in a manner that clears your head and releases endorphins, or receiving a massage (if that's something you're comfortable with).

- Move your eyes side to side while walking, running, or cycling to disengage the amygdala. This is an everyday form of EMDR that alleviates anxiety.

So much of feeling as if you're living in power and possibility is about feeling a profound sense of ease. So much of being the person you want to be is feeling a profound sense of ease with the idea of being that person. Wealth is really only a feeling of ease about and around money. You feel wealthy when you lack tension about finances. Patience is a feeling of ease about time. Confidence is a feeling of ease about yourself and others. Intimacy is a profound sense of ease around another person.

Become comfortable with the emptiness of ease. Ease means you don't have to do anything else. You may have to force yourself to feel the ease, to let it wash over you, and breathe into it instead of resisting it. You may have to pretend you like how it feels until one day, you actually do.

Emanate Confidence

Confidence tends to be an outer reflection of an inner sense of self-worth. If we emanate confidence, other people will sense that we believe we're worthy, and they'll believe it too. Other people will be more likely to believe in us, trust us, and respect us. All of these are reactions that lead to benefits from the network of connection.

Of course, it's a process to progress for those of us who have limiting beliefs about ourselves from childhood. But being aware of how we're currently showing up in the universe versus how we'd like to show up in the universe, and behaving in alignment with the latter, transforms our presence. Pretending we're confident even when we're not *will make us feel* more confident and help us emanate more confidence. Presenting the physical self as confident encourages the mind to integrate confidence. It works because the subconscious mind and the body don't like being out of sync. Our mind will change its beliefs to reconcile what the body is doing.

The following are some highly specific physical acts you can perform to emanate confidence:

- Walk at a healthy pace. Walking too slowly can signal a lack of dynamism. Walking too fast, as if you're in a hurry, can signal a lack of control over yourself or time.

- Keep good posture, with your shoulders back and your head up.

- Keep control of your body: don't fidget or make rapid or jittery movements or engage in distracting physical habits like hair twirling or nail biting. These habits convey nervousness, which makes other people uncomfortable.

- Stay big. Don't cross your legs and make yourself small.

- Stay open. Don't cross your arms and make yourself closed off. Keep your hands visible, with slightly open palms.

- Make eye contact to convey engagement and security (avoiding eye contact can signal that you feel weak, inferior, or afraid).

- Speak clearly and at a measured but energetic pace, with steadiness and appropriate inflection. I had a therapist who requested to share a recording of our session with some colleagues. The colleagues noted that they could sense trauma in my voice. It was sad to hear, but I knew it was true. I had the same unusual, damaged, monotone voice, with awkward inflection, as my siblings. Simply being aware of it has led me to normalize my voice (at least I think so).

- Unfurrow your brow. Even as I introduced ease into other parts of my body, I found my brow was often furrowed (especially when writing). The area in the middle of the forehead is sometimes referred to as the third eye. It's an easy muscle to relax once you're aware of it.

- Always emanate confidence when speaking about your dreams, physically and with word choice. This doesn't mean being arrogant, which is a frequency opposed to confidence (and which tends to be a cover for a lack of confidence).

Never, ever convey desperation with your body or words. The precise opposite of confidence in your dreams is desperation, and it's far worse than arrogance. Desperation is often defined as the "loss of hope and surrender to despair" or "a state of hopelessness leading to rashness." Desperation is wanting something badly, but having no real hope of obtaining it, creating a deep and troubling anxiety. Emanating desperation undermines the practices in this book. Desperation is the death of attraction. Desperation is the death of attainment.

Find a way to emanate confidence in your dreams and your capacity to heal. If you're not emanating confidence, take a break. Go back to the mind-body integration therapies. Go back to your authentic self, your imagination, and your belief in abundance. Know that desperation is profoundly unhelpful. Know that you have time, and that you have never-ending paths to your dream.

Desperation arises from a fear of uncertainty or a fear that you're not good enough to have options. Fear never fuels anything good. Desperation is so paralyzed by fear that it becomes a horrific negotiator, willing to sacrifice everything. *No sacrifices are required.*

No negotiation with God, spirit, or the universe is required. Believing that sacrifices and negotiation are required degrades our confidence and gives rise to an anxiety spiral, a lack of composure, and a sense of limited options, leading us to premature, hasty, unwise, or unethical decisions—decisions that often haunt, delay, or obstruct us later. Desperation erodes ethics, rationality, empathy, and authenticity.

I disagree with manifesting practitioners who advocate a feeling of desperation to feed inspiration or innovation, conceiving it as analogous to "burning the ships" or giving yourself no other option but success. Committing to no other option but success doesn't make you desperate, unless you insist on only one path to your success. My only option as a child was to escape. My only option now is to write this book. I'm not desperate; I've cut off other options intentionally in service of my dream, which only brought me more certainty of purpose, the opposite of despair. And I know that I have never-ending paths to my dream. You do, too. Don't blunt the inherent generosity of the universe with desperation.

Desperation is never all or nothing. Many people may be desperate about one thing and confident about another. But the subject arousing desperation will be contaminated, severely limiting your options with respect to it, as others naturally pick up on the way it colors the way you move, speak, and present yourself. The egocentrics of the world who wield power in one way or another will sense an opportunity to take advantage, and they may harm you or use your desperation to manipulate you. Many people who could have helped you will avoid you, because your desperation reminds them of the desperation they have felt before or that they fight to keep at bay—and people who avoid you can't provide meaningful connection or opportunities.

An Aside: Desperation and the Pursuit of Romance

Desperation often arises with respect to one of the most common desires: romantic love. Far too many manifesting writers, bloggers, and influencers exploit the very human experience of unrequited love. They promise that enough affirmations will secure the love of one's object of affection. By doing so, they imply that an affirmation can control another person. It's an extremely lucrative message, and an extremely deceptive one.

As we've learned, controlling others is impossible, and the more time and effort you spend on the attempt, the further away from your dreams you'll be. You can't bring forth a particular person's love for you. They will either love you or not. Each individual is a real person with their own mind and heart, and they are worthy of their own dreams. Why we love who we do—and why some of us are more likely to develop crushes on or pine away for a particular person who doesn't show interest in us—is entwined with our pasts and our traumas. It doesn't always make sense, and it can feel very unfair and deeply painful.

You can fall in love with the person of your dreams and build a wonderful relationship, and the practice of self-possession is critical in such pursuit. But there is a significant part of the process of falling in love that is outside the scope of bringing forth your dreams. I believe that you can bring forth love, but you can't control the form (person or process) it takes. We can pursue, but the right person will be someone who feels the same way about us, and we can't trick them into it.

It's completely normal to desire a loving relationship and all that tends to go with it. It's also completely normal to feel drawn to a particular person, to have a crush, intense attraction, or other feelings of connection that consume our thoughts. You can nudge that person, charm them, and seduce them (and, from experience, the less desperate you are, the more likely you'll do any of those successfully).[73] But you can never force someone to feel, think, or act in a certain way. You can't make a specific person fall in love with you or want to be with you. We are all free. Trying to control someone is not ethical, nor does it tend to work out the way we intend.

Obsessing over making a specific individual fall in love with you is unproductive with respect to your own time and energy and disrespectful with respect to the autonomy of your beloved.

Think about how you would feel if someone were putting that energy into obtaining your "love." How creepy would that be? Next, think through what the fixation is really about. A fixation on a particular person tends to be more about you than them. Ask yourself what this person represents or expresses that's missing from your life. How do you feel with this person? Do you feel safe? Accepted? Understood? Respected? Excited? Maybe this person makes you feel energized by triggering something related to your past, your trauma, or your sexual development. Understanding what they represent is key to understanding your patterns and breaking out of them.

Apologies if this is all very unromantic. I learned the hard way.

I believe the truth is just as romantic: gentle persuasion with uncertain results. Accepting the uncertainty of results in love is an act of love in itself, deeply generous.

Think of the Disney version of *Aladdin*, when the Genie tells Aladdin what types of wishes he isn't able to grant to him: he can't bring someone back from the dead, he can't kill someone, and he can't make someone fall in love. Jasmine does in fact fall in love with Aladdin. Aladdin had already encountered Jasmine, and they had chemistry. Chemistry isn't enough by itself, but it's a foundation. Aladdin then pursued persuasion with fantastic results. Notably, toward the end of the movie, their relationship almost falls apart.

Aladdin doesn't hold on desperately, though; he lets go, before his (and Jasmine's) dreams come together.

Desperation—that grasping, sad, covetous energy—is the death of gentle persuasion. It's the death of love. It will infect every action, look, or word with depletion rather than vitality. Pretend what you intend: Behave as if you love yourself the same way you imagine your romantic partner will, and radiate an engaged, loving, and open confidence. Behave as if you're whole and as if you have options in your path to love, because you are, and you do. Keep a genuinely open mind with respect to prospects. Relaxed energy is attractive and will paradoxically increase the chances that your original beloved may become interested, as well as so many others.

If you're looking for a partner, I recommend the following ritual (this is the only ritual in this book, but many aspects of it can be replicated to bring forth other types of intentions):

- Make a list of the top five to ten qualities important to you in a partner. Focus on what you really care about, your non-negotiables, because anything you don't mention could be a surprise. Everyone has flaws and baggage, and your partner will not be perfect, but some flaws may be more agreeable to you than others. I've known people who found their dream partner but missed critical pieces like "loyal" or "family-oriented." Write this list down, pencil to paper—or if you type it on the computer, please print it out. Spend time crafting it with confident and positive energy. Anything and everything is possible.

- Put the list in a drawer or box in your home. Look at it from time to time.

- Stop engaging with your exes or previous romantic interests. You don't have to be celibate, but don't waste your emotional and sexual energy on old attachments.

Their history is too strong, the connection is too easy, and the certain rhythm creates an illusion of safety. I remember finding comfort after the end of any romantic relationship by turning to someone I knew well. And since I wasn't in a relationship with that person (with all of the attendant expectation), intimacy was easier. But it wasn't fair to me, and it wasn't fair to them. Don't give yourself the backup option. Shortly before I connected with my husband, I deleted the phone numbers of all my exes.

• Go out, live your life, and try new activities, always being authentic and emanating confidence, composure, and an open heart. This is your project. Take risks. Try. Make new friends who can introduce you to others.

• Don't be jealous of friends in happy relationships; instead, celebrate and compliment them. Have fun being single. Have fun because you believe that this is the last time you'll be single. Don't complain about dating. Be super supportive at weddings.

• Meet people. Get to know them, but *don't settle*. If you find someone who lacks the traits that are important to you, politely move on. By settling, or even flirting with the idea of settling, you send the universe mixed messages. Settling conveys that the traits you listed aren't critical to you, so the universe becomes confused and ignores your initial request.

• On the other hand, it's completely understandable to change your mind about one trait or another. Let's say you thought something superficial, like eye color, was important to you, but it turns out it isn't. Roll with it, always with awareness of what you're doing. Keep an open heart. An open heart looks past the superficial. When you're in love, the minor things are negotiable.

- Meet your love. Let go. Be vulnerable. If the relationship aligns with your highest self, commit. Things will never be perfect, but they will be more wonderful than you ever thought possible. If you're able to execute on this specific list, while continuing to engage in the practices in this book, healing your interfering wound and transforming your limiting beliefs, it *will* happen for you.[74] A healing, positive, brave, confident, relaxed, and open-minded person who knows what they want and doesn't waste their time on the disinterested or toxic will find love. Pretend to be these things until you *are*.

Emanate Optimism

Optimism is believing in the best possible outcome. I think it's unfortunate that some writers have rejected optimism as a universal value on the grounds that it's unrealistic. Optimists are not unrealistic at all, but rather tend to exert more effort than the less optimistic, motivated by beliefs that their effort makes a difference and that exceptional results are possible. This often leads to better results. In one study, greater optimism two weeks prior to an exam predicted more study hours, greater overall satisfaction with the quality of studying, and a better grade. Students also experienced minimal negative consequences if their expectations were not met. If, instead, students lowered their expectations the day before the exam, they tended to study less and received a worse grade.[75] Several other studies have demonstrated that people who are naturally optimistic are more likely to choose continued effort over giving up on their goals, which fosters commitment, persistence, progress, and well-being.[76]

Expectations of success motivate us to renew our efforts when obstacles or difficulties arise. Optimists are more resilient, as they tend to view adversity as a discrete and temporary state. In another study that involved medical school matching, those with high optimism of matching with their top choice had higher levels of happiness and lower levels of stress during the process, as well as a greater likelihood of actually matching with their top choice. Medical students who were optimistic, but didn't match, didn't demonstrate greater distress; instead, optimism seemed to buoy resilience. Optimists are less likely to blame themselves for a bad outcome and more inclined to view a bad situation as temporary. Optimists also tend to be flexible with their goals and adjust them as they go along, making it more likely the goals will be achieved. As a result, optimists experience lower levels of stress and distress, among other physical and mental benefits.[77]

The aim of pretending what you intend is not perfect control or suppression of feelings perceived as negative. It's knowing that your feelings are not you—only sensations passing through. They don't get to distort your perception. They don't get to dictate your possibilities. Critics of optimism argue that it requires us to act cheerful and upbeat, no matter how we're feeling. We feel our feelings fully, but by choosing optimism after the pain begins to ebb, we further pull ourselves out of the pain. We don't let a painful experience limit or disempower us. Walking around anticipating failure and heartbreak doesn't do us or anyone else favors.

We all vary in our natural inclination towards optimism, but we can all cultivate greater optimism. Optimism is not a static personality trait but rather a practice, just like confidence. Cultivating optimism includes many practices set forth in this book: envisioning a future self that is living a life as good as the best, journaling to acknowledge gratitude, identifying our strengths, living in the present moment, accepting what we can't control, exercising, spending less time with our phones and computers, and using an affirmation like "I expect everything to go well." We train ourselves to be optimistic. Research by Martin Seligman (the "father of positive psychology") found that twelve weeks of optimism training was more effective and longer-lasting in treating clinically depressed patients than standard clinical protocols (i.e., medication).[78]

Smile (or at least relax your face)

While you're cultivating optimism, start pretending. One way to do this is by smiling. You don't need to smile when you're angry or sad, but try smiling when you're feeling less intense negative feelings like nervous, frustrated, or bitter, or even neutral. Smiling at someone makes them feel special and liked, feeding a desire to be around you and bask in the glow of that smile for longer periods of time. We can use our smiles to make new friends and acquaintances, charm investors and interviewers, win votes, and accomplish other steps toward our dreams. Smiling will also eventually lead to us feeling more optimistic, because our body and mind want to be in sync.

I understand that smiles are complicated. You can't walk around with a huge smile on your face all the time and expect people to treat you seriously or appreciate you, regardless of gender—and smiling is heavily gendered. Women are taught to perform smiles, while men are implicitly discouraged from smiling very much. Neither is helpful. It's not always appropriate to smile.[79] The resting bitch face is powerful, especially when walking alone at night or being hit on at a bar.

Instead of smiling all the time at everyone, try an "easy smile"—simply turning up the corners of your mouth. The easy smile should never feel forced or fake, but reaching the point where it won't feel forced or fake may take pretending. I like to stretch my mouth into a smile right before interviews, parties, and other events where I'll be interacting extensively with others. It contributes to the relaxation of my face and seems to flood me with positive energy. Then, once I'm engaged with others, I find my smile to be ready, powerful, and appropriate.

Here's how to practice:

- Try smiling right now, as big as you can. Stretch your mouth out, show your teeth, and let your face wrinkle. Settle into that smile. Hold it, even if it's awkward and uncomfortable. Notice your feelings. Are you angry, happy, or annoyed? Do you feel absurd?

- You may feel tension as your face and mind may be in conflict. If you keep holding a smile, or reinitiating a smile, the tension will slowly dissipate. The thoughts may turn positive on their own, or you may want to intentionally think of happy or funny ones.

- It may be nearly impossible to hold your smile, but it's also nearly impossible to hold on to low-frequency thoughts while you're holding your smile. *Let the smile win. Let the smile take you to a better place.* Feel your resistance melt. This smile is ultimately for you. It's not disingenuous because smiles feel good if you let them.

Use Bright Language

We become our language. The language we choose to use—aloud, in writing, and internally—defines us and defines our context. This includes the words we select, our grammar, and what we actually say. Here are some helpful ways to deploy language to facilitate an optimistic outlook:

- Use proper grammar.

- Use bright, cheerful, and favorable words to describe others.

- Give compliments whenever you can.

- Be interesting so that you give to the universe and people receive something valuable from you. For example, share stories that are relatable or funny, or show passion for a topic (even a controversial one). Being real is rarely boring.

- Never miss an opportunity to say congratulations or express sympathy.

- Be aware of how you use the words *I am*, and use words/phrases such as the following, or words that radiate similar frequencies: *I aspire, bright, amazing, exceptional, appreciate, grateful, optimistic, original,* and *fortuitous*.

- Don't use words or phrases with negative framing, such as *can't*, or words that show a lack of certainty of a positive outcome, such as *hopefully, unlikely,* or *possibly*. These convey that you're scared to believe.

- Don't casually say *sorry*; try to use this word only in the form of a sincere apology.

- Never call people names. Don't speak ill of people unless absolutely necessary, such as warning someone of danger or manipulation.

- Don't take things personally, because they usually aren't

personal.

- Never complain and never explain (publicly).[80]

Look and Act the Part (of the Self to Which You Aspire)

A sense of ease, confidence, and optimism is appropriate for everyone, but it's also helpful to project traits specifically supportive of your dreams and the person you want to be—your highest self. Know who you want to be, and perform the part of such a person. Ask yourself: How would a person with the job or lifestyle I want behave? What would a loved/healthy/wealthy/confident/popular person do? How would they interact with others? How would they dress? How would they live in their body?

For example, a popular person would probably be on good terms with many people in their community. They'd probably be friendly and communicate well, but also maintain a bit of mystery. They would never be annoying, arrogant, or rude. They would dress in trendy, socially acceptable styles, but perhaps have some signature (but not alienating) aspects to their style (an artist, on the other hand, would probably dress in a unique way and not care whether they were alienating or not). They would attend parties and events. The best way to be invited to parties and events is to start throwing them yourself, inviting many people, and showing social awareness during those events. The best way to become popular is to perform the part of a comfortably popular person.

A large part of projecting the self to which you aspire is looking like the self to which you aspire on the outside. Somewhat unfortunately, the appearance we project matters. It may seem incongruous to bring up the seemingly superficial in a book that otherwise dismisses it, but it's necessary because our brains are hopelessly attuned to appearances. Instead of lamenting that it's unfair (and it certainly is), we can remember that our appearance is not us, only a projection, and we can use that projection to our advantage.

Beauty is only one element of our appearance. Our inclination to notice and judge superficial beauty may be an inborn product of evolution or socially constructed, but it's unavoidable. Numerous studies have demonstrated that people tend to associate beauty with positive traits, which gives the beautiful an advantage. The definition of beauty—what's appealing, and why—is an unresolvable philosophical question. The classic Greeks thought beauty arose from symmetry, harmony, and coherence, and studies regarding attractive faces tend to define them as symmetrical and close to the overall average for a particular ethnicity. I disagree because I believe some of the most striking people have an unusual attribute—a gap in their teeth, a large nose, strong eyebrows—that make them appear authentic, complex, and spirited. Beauty is like art in that sense: Beauty has a uniqueness that separates it from the merely pleasant. Confidence combined with ease also tends to give people an "it" factor that transcends conventions. Confident people appear effortlessly attractive, while people chasing cosmetic treatments to reach an image of perfection often appear effortfully uncanny.

No matter how symmetrical our face, no matter how much conventional beauty we were born with, we can cultivate a striking and attractive appearance. We can take care of our skin, hair, and body. We can smile. We can emanate ease, confidence, and optimism. We can use fashion and style in a manner that is true to us yet aspirational. We can use intention to mold our appearance.

Clothing is one of the most basic forms of personal expression and one of the first ways we convey our personality to others and to ourselves. It's a way to affirm our identity, authenticity, and worth. It's a way to help ourselves feel good. For example, according to, one study, women who wore special undergarments reported feeling more confident and attractive, and the trick was choosing them in accordance with personal taste.[81]

Style reflects so much of what is internal to us and how we view ourselves. Personally, I love the softness and comfort of organic cotton and try to incorporate as much as I can in my wardrobe. As a child with sensory issues (either innate or caused by C-PTSD), I was constantly uncomfortable in the itchy, cheap materials I wore most of the time. Feeling like I'm not wearing anything (while still actually wearing something) is freedom and ease to me. Today, I very rarely wear synthetic materials, no matter how special the design itself is.

Have fun wearing beautiful, stylish, flattering, and well-made clothing when you can. Consider buying less clothing and spending more to ensure it fits your intentions. Actor Jeremy Strong's friends noted that when he was building his nascent acting career, he only owned four or five articles of clothing, and they were all designer.[82] This is a great example of a combination of aspiration and authenticity—Strong knew he was a star and performed the part with aesthetic precision.

Think of someone's style that you appreciate and break down what you appreciate about it. Sometimes a style icon can give us guidance if we're at a loss with respect to style, although we should never copy them too precisely, as that risks inauthenticity. Find inspiration in the way they pull their look together. Pretend it's effortless, even when it's not.

Only focus on designer labels if it feels authentic to do so, and if it somehow facilitates the unfolding of your dreams. It's unnecessary for most of us (and can even be counterproductive), but in certain contexts it can have dramatic effects. Be careful, as wearing high-end designers with no thought as to what's flattering or fits well prioritizes perception of status above all else, and often backfires by presenting as awkward and try-hard.

More importantly:

- Wear clothing that is clean, fits well, and makes you feel good in your body. Doing the opposite (wearing clothing that is dirty, poorly fitted, unflattering, and makes you feel bad about your body) can foster depressive feelings, exacerbating a rut that's hard to escape from. Common advice for managing depression is to trade pajamas for a clean, well-fitting outfit.

- Use color to your advantage. Wear a color to which you connect, such as red for assertiveness or passion, or choose colors that complement your own coloring.

- Consider paying twice as much and buying half as many. Choose quality over quantity (not necessarily based on luxury labels unless they are clear winners in that regard). Choose utility, robustness, durability, and pleasurable tactile sensations.

- Consider adding a dopamine kick to your outfits, even if it's relatively minor—fun socks or interesting jewelry. You'll receive a surge of good energy by wearing it, and others will by viewing it.

- Never look like you're trying too hard. Trying too hard may entail wearing overly expensive accessories or inappropriate clothing. Trying too hard conveys unnaturalness, a lack of confidence, and insincerity.

- Be a conscious consumer. Think about how your clothing is sourced, where it is made, and whether the materials are natural.

- Dress for the results you desire. One study found

that participants who wore formal business attire while completing a series of cognitive tests felt significantly more powerful and in control of their situation than their underdressed peers, which in turn shaped their cognitive processing and decision-making; they demonstrated enhanced cognitive control and more abstract thinking.[83] Another study separated three groups of men into negotiations (one dressed in sweats, one in suits, and one in their own clothing), and the men wearing suits did best.[84] The men in sweats showed lower testosterone (as an aside, the higher testosterone that might be helpful in a negotiation can be unsupportive in other contexts).

- Wear happy clothing—dress how you'd like to feel and how you'd like others to think you're feeling. Wear clothing that has received compliments in the past or brings back good memories.

***

Experiment and see what works for you. Have fun looking and acting the part. Have fun learning to radiate self-possession. You'll receive feedback from the universe that will let you know if you're on the right track. Over time, your insides and outsides will align and integrate, and you won't be pretending anymore.

Chapter 10

Practice Breaking Through Time

A straight line is not the shortest distance between two points.

Madeleine L'Engle, A Wrinkle in Time

The distinction between the past, present and future is only a stubborn persistent illusion.

Albert Einstein

This is the chapter where I risk losing you. This is a chapter more vulnerable to me than any other. This is the chapter where you may decide I'm verifiably insane—or, worse, that what I've asked you to do is too much, too painful, too intense, too odd, and too risky. This chapter includes no data whatsoever, but it is inspired by geniuses and free thinkers who have conveyed one of the most important secrets of the universe:

Time is an illusion.

The practice of breaking through time proposes that our perception of time is the result of our cultural conditioning and personal inclinations. Time travel is possible (if not

physically, then mentally and spiritually), and it can be tremendously healing, supportive, and inspiring.

The end of your life and the beginning of your life are baked into every single present moment. *It's all happening at once.* You can visit and become familiar with your past and future selves, and integrate them with the present. You can create harmony among who you were, who you are, and who you will be, a harmony in which your future self (who has healed and has realized their dreams) always carries the melody.

Time travel is a popular subject of books and movies because somewhere, deep in our collective subconscious, we recognize the elasticity of time. Time is just a social construct that is imposed on us subtly but relentlessly. From the moment we're born, our culture enforces the linearity, rigidity, and consistency of time, shaping our perceptions so uncompromisingly that it's difficult to imagine any other way of thinking.

Western culture venerates boundaries that distinguish and demarcate, and time is an easy prisoner. As young children, our perceptions are free, flexible, rambling, nonlinear, noncategorical, and creative. We don't understand hurrying, or waiting, or sequences of events. My three-year-old son will often mix up tomorrow and next year, for example. We don't understand why time requires our constant attention. We see people wondering what time it is, we see people running late, and we're told "not now," or "we'll do that tomorrow."

This preoccupation with time is relatively recent. Only with the Industrial Revolution and railways did watches and clocks become more common. With technological innovation, globalization, and the hyper-connection and homogenization they have wrought, time has become ever more present, through digital clocks on all of our technology, planes and trains to catch, maps estimating our arrival time, and appointments for virtually everything.

Biologically, our minds are inclined to prune away the chaos of the world into something more orderly. Synaptic pruning happens very quickly between the ages of two and ten, when about 50 percent of extra synapses are eliminated, and continues through adolescence at a slower pace. The free form and elastic is lost, and time is constructed for us.

We're taught that without boundaries, categories, and one-dimensionality, everything would turn to chaos—but the opposite of linearity is cycles, not chaos. Cyclical time means viewing time in terms of eternally repeating cycles of events, rather than a straight line moving from the past to the future. While Western culture sees time as monochronic (tangible, linear, finite, with one event happening at a time), certain other cultures have viewed time as polychronic (of an infinite supply, with many events happening at once, cyclical and even rhythmic).[85] For example, the Hopi and other Native languages lack past and future verb tenses, rooting everything in the present. Other cultures have viewed time as being in a vertical relationship with the present, where the present is a "hub" in which past and future exist simultaneously or in layers, interwoven in a way that transcends conventional linear time.

Similarly, the Buddhist concept of dependent origination posits time as a series of interrelated moments, where all phenomena are dependent on multiple causes and conditions, and nothing exists independently or in isolation. Causes and effects are not simply arranged in linear sequence but are part of a complex, nonlinear web of interdependent relationships and a perpetual flow of interconnected events. The present is only a central moment existing simultaneously in relation to the past and future, making forward and reverse causality possible. The "self" is not fixed, but rather a dynamic collection of changing conditions.

Einstein also questioned the linearity of time. In his theory of relativity, no universal "present" exists, nor does time pass at a uniform rate. Time is interconnected with space in a way that's dependent on the observer's frame of reference, rather than being absolute, universal, and unchanging. As such, no single, universal "now" exists. The theory of relativity has practical implications: One of the key aspects of relativity is time dilation, which states that time moves at different rates for observers in different relative states of motion. Satellite GPS has been built around its assumptions—that time slows down and stretches out.

It may seem paradoxical, but freeing our view of time from culturally imposed boundaries allows us to have an even greater command over it and to make sense of our own rich and complex experiences with it. Many of us have had the sense of experiencing time differently from others. We may feel like time is moving fast (in flow states, during adrenaline rush activities, or while binge-watching a television show) or moving slow (when experiencing boredom, pain, or awe). We can experience ourselves as a hub of overlapping and interconnected events when we consider memories or visions of our future. Memory is not linear, and memory is all we have of the past; dreams are not linear, and they are all we have of the future. To put it another way, the past is flexible because the past is based on memory, and the future is flexible because it's based on imagination. Both memory and imagination are perceptions, and they activate the same part of our brain. For example, people with amnesia can't plan for the future, because they can't access memories. Memory and dreams are two sides of the same coin.

Memory is truth, but never pure or objective. For many of us, a memory from long ago can feel like it happened yesterday. If painful, it can increase our blood pressure in the present. And we may remember a particular past event very clearly while completely forgetting other events that other people might find meaningful and memorable. Some of us tend to remember moments we feel badly about—whether because of regret, guilt, embarrassment, or something else—while the people who shared those moments with us may forget them completely. Several years ago, I shared an opinion on social media that basically amounted to: Don't demean or vilify people who didn't vote the same way you did. Friends who shared my general political stance were very upset with me over this; they were angry, and they read it as a dismissal. They attacked me online (only briefly, as the drama soon petered out). We were on the same side but not taking the same approach. I stand by my statement; it's consistent with the philosophy of this book. You'll never win an argument with yourself, another person, or the public through personal insults. However, I grew to regret sharing a knee-jerk opinion while many of my friends were hurting.

When I saw one of these friends at a reunion, the memory became as salient as if it had happened yesterday. I expressed my regret and even told him he had been more right than I had. And he said he didn't remember the interaction, but in any event, he agreed with my original argument (which felt very validating). The interaction was both confounding and cathartic. I think I carried that particular memory, while he didn't, because I hadn't forgiven myself for it. Maybe sometimes forgiving yourself requires talking to the person who participated in the conflict with you, and maybe sometimes it simply requires revisiting that moment and letting go.

Memory is a form of perception acutely vulnerable to our trauma. Some people who have suffered severe trauma repress their memories, while others are haunted by them. All of us make less than ideal choices based on memory every day, taking us away from a life as good as the best. We can't rid ourselves of our memories, but we can't let them define us either. We can heal memory so that it gets out of the way, while we fully exist in the present as is. Instead of making choices based on the memories of our injuries, we can make choices based on what is authentic, imaginative, and aspirational—in other words, our highest self.

Our future informs our present because as soon as we make a decision, we put ourselves on a new timeline. As soon as we make a decision, we define our present and what futures will be available to us. Before you get worried, realize that it's not like a maze with one way out. We can reach the same destination through multiple paths, although some may be more pleasant and require less work.

I believe that healing is polychronic. So much is happening at once. We simultaneously use the future as an indication of how we should live our lives in the present, and the past as a springboard for healing and growth in the present. The past is not clear, and the future is not unpredictable. Our actions in the future could affect our circumstances today, and our actions today could affect how we view what happened in the past (which is only knowable from our present). You can work through and reprocess memories based on what you know now, thereby changing the past (in the sense of changing your perception of the past, which is all you have anyway).

We can't control time, but we can experiment with it and start to be in relationship with it. We're so indoctrinated that it's impossible to deconstruct our perception of time completely, nor would we want to. We can still cultivate a nonlinear view of time and engage in mental time travel for specific empowering and healing purposes. Time is not imposed on us but rather springs from us, and we can use that to our intellectual and emotional advantage.

Heal the past and dream of the future in tandem, while moving with gratitude within the present. *It's all happening at the same time.*

Visiting Your Future Self

Einstein believed time travel to the future was theoretically possible, so let's start there.

Ask yourself: *What life is the future you living?*

Your future self is something like your child: You're gestating it. Every choice you make today shapes that future self's existence. It's an obligation, but it's also freedom. The future self is the self of endless potential and possibilities.

Find a meditative posture, or engage in active meditation such as yoga or running. Close your eyes (or don't, if you're in active meditation) and slowly allow a vision of your future self to emerge. Pick an age—thirty, forty, eighty, ninety. This future self should be you, but wiser, calmer, and more content. More regulated and more integrated. Your future self has realized their dreams. Don't worry about how you'll get from point A to point B, or about what's realistic for you, or about what you think you deserve. Just imagine your future self as your highest self, living a life as good as the best.

Focus on where you are and how you feel—all the senses of the moment. What comes to mind? What are you doing with your day? Where are you? Who is in your life? How do you feel in your mind? How do you feel in your body? What dreams are you living?

There are no rules, other than reserving judgment and feeling good while viewing this future self. For example, I've enjoyed visions of myself at an older age celebrating a birthday on a yacht in the Adriatic, off the coast of the land of my ancestors, surrounded by friends and family; sitting on a balcony overlooking the beach, writing and drinking a mojito or tea (depends on the day), feeling the sun on my skin and listening to the waves of the ocean; and giving a talk to a lively audience about this book and its ideas.

Take your time and allow your future self to reveal themselves. It may feel like you're adding random details to the vision, but if you're rooted in authenticity, they aren't random. These details will emerge and color your vision with energy and dynamism. Be limitless, no matter how crazy or unrealistic your vision may seem to you right now. If a detail you've conjured feels uncomfortable in any way, change it.

Once your vision is fully formed, talk to your future self. Tell your future self how you're feeling now: dreams, fears, anxieties, and questions. You can be completely vulnerable, because your future self accepts you as you are. Share the limiting beliefs that are holding you back. Share your doubt. Share your fear. Your future self already knows the severity of your limiting beliefs and how restricted by them you might feel, because they've survived it. Your future self is an empowered and limitless version of your authentic self, sourced from a deep part of you that knows what wonderful things you're capable of. Your future self is the best of you.

Allow your future self to respond. Allow your future self to believe in you in a way that your current self may not. What does your future self want to tell you? What is their advice? What are their words of comfort? What are the words of inspiration?

This practice is particularly helpful for those of us who struggle to show compassion for ourselves. Our future self can do it instead. Our future self also treats us with dignity and respect, which might mean calling us out on our missteps. Create the space for that guidance. Allow intuition to surface from deep within you.

If you want to make the exercise more concrete, you can also have your future self write a letter to your present self. Write what you would say if you were in their lovely position advising yourself. Don't lose the visual details. Imagine the precise context in which your future self is writing such a letter.

My future self thanks me for taking risks, eliminating negativity from my life, taking care of my mind and body, and never giving up. My future self tells me that finding regulation and peace today will lead to transcendence tomorrow. My future self tells me that all of the acts of connection I've performed have led to a brighter existence for others and a network of loved ones. My future self tells me I'm a writer—that I was born a writer. My future self is blissful, with a contented mind and a full heart, like an elderly lady Buddha.

We're using the future as an indication of the present. Our future self is our touchstone, guiding us to make the choices that will lead us to them. By visiting our future self, we define ourselves today. When uncertain, we can tap into our future self and wrestle our autonomy away from our memories. Engaging with our future self is a way to excavate the truths deep within us that might be otherwise inaccessible. We're forced to think about who we are and who we want to be, and how those two connect. If we're confused as to which path to take, we can ask our future self for signs to look out for. It's a profoundly defining and integrating act, particularly helpful when we feel lost.

In a moment so challenging it's hard to envision anything better, remember: *What is now is not what must be.* Each moment contains within it endless possibilities. Each moment provides an opportunity to decide what comes next. Everything in the present can be changed to reflect the future we envision. We have endless opportunities to become who we want to be.

Visiting Your Past Self

Let's move to the other end of the spectrum. Similar to the way your future self reassures and provides clarity to your present self, your present self can reassure and provide clarity to your past self. Our past self needs us to be the future self—to comfort and advise.

Visiting our past self may initially be unwelcome for those of us with childhood trauma. Why revisit deep sorrow, trauma and shame, hurt and terror? We're doing so much better now; we're healing, so why would we want to go back? Why would we want to be triggered?

I love visiting my future self, and I hate visiting my past self. It's one of the reasons I struggled with EMDR. The truth is, I hated my past self for being so helpless, lonely, and vulnerable. Even though my past self was a child, and I understood that rationally. That child was really, really heartbreakingly vulnerable. That child is so many of the things I worked so hard not to be, embodying so many natural sensations that I eventually stopped allowing myself to experience because they were rejected, ignored, or a physical or emotional liability.

Our past self is real, whether we like it or not. Our past self—all of our past selves—live within us, forever. They aren't going away, even after we heal. We can't abandon our past self, that young person, the way others did. Our past self needed to be saved and wasn't. The pain of it is almost unbearable. Our past self needs to know they're not bad, shameful, or unworthy. Our past self needs to know they're loved, that life will get better, that they have a right to participate in that better life, and that we are always there for them. Only by validating our past self can we quiet the voice of the wounded narrator.

Think of a moment in the past where you felt helpless or alone, in need of comfort or guidance. Think of a time you felt unseen or unheard, or violated, broken, or fractured. It could be the day someone excluded you at school, or the day your parents told you they were divorcing, or the day your dog died. Or, it could be the moment you were mistreated, abused, or assaulted. Address these unhappy moments with uncompromising clarity. Address those moments with empathy and compassion for yourself.

When and where does your past self need your help?

It is an incisive, surgical revisit. We must be in and out.

I know the exact moment for me, and it's a moment I'm only able to feel calm enough to write about because I first reprocessed it through EMDR (I suggest that if a memory causes dysregulation or a strong emotional or physical response, address it in therapy first; the practice described here goes beyond EMDR and is best done from a regulated state). It was the first time my father hit me, when I was two years old and had wet my pants. I can't be entirely sure the memory I hold is of the first time or a conflation of the many times that followed, but it has been substantiated by my mother. I was a toddler, and my father hit me over and over again, with what felt like inexplicable rage. My mother neither tried to stop him nor consoled me. I cried myself to sleep that time and the many times that followed.

That toddler was confused and so very vulnerable. Someone she trusted, who was supposed to care for her, was hurting her over and over again. That toddler was small, weak, and helpless physically, with no autonomy and no freedom. That toddler had not yet built up the many defenses she would build over time in service of her survival. That toddler knew it was cruel and unfair. That toddler knew it was wrong. And so that toddler knew she was trapped in an environment where people did the wrong things, and where she would never, after that moment, feel safe.

I'm still terrified to write the words: that child was helpless.

It's okay to admit that the child was helpless. I remember *I'm no longer helpless.* I'm an adult, with emotional and physical resources. The memory is excruciating, but that child needs me.

I visit that sweet child, that *me.* I imagine my present self arriving on a flying dragon, scooping up her up, holding her tight, telling her I love her and that the universe loves her. It's hard for her to believe, because it doesn't make sense—nothing makes sense. I tell her she's right: It's not right, it's not good, it's not normal, it's not love, and it's not her fault.

It's not love.

It's not love, and it's not her fault.

That treatment of her is, was and always will be unacceptable.

One day she will start to feel safe, worthy, and empowered.

One day she will know love, and the contrast will be stark.

What was done to her, the environment she was born into, has nothing to do with her or the light she has inside. That light will guide her. She can't lose it.

I hope that a piece of what I say lodges inside of her, to see her through, to lead her to me.

The memory remains excruciating every single time I revisit it. So many of us with C-PTSD have experienced the desolation of having no one to help us. So many of us have spent our entire lives protecting ourselves with layers of fabrication that saved our existence but hinder not only our dreams, but our ability to feel whole, regulated, and integrated.

We were helpless and no one helped, but that's in the past now. We are adults now. We are no longer helpless. We have the power to heal and transcend. We can guide that child to the present. We honor our connection to that child while recognizing we are distinct from that child.

If we need to feel more grounded in the present and more separated from the threats of the past, we can practice bilateral stimulation as in EMDR. We can move our eyes side to side as we engage with the past.

And then we can envision ourselves walking away with complete confidence that the child will transcend. That child will become someone with resources, love, and realized dreams. Cruelty will not define that child's power and possibilities. We guide that child to the present.

By traveling to our past self, we make the contrast between our adult and young self incontrovertible. We're adults who can be there for our child selves. We can love that child. That child will transform with every choice she makes as she finds her way to you. When you sense that child coming to the forefront of your thoughts, beliefs, and actions, remind her that you're in charge now. You will take care of things. She is forever safe now. It was not her fault, and nothing she did or didn't do could have ever changed it. The time for change is now.

That moment will never repeat itself, except by your own design. You will never be helpless again. Even if you open yourself up to being vulnerable, even if you tell the truth, even if you make mistakes. You will never be helpless again.

That child is not the wounded narrator, who came later based on the beliefs that child felt compelled to believe to make everything make sense. That child had a purity of emotion and existence, an openness to trust and vulnerability. We can still tap back into that purity and openness. By doing so, we weaken the wounded narrator, who otherwise threatens to take control of the direction of our lives. The wounded narrator will complicate, sabotage, run away, or engage in any number of other defense mechanisms because she is scared of something so painful happening again. She will think she is protecting you, but she will make everything harder.

The love, comfort, reassurance, and inspiration you give your past self will immediately empower your present. The unconditional love you give that child will heal them. I'm trying so hard to unconditionally love that child as I write and rewrite this section, in real time. I spent so long fighting the vulnerability of that child. Only by folding her—perceived weaknesses and all—within myself can I be whole and let go. All versions of us are a part of us.

Once you've visited the memory, determined what limiting beliefs it gave birth to, and integrated the past self living in it, let it go. Accept your past self. Forgive your past self. Once the past self is loved and accepted, our job is done.

Leaving is a critical part of this exercise; we can't stay in the past. Even with healing, those feelings can never be made good, but once you've gone through this process, you have put the past in its place. This recognition of when to leave the past takes great awareness. I don't believe in sitting with the past for too long, and that's why I don't have much faith in ongoing talk therapy that doesn't lead anywhere. Everything that happened, happened. The past is ultimately a limiting state. You were a victim then, and you're not a victim now. You can be a hero now. Your past is only relevant in terms of healing your interfering wounds and transforming your limiting beliefs. The more you heal and transform, the less you'll think about it.

Never Hurry, Never Worry, and Allow Momentum to Emerge

We don't necessarily perceive time the way it is. Like everything else subject to our perceptions, we only see what we want to see and hear what we want to hear. Time's interpretability can be used to our advantage.

Time is full of contradictions, just like we are. Time is a boss, and time is your ally. Time is inexorable, and time is accommodating. Anxiety about time is fruitless. Being in a hurry is being desperate for time. Being worried about having enough time is being desperate for time. You're playing a game of control that will never work out. This applies to your dreams and it also applies to your day.

One day I was worrying about time as I juggled the morning routine. I'd be dropping my older children off at school and then taking my younger son to a toddler class. It was a long drive all the way across the city, and we had been late before. So, as soon as we were in the car, driving to school, already behind schedule, I started repeating "I own time" while focusing on long breaths in and out. I ended up arriving five minutes early to the class that day. It felt like magic. Was traffic particularly light? Did I drive faster? Was I more efficient in all the little moments making up the journey? I didn't speed or run through red lights. Maybe luck was on my side. Since then, I've often used similar statements—ones that may or may not be true in themselves, but that dismantle a particular interpretation of time—to great effect. If I'm running late, I end up being much less late than originally expected. Sometimes I'm even early. I feel calm and steady. I feel in relationship with time.

Many of us with C-PTSD are preoccupied with and hypervigilant about time. Perhaps we had to worry about what time a parent came home (so we could anticipate their rage), or we watched the clock tick by when our parent was late picking us up from school. Maybe we felt so awful about ourselves that the self-imposed shame of being late just made it feel all the worse. Maybe being considered timely and aware of time felt validating and gave us a sense of control amid the chaos of our environment. The rigid management of time promised the illusion of control, but it left us flailing; holding on too tight to time can make us feel out of control, anxious, and desperate. We believe we're running late, we're falling behind, or we've missed our chance.

In the past, I was preoccupied with timeliness. Being on time and having a plan made me feel in control. It started in high school when I purchased a planner and took great comfort in writing out my extracurricular schedule and to-dos. I continued to use a planner in college, until one day I looked at it and felt utterly overwhelmed. I knew I could do all the things, but I didn't like seeing them there. The intensity of it drained me. The illusion of control was beginning to disintegrate.

While some of us with C-PTSD are hypervigilant in a way that leads to being overly concerned with timeliness, others with C-PTSD react to trauma by being late on purpose (consciously or subconsciously). This is a problem to the extent it's disrespectful of another person or a group's time. Some people choose to be late because they assume no one would care, or they're looking for an expression of caring from the person waiting for them. Or, they may want to rebel due to a subconscious desire to reject authority, resisting a form of control. Others may feel paralyzed by the pressure to be on time. People with perfectionism may take longer to get ready or complete tasks, leading to lateness. Still others may seek the adrenaline boost of rushing to deal with the consequences of being late. They may overschedule because they feel like they must do a lot and appear busy to convey their worth to themselves or others. They may become procrastinators with anxiety about shifting from one activity to another, or making a mistake and being judged for it.

Both approaches to time are ultimately futile. We aren't exerting the power over people or institutions we think we are. Time is just time—important and also trivial.

Respect time. Respect other people by being on time when possible. Respect your commitments. But if you're late, you're still worthy. It's okay. You can let go of the need to control and the need to be perfect, or the need to show how much you don't care.

Take responsibility for your view of time and keep a relationship with time that is both thoughtful and relaxed. We can't control the speed by which an idea or plan takes shape, or how or when our dream is brought forth. Choose to perceive time as your powerful ally that sometimes knows better than you and will certainly reveal all. Trust time, work with time, and know you have enough time. If you're looking for answers, be patient and let time show you. Time will always pass. Uncertainty will always clear.

Don't worry about the future, and don't hurry toward the future. *Have fun with the future.* Your future self is so patient.

Move forward, knowing time is available to you. If you feel short on time, take a step back and examine how your time is spent, and whether your subconscious is driving your choices rather than your conscious mind. Letting the subconscious rule can make us feel at a loss. Acknowledging what the subconscious is struggling with leads to release. For example, I recently experienced feeling that I didn't have enough time. My toddler had been sleeping poorly, and I'd been short on time for writing. I tried to accept that I couldn't control certain elements of the situation, but I felt internal resistance. My resistance reflected a scarcity mindset, a comforting sense of panic, a familiar feeling of helplessness. I decided to tell myself that the time I needed would become available to me, and I simply had to find it. *I had to want the time. I had to value the time.* So here I am, writing these words at five-thirty in the morning, on a day my son didn't happen to wake up early.

When such opportunities come to you and you take them, the universe will know what you want ever so clearly, and the universe will grant you more of it. When you don't squander the time you have, you're rewarded. Not squandering doesn't mean staying perpetually busy or working yourself to the bone. It means respecting time and using time for a purpose—whether that is healing, imagining, connecting, creating, or just having fun. It means being grateful for time. It means knowing time is possibility. It means giving time permission to unfold in your favor.

CHAPTER 11

THE UPWARD TRAJECTORY OF EMPOWERING BELIEFS

*The only way to deal with an unfree world is to become
so absolutely free that your very existence is an act of
rebellion.*

attributed to Albert Camus

*The pleasures of heaven are with me and the pains of
hell are with me / The first I graft and increase upon
myself, the latter I translate into a new tongue.*

Walt Whitman, Leaves of Grass

I know what it's like to want to give up. To collapse. To submit to
a deluge of abuse, lies, and chaos. To spiral. To be so worn down
from emotional and intellectual exertion that you consider giving in
to the despair, letting it win.

I was working through the final draft of this book when the father
from whom I was estranged died. He knew he was ill, and so did I.

When I first learned he was ill, a flooding panic seized me.
A heavy weight on my chest, a racing heart, and quick and
erratic thoughts consumed me. I was immediately compelled to
do something, anything, to make the flooding subside. Instead of

doing something—which in the past would likely have entailed being the dutiful daughter, pretending like the past never happened, submitting to poor treatment so I could feel like I was doing "the right thing" in society's eyes—I did nothing. I sat with it, letting myself feel the flooding until it gradually subsided. I stayed with my emotions and worked through them in somatic therapy, which allowed the fragile echoes of my wounded narrator to fade away. And everything gradually calmed, and I circled back to the truth: that the illness changed nothing. I felt empathy for my father's physical suffering, and I moved on.

My father died a few months later. He had never apologized. He had never gone to therapy as I'd asked. The last text I read from him said that he was ashamed of me (to be fair, texts attacking me were interspersed with generic love-bombing texts, in typical narcissistic fashion). He knew he was ill, and he chose to do nothing. It was the death of a person, and it was also, for me, the demise of a castle in the sky—a castle in which I was loved as I should have been by my father. *It hurt so much.* I thought I had already mourned the absence of an emotional safety net, of secure attachment, of a relationship as it should be, but I mourned again because this was the ultimate destruction of hope. The destruction of possibility. My father would never acknowledge what he had done, let alone apologize. Where a loving relationship should have been, there lay a deep and unsettling hollowness.

And *I mourned him*, much to my embarrassment. I was sad, and I hated myself for it. How could I possibly have love for someone who hurt me and others so much? I don't know. I had never stopped hoping he'd find a way to live a life as good as the best.

While I was still processing my feelings, rather than rushing to make logical sense of what made no sense—as I would have as a child—a gaslighting, radically narcissistic obituary was published. It portrayed my father as the man my mother had spent my entire life trying to convince me he was, despite all evidence to the contrary. And it referred to my life—what I had fought tooth and nail for, against their resistance, attacks, blindsides, and betrayals—as my father's commendation.

It seemed impossible that anyone who actually knew him, anyone who saw me as a child, anyone who understood narcissism, would believe the words, but they still destroyed me. The pain of the only thing I had ever owned when times were bad—my story, shaped through the practices in this book—being distorted and exploited was overwhelming. All of the insights of this book (including that no one else's imagination could possibly define me or dictate my reality) dissolved, and I felt crushed. Completely and utterly destroyed. Here I was again, being used as a punching bag one minute and a trophy to service fragile selfhoods the next. My survival was somehow a reward for the very people who had made it so hard for me to survive. The obituary felt like an anti-apology, a fuck you, and a seizure of my selfhood. It didn't matter that no one would read it. The truth felt buried in service of the illusion that formed all of my limiting beliefs—the illusion that my father unconditionally loved me, and that his unconditional love meant being unseen, unaccepted, and unsupported, being attacked repeatedly physically and emotionally, and being forced to lie to the world about it.

I felt submerged, and I feel submerged writing about it right now.[86]

Everything I had written, and all of my supposed healing, left me, and I was a child with nothing again.

Disintegrated and dysregulated.

Annihilated.

I couldn't write.

I couldn't think.

I couldn't be me.

I was stuck in an ugly state of sorrow, anger, confusion, and loss, and I was so tired of fighting for truth, healing, and wholeness. And then I felt guilty being stuck, as I was supposed to be healed. My wounded narrator overwhelmed me: I was not healed, I would never be healed, I was a failure, I was wrong about everything, and I was meant for a life of pain. Who was I to think I deserved anything better than this? Who was I to advise others, when I couldn't even be resilient?

As an aside, people who have survived trauma are often told how resilient they are, with a sort of condescending admiration, but I hate the word "resilience" because it rewards a quick resolution of intense emotion (too quick for real healing), and it glosses over how challenging each moment of having to overcome can be. Resilience can come from an overactive fight response, a programmed drive to survive. I've had this type of resilience for most of my life. If something bad happened, or I faced a setback, I moved on quickly by entering hyper problem-solving mode, or engaging in distractions if solutions weren't available. *Anything but feeling.* This response helped me survive, but it left my interfering wound buried in raw form. It often led me to make hasty decisions that weren't ideal long-term. I had to learn to sit with the awful feelings and unfairness, to examine why it hurt so much, to not exhaust myself. I had to let go of the illusion of control over my feelings, and the illusion that control would give me the upper hand over trauma.

The feelings I experienced around my father's passing were gut-wrenching, and perhaps worse because in the midst of my healing, I had retained the fantasy that I could create a life where I was never hurt again, where there were no surprises and no challenges to work through anymore. I always hated being surprised. It was so scary to be surprised when I was a child, and I still felt that way. And it truly is easier to hold empowering beliefs in the moments when you feel good and free, and aren't reminded of your past.

That's not reality. I wanted perfection, and perfection is impossible. I wanted things to make sense, and they often don't. Life is often messy. At times, it is also really, really unfair.

I find calling out the unfairness of life deeply reassuring. As a child, I wasn't permitted to call out the unfairness of the way I was treated, or my position in the world, or the stressful events that kept occurring. Because no one validated me in this way, I was forced (by my own survival mind) to make sense of unfairness, and my mind did so by turning to limiting beliefs. Unfairness suddenly made sense if it was all my fault and therefore actually fair after all. But as we've learned, the easiest answer isn't necessarily true, accurate, or conducive to a life as good as the best. The easiest answer often feeds a destructive narrative.

It's okay to admit that life is unfair. The truth isn't simple or neat, nor does it always make sense. Bad things didn't happen to us because we're unworthy, limited, or powerless. Sometimes they happened because life is unfair.

Acknowledge life's unfairness, but don't squander your time resenting it. It just is. No one, and certainly not the universe, owes you anything. Only you owe yourself a life as good as the best.

I trust we can hold two seemingly contradictory truths in our heads: life is unfair, and we can create the life of our dreams. I believe that admitting that life is unfair respects life, in all its messy and radiant imperfection, as you should be respected in all of yours.

Life can be unfair in a negative way, and it can be unfair in a really positive way. On your journey, terrible moments that have nothing to do with anything you did or didn't do will occur. Also on your journey, wonderful moments that have nothing to do with anything you did or didn't do will occur. You don't embrace the terrible, but you do work through it (a range of responses may be appropriate, including future avoidance, acceptance, or resistance); you embrace and exploit the wonderful. *That's all you can do, and that is tremendous power.*

Doing everything this book says perfectly—even if that were possible—wouldn't give you a life without pain or loss. We live in a reality where everyone is navigating all kinds of things and dreaming of all kinds of things while navigating challenges and opportunities, creating complexity. We also live in a reality where none of us can live forever. Delays, losses, setbacks, and struggles are inevitable.

Neither a perfect life nor a perfect self exists.

You are messy and imperfect, and you will never be 100 percent healed. And you are lovable and lovely, worthy of a life as good as the best. Accepting your full self—all the parts, including the ones that are neglected, sullied, barely healed, or anchored in emotions such as shame (against your best intentions)—takes you across the only finish line possible. It may seem paradoxical, but accepting this reality of imperfection is precisely what permits power and possibility to unfold. It's what allows you to believe that you are worthy of a great life, with your wildest dreams brought forth, *and makes it real.* This acceptance will give you the best type of motivation, the truest confidence, and the healthiest perspective.

Love yourself unconditionally. Love yourself the way you should have been loved as a child, and the way you would love a child now, knowing all you know. When you love someone, you show them compassion and patience. When you love someone, you believe in them, so you hold them accountable to be their best. You're honest, and you have high expectations. And when you love someone, you also give them a break when they're having a hard time.

It's not failure.

You can take breaks. You can mess up.

You will not drown or disappear.

You will not be doomed.

The line won't be straight. But the trajectory will move forward. The trajectory is your direction over time, and it should move toward wholeness, authenticity, connection, and possibility.

There is no fairy tale, or paradise, or promised land. There is only you, and the privilege of being you—fully, freely, and completely.

Life is always in flux. Nothing is final—not the moments you bring forth a dream and not the moments of temporary delay (my preferred term for what others call "failure"). Temporary delays and breakthroughs, setbacks and successes, are all ephemeral. Success is the exact moment it all comes together, and it's over in an instant. The temporary delay is the exact moment when it all seems to fall apart, giving way in an instant to a moment of potential rebirth. All will happen, and all are just moments. "You" are not even final, ever. Your entire sense of self can be transformed in a moment, with a particular act or a choice not to act.

Many of us with C-PTSD have a difficult time embracing moments of temporary delay because they make us feel exposed and vulnerable, like we were when we were first hurt. Then, we may have propped ourselves up with limiting beliefs, perfectionism, or self-denigration. Now, everything feels like our fault. We experience temporary delays, mistakes, and missteps as assaults on our worthiness and lovability, our sense of what we could be capable of. If we could only avoid failure by being perfect, we'd never be discovered as less than. If we fail, we are obliterated. The feelings of shame and defeat can be terrifying.

Many of us blame ourselves even when a difficult event occurs that very obviously has nothing to do with us, because it's a reflex—how we made sense of our childhood trauma. If it was all our fault, we still have parents who loved us, right? Because what kind of person doesn't have parents who love them? No one would even believe us if we told them. We strive to find a cause for painful events—some minor misstep we made, a supposed transgression we perpetrated that is now being punished, or a sign from the universe. We struggle so hard to make it make sense that we lose out on an opportunity to learn something real. It doesn't always make sense. Sorry, I can't promise you (or myself) sense or logic or fairness in the universe we live in. Many times, temporary delays have nothing to do with anything you do (or don't do), think, or feel. We live in a universe of complexity, where multiple dreams and traumas are intersecting, merging, and breaking apart simultaneously. The universe is working out the timing.

Temporary delays—failures—are not as big a deal as we make them out to be in our minds. Honestly, no one else really cares as much as we do. Other people aren't walking around harshly criticizing us the way we're criticizing ourselves. It's all in our heads, which means that the power over it is in our heads as well. We allow our experiences with temporary delays to take us down, or we use them as an opportunity for transformation.

Sometimes all we can do is move forward, continuing to participate. Temporary delays are not personal, but we must take personal responsibility for how we react to them. We can participate by considering that bad things don't happen for a reason, but bad things do communicate information. Temporary delays are sometimes suggestions from the universe, hints that you might approach a situation differently. A temporary delay may cause you to consider another path to your dreams. Approach a temporary delay with curiosity: Did you try something new? Maybe it didn't work. Or maybe it will work next time. Think critically about it. Change your plan if it's not working. Are you stuck in an old routine or mindset? Are you uncertain? Are you desperate? What can you do to regulate your mind? Use practical lessons from these temporary delays to learn about how the universe works and to make your future decisions more effective.

Almost every path contains within it a temporary delay, or ten. Being laid off from a job is a temporary delay to having the career of your dreams. Being out of money is a temporary delay to being extraordinarily wealthy. Losing a competition is a temporary delay to winning a different one.

Importantly, being pulled back into the pain of the trauma you experienced in the past is a temporary delay to even more profound healing. It's temporary if we treat it as such, if we don't block the potential for healing with our limiting beliefs.

We may be shut out from doing things in a particular way, but we can find another way. The "way" is not important. The "way" is not something we're seeking to bring forth. The dream is. You can't control the way, but the dream is yours. This is tenacity. Tenacity takes us to the forward trajectory.

Tenacity is distinct from resilience. Tenacity is like magic. Tenacity is choosing to move forward, to transform, to pivot toward our dreams in any moment we can. Tenacity is existing without giving up. Tenacity is hacking away at limiting beliefs, one moment at a time, until you reach the moments of empowerment and limitlessness, and they grow in frequency, and then you reach the moments your dreams are made real—and they grow in frequency, too.

The delay is temporary. Moving forward is forever.

Just move—or, in other words, exist without giving up.

If your first plan doesn't work, create a new one, or a dozen new ones. If you don't make it on the first audition, do a hundred more. Accept the reality of the delay, examine its causes, take a break if you need to, and be brave again. And again. And again. Engage in integration practices. Converge on the forward trajectory. Converge on wholeness, authenticity, and connection. Converge on abundance, creativity, and possibility.

The only way I overcame the overwhelm of my father's death and related events was to let myself feel submerged. And then to realize I was still breathing. It's a practice I learned in somatic therapy. If you're feeling emotional pain in your chest, for example, you can stretch your chest out and make yourself big—or, you can huddle your arms over your chest and make yourself feel even more constricted. Sometimes, letting the scary feeling go all the way and reaching the epiphany that you're still standing, still breathing, is incredibly freeing and integrating. You've taken the feeling to its maximum and you're still there. You realize: *Even though I feel submerged, I'm not. I'm an adult, and they can't do that to me anymore. No one can take away my imagination, my authenticity, my freedom to choose what I do and how I react, or my dreams.*

Eventually, those revelations led me to write this.

When we're stuck in the moment of delay or a rut, feeling depressed, hopeless, or without motivation—as I was—we're experiencing a freeze/collapse trauma response. We're trying to protect ourselves from overwhelm, just as we did in childhood. But we can't move forward, and we can't quiet the wounded narrator and regain a grip on our highest frequency beliefs, until we move into the void, the space of the awful and untethered. We can be brave and trust that the void can't swallow us. We can be curious, feel fully, and release. We are solid. We have weight in the void.

Allow yourself to feel the pain of your experience, without suppressing it. Take the time to work through the feelings with honesty and compassion. Giving way to the experience of any and all feelings is a workaround that saves us from being dragged back into our traumatic programming. We can handle it now. We don't have to turn the feelings into limiting beliefs to survive anymore. We can move through the waves of distress. We can recognize them as profoundly unwelcome while giving them the space to recede. The waves may ebb and flow. We will not drown. We ride the wave while continuously reminding ourselves of its temporary nature. The pain never feels temporary, but it always is.

I still live with my C-PTSD. The wounded narrator's voice has faded, but it still emerges from time to time. I'm still surprised by my triggers and the moments when I struggle to regulate my emotions. I've had to learn to stop being so hard on myself.

Stop being so hard on *yourself*. Treat yourself as the best version of you would treat someone else going through the same setbacks. Trust yourself. Don't be afraid of taking a moment that looks like standing still but is, in reality, tremendously transformative. You're worthy of your own trust. You're not too much. You're not too little. You're as good as the best. When you're ready, moving forward will be like breathing.

You know how to swim through the setback.

You were born knowing how to be yourself.

Keep engaging in the integration therapies and practices in this book. Or not. You can also just *be* for a little while, a feeling, sensing, thinking person who is aware of themselves.

The struggle doesn't prove you can't heal; the forward trajectory proves *you are healing*. You'll know you're on the forward trajectory not based on how many boxes you've checked, how successful you are, or how many of your dreams are realized. You'll know because of how you feel, especially in the moments after a setback. You may be surprised by the wounded narrator's emergence after so much healing. You may struggle to regulate your emotions. But you'll recognize what's happening. You'll allow yourself to feel and validate your own feelings the way no one did when you were a child. You'll make a choice to engage in a mind-body integration therapy. You'll be able to accept that you are both fallible and worthy, that the world is both unfair and full of opportunity, and that you are permitted grace and compassion. You'll move towards power and possibility, and the wounded narrator will begin to rest.

There is happy, but there is no ending. Healing has no resolution. Dreams have no resolution. Everything is a moment in time. But string enough moments of well-being, power, and possibility together and you'll have a life as good as the best.

On the other hand, things may work out so well that it defies even your most empowering beliefs.

You may not like the way happy feels. Some of us with C-PTSD feel unsafe when we start to live as our highest selves. Exhibiting a healthy response to our emotions may not feel normal to us. The absence of drama, pain, a racing heart, or a queasy tummy may lead to a frightening feeling of emptiness. We may feel an aching at the healing wounds, a reminder of what was.

Feeling whole, at peace, and fulfilled can feel profoundly wrong, uncomfortable in a way that seems to compel us to resist it. It can also feel boring, consciously or subconsciously.

Nothing is wrong. Your mind is just attempting to recreate (a now irrelevant) illusion of safety, the illusion that saved you as a child, the illusion sustained by limiting beliefs. Those seductively familiar patterns of the past promise comfort, but the past is boring and limiting. Our wounded narrators are boring and limiting. Our wounded narrators live in a past that is monotonous—a cycle of trauma repeating endlessly into infinity. The past doesn't give life to our dreams. The past only gives birth to preservation of the past.

That present peace may feel overwhelmingly calm, but it's not numbness. If you've engaged in the practices and integration therapies described in this book, you're not detached; you're more attached to your body and the moment than you ever have been before.

That odd feeling is presence. You are here. You don't have to run away again, to retreat into the sham cocoon of limiting beliefs.

You have the tools to accept this emptiness and see it for what it actually is: contentment, peace, and integration. Wholeness, freedom, and space for expression. A life as good as the best.

AFTERWORD

If I've missed something, I want to know.

Even though I aim to reach and embrace multitudes of perspectives, I can only write from my own. In many ways, I find this disheartening.

But your journey can inform my perspective, just as I hope my journey has informed yours. I'm curious about your journey. I'd love the chance to learn more and draw closer to the truth, and you and your journey are a beautiful part of that truth. If you think I've missed a critical challenge, or a nuance, or a practice that could help others—anything that led you to a breakthrough—please let me know.

I welcome discussion, but reject desperation and self-pity. Do not surrender your worth, power, and possibilities to prove that the universe isn't perfect. I already know that.

I also know this:

You are light.

You will heal.

Your possibilities are limitless.

A life as good as the best is yours.

Acknowledgements

Thank you to J., my partner in life and design, for everything. In relationship with you, I am both elevated and grounded, steadied and endlessly inspired.

Thank you to my children, for being children, for being themselves, for being love.

Thank you to K., for proving miracles are possible.

Thank to my friends from all different parts of my life, for, over the years, showing me empathy, nonjudgment, and the life-affirming distraction of a hell of a good time.

Thank you to the teachers who saw me, the therapists who calmed me, and the mentors who showed me that there's always a way.

And thank you, dear reader. I have rendered these words, but their meaning belongs to you.

ENDNOTES

1. Even the so-called "Dark" Age was a time of significant technological advancements, including mechanical clocks, towering cathedrals, agricultural machines, and eventually the printing press.

2. Children of narcissists, in particular, are made to feel selfish for having any needs, let alone wants. Narcissists demand all our physical and emotional resources. My parents always found a way out of their self-inflicted financial emergencies, whether I helped them or not, but they demanded I give them all of the financial and emotional support I was capable of. This cycle played out repeatedly, and yet it took a massive unlearning process to rid myself of the deep-seated fear of keeping anything for myself. I've also seen a different version of this dynamic play out in wealthy families, where there can be an unspoken expectation that children not outperform their parents and a requirement that they protect their parents' egos at all costs.

3. There's nothing wrong with serving the public; it only becomes a problem if you sacrifice your well-being.

4. These feelings fuel growth under capitalism. Beyond any impact our trauma may have had on us, those of us in capitalist or pseudo-capitalist systems are conditioned to believe in scarcity and that our low self-worth can only be cured by consumption.

5. Bursts of competitive energy aren't bad if we choose to view others' performance as a standard of excellence to which we can aspire—and if we don't take winning or losing personally. Participating in a competitive arena such as sports or electoral politics means there's always someone to beat. In other realms, first place typically doesn't exist. Even when it does, it's always temporary. Living in the arena of contagious success can be forever.

6. Venkat Kuppuswamy and Ethan Mollick. "Second Thoughts About Second Acts: Gender Differences in Serial Founding Rates?" Working paper, Wharton, University of Pennsylvania, 2016.

7. Antonio Chirumbolo, Stefano Livi, Lucia Mannetti, Antonio Pierro, and Arie W. Kruglanski, "Effects of Need for Closure on Creativity in Small Group Interactions," *European Journal of Personality* 18 (2004): 265–278.

8. Julia Gärtner, Lisa Bußenius, Sarah Prediger, Daniela Vogel, and Sigrid Harendza, "Need for Cognitive Closure, Tolerance for Ambiguity, and Perfectionism in Medical School Applicants," *BMC Medical Education* 20 (2020): Article 132.

9. David Disatnik and Yael Steinhart, "Need for Cognitive Closure, Risk Aversion, Uncertainty Changes, and Their Effect on Investment Decisions," *Journal of Marketing Research* 52, no. 3 (2015).

10. Djikic, Maja, Keith Oatley, and Mihnea C. Moldoveanu. 2013. "Opening the Closed Mind: The Effect of Exposure to Literature on the Need for Closure." *Creativity Research Journal* 25, no. 2 (2013): 149–154.

11. Evan F. Risko, Nicola C. Anderson, Sophie Lanthier, and Alan Kingstone, "Curious Eyes: Individual Differences in Personality Predict Eye Movement Behavior in Scene-Viewing," *Cognition* 122, no. 1 (2012): 86–90. Jacqueline Gottlieb and Pierre-Yves Oudeyer, "Towards a Neuroscience of Active Sampling and Curiosity," *Nature Reviews Neuroscience* 19, no. 12 (2018): 758–770

12. David M. Lydon-Staley, Perry Zurn, and Danielle S. Bassett, "Within-Person Variability in Curiosity during Daily Life and Associations with Well-Being," *Journal of Personality* 88, no. 4 (2020): 625–41; Alexandra Drake, Bruce P. Doré, Emily B. Falk, Perry Zurn, Danielle S. Bassett, and David M. Lydon-Staley, "Daily Stressor-Related Negative Mood and Its Associations with Flourishing and Daily Curiosity," *Journal of Happiness Studies* 23, no. 2 (2022): 423–438; Veljko Jovanović and Dragana Brdaric, "Did Curiosity Kill the Cat? Evidence from Subjective Well-Being in Adolescents," *Personality and Individual Differences* 52, no. 3 (2012): 380–384.

13. Jonah Paquette, Awestruck: How Embracing Wonder Can Make You Healthier, Happier and More Connected (Boulder: Shambhala, 2020).

14. Jia Wei Zhang, Ryan T. Howell, Pooya Razavi, Hadi Shaban-Azad, Wen Jia Chai, Tamilselvan Ramis, Zena R. Mello, Craig L. Anderson, Maria Monroy, and Dacher Keltner, "Awe Is Associated with Creative Personality, Convergent Creativity, and Everyday Creativity," *Psychology of Aesthetics, Creativity, and the Arts* 18, no. 2 (2024): 209–221.

15. Jennifer E. Stellar, Neha John-Henderson, Craig L. Anderson, Amie M. Gordon, Galen D. McNeil, and Dacher Keltner, "Positive Affect and Markers of Inflammation: Discrete Positive Emotions Predict Lower Levels of Inflammatory Cytokines," *Emotion* 15, no. 2 (2015): 129–33; Paul K. Piff, Pia Dietze, Matthew Feinberg, Daniel M. Stancato and Dacher Keltner, "Awe, the Small Self, and Prosocial Behavior," *Journal of Personality and Social Psychology* 108, no. 6 (2015): 883–899; María Monroy, Michael Amster, Jake Eagle, Felicia K. Zerwas, Dacher Keltner, and Javier E. López, "Awe Reduces Depressive Symptoms and Improves Well-Being in a Randomized-Controlled Clinical Trial," *Scientific Reports* 15 (2025): 16453.

16. Gordon Neufield and Gabor Maté, *Hold On To Your Kids: Why Parents Need to Matter More than Peers* (New York: Ballantine Books, 2005).

17. I appreciate the irony that someone who relied so heavily on positive attention is now writing a book that she hopes will receive positive attention. I have to ask myself, do I want to help people, or do I want attention? Happily, it's more the former than the latter. It takes time to fully accept that our worth, power, and possibilities don't hinge on external validation.

18. Some might argue that you must at times engage with toxic individuals to get ahead. The toxic environments created by these people—which sometimes promise great reward, such as in big corporations or in politics—are enormously difficult for those of us with C-PTSD to navigate. We end up in a maelstrom of triggers, self-defense mechanisms, and dark energy. We can halt our healing and even reverse it by agreeing to participate in these environments. We should ask ourselves if we really want to be a part of them.

19. My father may have had severe borderline personality disorder combined with narcissism, which manifested itself through rageful attacks, fear of abandonment, reckless behavior, and addictions, although I'm not an expert and will never know for sure. Only about half of people with personality disorders recover from them, with the best care. Some people with personality disorders can abide by boundaries; many cannot. Narcissists typically don't change or respect boundaries because they don't take responsibility. In relationship with a narcissist, they and their feelings are the center of everything, and you don't exist except as a source of supply to make them feel real. They will never love themselves enough to love you, no matter how much you give them, unless and until they engage in extensive therapy, which few of them attempt.

20. Daniel J. Siegel, *The Developing Mind: How Relationships and the Brain Interact to Shape Who We Are*, 3rd ed. (New York: Guilford Press, 2020).

21. Jennifer E. Stellar, Adam Cohen, Christopher Oveis, and Dacher Keltner, "Affective and Physiological Responses to the Suffering of Others: Compassion and Vagal Activity," *Journal of Personality and Social Psychology* 108, no. 4 (2015): 572–585; Maria Di Bello, Luca Carnevali, Nicola Petrocchi, Julian F. Thayer, Paul Gilbert, and Cristina Ottaviani, "The Compassionate Vagus: A Meta-Analysis on the Connection between Compassion and Heart Rate Variability," *Neuroscience & Biobehavioral Reviews* 116 (2020): 21–30.

22. Marieke Verkleij, Erik-Jonas van de Griendt, Vivian Colland, Nancy van Loey, Anita Beelen, and Rinie Geenen, "Parenting Stress Related to Behavioral Problems and Disease Severity in Children with Problematic Severe Asthma," *Journal of Clinical Psychology in Medical Settings* 22, no. 2–3 (2015): 179–193; Junko Nagano, Chizuru Kakuta, Chihiro Motomura, Hiroyuki Odajima, Nobuyuki Sudo, Shigeko Nishima, and Chie Kubo, "The Parenting Attitudes and the Stress of Mothers Predict the Asthmatic Severity of Their Children: A Prospective Study," *BioPsychoSocial Medicine* 4, no. 1 (2010): Article 12.

23. James A. Coan, Heather Schaefer, and Richard J. Davidson, "Lending a Hand: Social Regulation of the Neural Response to Threat," *Psychological Science* 17, no. 12 (2006): 1032–1039

24. Steven W. Cole, John P. Capitanio, Katie Chun, Jesusa M. G. Arevalo, Jeffrey Ma, and John T. Cacioppo, "Myeloid Differentiation Architecture of Leukocyte Transcriptome Dynamics in Perceived Social Isolation," *Proceedings of the National Academy of Sciences of the United States of America* 112, no. 49 (2015): 15142–15147.

25. John T. Cacioppo and Louise C. Hawkley, "Perceived Social Isolation and Cognition," *Trends in Cognitive Sciences* 13, no. 10 (2009): 447–454.

26. Inmyung Song, Jin-Won Kwon, and Soo Min Jeon, "The Relative Importance of Friendship to Happiness Increases with Age," *PLOS ONE* 18, no. 7 (2023); Eliazar Luna, Milagros Ruiz, Sofia Malyutina, Anastasiya Titarenko, Magdalena Kozela, Andrzej Pająk, Ruzena Kubinova, and Martin Bobak, "The Prospective Association between Frequency of Contact with Friends and Relatives and Quality of Life in Older Adults from Central and Eastern Europe," *Social Psychiatry and Psychiatric Epidemiology* 55, no. 8 (2020): 1001–1010.

27. Christopher M. Masi, Hsi-Yuan Chen, Louise C. Hawkley, and John T. Cacioppo, "A Meta-Analysis of Interventions to Reduce Loneliness," *Personality and Social Psychology Review* 15, no. 3 (2011): 219–266.

28. James Hollis, *The Eden Project: In Search of the Magical Other* (Toronto: Inner City Books, 1998).

29. Per the Jungian view, we confront our own shadow aspects (unhealed and/or repressed parts of ourselves) when interacting with the person with whom we are in relationship. These aspects have to be acknowledged and integrated, and we have to be aware and authentic, to make the relationship function (instead of deteriorating into conflict and tension). Attachment theory also advocates for healthy, supportive relationships as therapeutic tools to heal from past experiences of insecure attachment. We can heal and develop a more secure attachment style by being emotionally vulnerable and communicating honestly with the person with whom we are in relationship.

30. It's complicated, and much of healing and transcending is deeply independent. Buddha and Jesus left their families to do intense spiritual work. And afterwards they gave multifold through acts of love, empathy, acceptance, service, and creativity.

31. Kiecolt-Glaser, Janice K., Peter T. Marucha, William B. Malarkey, Ana M. Mercado, and Ronald Glaser. "Slowing of Wound Healing by Psychological Stress." *The Lancet* 346, no. 8984 (1995): 1194–96.

32. Samuel P. Fraiberger, Roberta Sinatra, Magnus Resch, Christoph Riedl, and Albert-László Barabási, "Quantifying Reputation and Success in Art," *Science* 362, no. 6416 (2018): 825–829.

33. Here again, the advice of this book differs from typical manifesting, which might suggest choosing a happier or more positive thought to replace a negative one. I believe this is too rushed for some of us, leading to the suppression of our feelings. Suppression only appears to work temporarily. If the negative feeling remains trapped inside, it will find a way out through negative thoughts (that impact behavior) and even physical ailments. Suppressed thoughts, rumination, and negative thinking are also associated with shorter telomeres (protective caps of repetitive DNA on our chromosomes that influence aging and disease).

34. I worked through this section many times in an attempt to address the physical abuse head-on, instead of downplaying its severity (and my vulnerability), as I had my entire life.

35. My college had incredibly generous financial aid and gave me a very low interest loan to cover the missing payments. I learned to never again expect anything from my parents.

36. In the Bible, a scapegoat is one of a pair of kid goats that is released into the wilderness, taking with it all of the sins and impurities of a community, while the other goat is sacrificed. The scapegoat died an uncertain and slow death in the wilderness, and that suffering supposedly served as atonement for the people in the community. In modern times, scapegoating is used to refer to the singling out of a person or group for unmerited blame and consequent negative treatment. Projection and displacement are used to focus aggression, hostility, frustration, and other low-frequency energies upon an individual who has done nothing to deserve it.

37. The maltreatment scapegoats endure is often the impetus that drives them to escape their dysfunctional home. As a result, they have the best chance in their family to end the generational cycle of abuse.

38. While fight, flight and freeze have been understood as reactions for some time (and are self-explanatory), fawn is a more recent addition that entails pleasing, appeasing, or "merging" with the needs of the threat and becoming endearing or useful, decreasing the likelihood the threat will attack you.

39. This is also why affirmations are helpful but not enough—we're fully conscious we're making them, even as if we try to convince our subconscious to believe.

40. Becca R. Levy, Corey Pilver, Pil H. Chung, and Martin D. Slade, "Subliminal Strengthening: Improving Older Individuals' Physical Function over Time with an Implicit-Age-Stereotype Intervention," *Psychological Science* 25, no. 12 (2014): 2127–2135.

41. This study also supports "stereotype embodiment" (the theory that cultural stereotypes are internalized and become internal beliefs, influencing behavior, psychology, and physiology and thereby becoming self-fulfilling prophecies), which dovetails with of our discussion about the impact of limiting beliefs. Negative age stereotypes lead to detrimental outcomes, including worsening physical function.

42. These include CBT (identifying negative thoughts and changing behavior in order to modify them, thereby desensitizing yourself from triggers), parts work (which involves recognizing disowned parts of you and giving them a voice before integrating them within an embodied sense of self), and internal family systems (which similarly identifies parts, but in this case they are thought of as families within your mental system that may be in conflict, and the goal is to harmonize the dynamics of the system). While all three influence the concept of the wounded narrator, they are quite distinct. I don't believe the wounded narrator should be given a voice or harmonized, or that we can transform the wounded narrator solely through action. Instead, we recognize the wounded narrator as a vestige of our trauma, distinct from our authentic self, and profoundly unhelpful in our current context. We accept that we live with our wounded narrators while encouraging them to recede from the forefront, discharging them from the responsibilities they have carried for so long.

43. Integration doesn't mean that the mind alone can cure disease or that physical pain or injury is the result of a subconscious wish. We live in a world where we can't live forever. Good thoughts are not always enough to surmount injury or disease, but they do help, while bad thoughts don't help at all (and may hurt). Suppression of our feelings doesn't help either.

44. Alia J. Crum and Ellen J. Langer, "Mindset Matters: Exercise and the Placebo Effect," *Psychological Science* 18, no. 2 (2007): 165–171.

45. Simon Rosenbaum, Catherine Sherrington, and Anna Tiedemann, "Exercise Augmentation Compared with Usual Care for Post-Traumatic Stress Disorder: A Randomized Controlled Trial," *Acta Psychiatrica Scandinavica* 131, no. 5 (2015): 350–359.

46. Risako Fujikawa, Adam I. Ramsaran, Axel Guskjolen, Juan de la Parra, Yi Zou, Andrew J. Mocle, Sheena A. Josselyn, and Paul W. Frankland, "Neurogenesis-Dependent Remodeling of Hippocampal Circuits Reduces PTSD-Like Behaviors in Adult Mice," *Molecular Psychiatry* 29, no. 11 (2024): 3316–3329.

47. Britta K. Hölzel, James Carmody, Mark Vangel, Christina Congleton, Sita M. Yerramsetti, Tim Gard, and Sara W. Lazar, "Mindfulness Practice Leads to Increases in Regional Brain Gray Matter Density," *Psychiatry Research: Neuroimaging* 191, no. 1 (2011): 36–43; Adrienne A. Taren, Peter J. Gianaros, Carmen M. Greco, Michael L. Thompson, Juliana W. Ross, and Erica A. Picard, "Mindfulness Meditation Training Alters Stress-Related Amygdala Resting State Functional Connectivity," *Social Cognitive and Affective Neuroscience* 10, no. 12 (2015): 1758–1768.

48. Yoga is the only exercise discussed in this chapter, but other forms of exercise are considered somatic and can unlock deep healing. These include dance, pilates, and aikido.

49. Jyotsana Rai, Akash Pathak, Ruchi Singh, Girish Chandra Bhatt, and Nirendra Kumar Rai, "Effectiveness of Yoga on Depression and Anxiety in People with Chronic Primary Pain: A Meta-Analysis of Randomized Controlled Trials," *International Journal of Yoga Therapy* 35 (2025): Article 5; Catherine Woodyard, "Exploring the Therapeutic Effects of Yoga and Its Ability to Increase Quality of Life," *International Journal of Yoga* 4, no. 2 (2011): 49–54; Neha P. Gothe and Edward McAuley, "Yoga and Cognition: A Meta-Analysis of Chronic and Acute Effects," *Psychosomatic Medicine* 77, no. 7 (2015): 784–797.

50. Bessel A. van der Kolk, Livia Stone, Jennifer West, Amy Rhodes, Diana Emerson, Michelle Suvak, and Josephine Spinazzola, "Yoga as an Adjunctive Treatment for Posttraumatic Stress Disorder: A Randomized Controlled Trial," *Journal of Clinical Psychiatry* 75, no. 6 (2014): e559–e565.

51. James Nestor, *Breath: The New Science of a Lost Art* (New York: Riverhead Books, 2020),

52. Susan V. Marcus, Patricia Marquis, and Chiharu Sakai, "Controlled Study of Treatment of PTSD Using EMDR in an HMO Setting," *Psychotherapy* 34, no. 3 (1997): 307–315.

53. John G. Carlson, Charles M. Chemtob, Karen Rusnak, Nancy L. Hedlund, and Masako Y. Muraoka, "Eye Movement Desensitization and Reprocessing (EMDR) Treatment for Combat-Related Posttraumatic Stress Disorder," *The Journal of Traumatic Stress* 11, no. 1 (1998): 3–24.

54. Internal family systems posits that the true, centered self is the one who demonstrates the 8 Cs and 5 Ps: Curiosity, Compassion, Calm, Clarity, Courage, Confidence, Creativity, and Connectedness; and Presence, Perspective, Patience, Persistence, and Playfulness.

55. In reality, there is no "everyone else." We all have authenticity we can tap into. We all have secrets, gifts, and ideas we haven't shared. "Everyone else" is a projection of the multitude's surface-level conformity.

56. Women face a particularly difficult social environment with respect to conformity, which includes cliques, drama, alliances, rumors, gossip, and pressure to submit and seek acceptance, and never to be so exceptional that they invite jealousy. This tragedy is amplified by social media. Many women are conditioned to chase illusions of perfection and belonging rather than to know and love themselves. Real belonging is always based on the authentic (messy, radiant, imperfect, worthy) self.

57. While I find elements of socialism theoretically appealing, I don't believe there is a practical way out of capitalism (and other experiments have tended to be even more problematic). Capitalism is fueled by selfishness and is fundamentally unfair, but capitalism perpetually provides new loopholes of access. Reading between the lines and thinking outside of the box is permissible under capitalism. Make it work in your favor and find a way from within.

58. I believe that there are underlying strains of contempt for the poor deeply embedded in our culture and within most, if not all, political parties. It's a pervasive implicit condescension, whether it's in the form of castigating decisions or deeming the poor helpless without government assistance.

59. Ann Huff Stevens, "Transitions into and out of Poverty in the United States," Center for Poverty and Inequality Research, University of California, Davis, 2012.

60. I don't believe we can ever have complete control over who we fall in love with, but with healing and the practices in this book, we are more likely to fall in love with people who won't break our hearts. Being an authentic human means always being a bit fallible, though.

61. This doesn't mean you need to ignore your depressed friend or avoid your pessimistic relative, or give up working in a profession where people tend toward combative. It does mean being aware that their way of being influences you, and trying to mitigate it as much as possible by surrounding yourself with the optimistic, imaginative, and supportive otherwise. You can be there and shine light on your loved ones, but never become anyone's companion in the darkness. Someone who attempts to drag you down is beyond saving (at least by you). In professional settings, curate a context full of individuals who can find balance—laughter along with conflict or controversy.

62. Jean E. Rhodes, *Stand by Me: The Risks and Rewards of Mentoring Today's Youth* (Cambridge, MA: Harvard University Press, 2002), 35–60; James J. Heckman, "Skill Formation and the Economics of Investing in Disadvantaged Children," *Science* 312, no. 5782 (2006): 1900–1902; Emmy E. Werner, "Risk, Resilience, and Recovery: Perspectives from the Kauai Longitudinal Study," *Development and Psychopathology* 5, no. 4 (1993): 503–515.

63. Girija Kaimal, Kathryn Ray, and Juan Muniz, "Reduction of Cortisol Levels and Participants' Responses Following Art Making," *Art Therapy* 33, no. 2 (2016): 74-80. Kaimal, Girija, Hasan Ayaz, Johanna Herres, Rebekka Dieterich-Hartwell, Bindal Makwana, Donna H. Kaiser, and Jennifer Nassar. "Functional Near-Infrared Spectroscopy Assessment of Reward Perception Based on Visual Self-Expression: Coloring, Doodling, and Free Drawing." *The Arts in Psychotherapy* 55 (2017): 85–92.

64. Mona Lisa Chanda and Daniel J. Levitin, "The Neurochemistry of Music," *Trends in Cognitive Sciences* 17, no. 4 (2013): 179–193.

65. Christopher J. F. Tsoi, Hannah L. Smith, and Michael R. Johnson, "Listening to a Popular Upbeat Song Can Lead to More Adaptive Cognitive Inferences for Stressful Events in Non-Clinical Adult Populations," *Psychology of Music* 51 (2023); Yuna L. Ferguson and Kennon M. Sheldon, "Trying to Be Happier Really Can Work: Two Experimental Studies," *The Journal of Positive Psychology* 8, no. 1 (2013): 23–33.

66. David Huron, "Why Is Sad Music Pleasurable? A Possible Role for Prolactin," *Musicae Scientiae* 15, no. 2 (2011): 146–158.

67. For most of us, most of the time. Mental health disorders like depression may require more intensive therapy and/or medication.

68. Elliot Greene and Barbara Goodrich-Dunn, *The Psychology of the Body* (Philadelphia: Lippincott Williams & Wilkins, 2004).

69. For example, I thought I had debilitating shyness as a child, when I really had selective mutism resulting from C-PTSD. I'm naturally an outgoing person, but that authentic core was hidden (including from myself) for a long time.

70. Not all the time, of course. Some people have C-PTSD, autism, ADHD, anxiety, or other challenges. Some symptoms of C-PTSD mirror symptoms of autism, such as hyper-reactivity to sensory output and atypical social skills. Unfortunately, sensitivity to neurodiversity doesn't change others' frequently automatic subconscious assessments.

71. The British children's book *The Gruffalo* is an extraordinary example of playing a part to shape your life successfully. A mouse, to scare away predator animals (fox, owl, and snake), claims to be en route to meeting a scary creature (the "Gruffalo"). The Gruffalo is implied to be the product of the mouse's imagination. Eventually, the Gruffalo actually shows up and threatens to eat the mouse. In an ultimate show of self-possession, the mouse walks back through the forest with the Gruffalo, and every time the pair interacts with one of the predator animals and the predator animal shows fear of the Gruffalo, the mouse convinces the Gruffalo they are actually afraid of the mouse. This convinces the Gruffalo that he also should be afraid of the mouse, and he runs off. The mouse ends up safe and happy—purely through the art of unflappable pretending.

72. R. P. Tsachor and T. Shafir, "A Somatic Movement Approach to Fostering Emotional Resiliency through Laban Movement Analysis," *Frontiers in Human Neuroscience* 11 (2017): 410.

73. By the way, sexual desire is not love. It's only desire. It's easy to mistake desire for love and meaning. It's never those things, but it can be appreciated for what it is—a great feeling.

74. This has nothing to do with living happily ever after. You live in a universe with many people with many different desires interacting, succeeding, and failing, and you can't control the unpredictable symphony. A relationship is complicated by your entanglement with another person and their own aspirations and healing journey. You may find love and it may last forever—or not. You don't know, but you should go for it anyway and invest in your acts of connection every day you're in relationship.

75. H. C. Lench and Z. K. Carpenter, "Optimistic Expectations Have Benefits for Effort and Emotion with Little Cost," *Emotion* 21, no. 6 (2021): 1213–1223.

76. Andrew L. Geers, Justin A. Wellman, G. Daniel Lassiter, and Nicole P. Fowler, "Dispositional Optimism and Engagement: The Moderating Influence of Goal Prioritization," *Journal of Personality and Social Psychology* 96, no. 4 (2009): 913–932.

77. Multiple studies have indicated that optimists live longer. For example, a study by Boston University researcher Lewina Lee published in the Proceedings of the National Academy of Sciences found that optimists tend to live 11–15 percent longer than pessimists and have an excellent chance of reaching age 85 (considered "exceptional longevity").

78. Martin E. P. Seligman, Tayyab Rashid, and Acacia C. Parks, "Positive Psychotherapy," *American Psychologist* 61, no. 8 (2006): 774–788.

79. Smiling is also culturally influenced. In many cultures outside of the United States, smiling too much (or much at all) is viewed as insincere, untrustworthy, unserious, or unprofessional.

80. Thank you to the late Queen Elizabeth II.

81. Christiana Tsaousi, "'What Underwear Do I Like?' Taste and (Embodied) Cultural Capital in the Consumption of Women's Underwear," *Journal of Consumer Culture* 16, no. 2 (2016): 553–571.

82. Michael Schulman, "On 'Succession,' Jeremy Strong Doesn't Get the Joke," *The New Yorker*, December 13, 2021.

83. Michael L. Slepian, Simon N. Ferber, Joshua M. Gold, and Abraham M. Rutchick, "The Cognitive Consequences of Formal Clothing," *Social Psychological and Personality Science* 6, no. 6 (2015): 661–668.

84. Michael W. Kraus and Wendy Berry Mendes, "Sartorial Symbols of Social Class Elicit Class-Consistent Behavioral and Physiological Responses: A Dyadic Approach," *Journal of Experimental Psychology: General* 143, no. 6 (2014): 2330–2340.

85. This includes Hindus, Buddhists, Aboriginal and Indigenous peoples, and the ancient Greeks.

86. Although less so with every re-read.

www.ingramcontent.com/pod-product-compliance
Lightning Source LLC
Chambersburg PA
CBHW050853150626
46549CB00013B/1611